B+T 2/12

Fire Your
Stock Analyst!

Fire Your
Stock Analyst!
Analyzing Stocks
On Your Own

Harry Domash

Vice President, Publisher: Tim Moore
Associate Publisher and Director of Marketing: Amy Neidlinger
Executive Editor: Jim Boyd
Editorial Assistant: Myesha Graham
Operations Manager: Gina Kanouse
Senior Marketing Manager: Julie Phifer
Publicity Manager: Laura Czaja
Assistant Marketing Manager: Megan Colvin
Cover Designer: Alan Clements
Managing Editor: Kristy Hart
Project Editor: Anne Goebel
Copy Editor: Gayle Johnson
Proofreader: Sheri Cain
Indexer: WordWise Publishing Services
Senior Compositor: Gloria Schurick
Manufacturing Buyer: Dan Uhrig

This book is sold with the understanding that neither the author nor the publisher is engaged in rendering legal, accounting, or other professional services or advice by publishing this book. Each individual situation is unique. Thus, if legal or financial advice or other expert assistance is required in a specific situation, the services of a competent professional should be sought to ensure that the situation has been evaluated carefully and appropriately. The author and the publisher disclaim any liability, loss, or risk resulting directly or indirectly from the use or application of any of the contents of this book.

FT Press offers excellent discounts on this book when ordered in quantity for bulk purchases or special sales. For more information, please contact U.S. Corporate and Government Sales, 1-800-382-3419, corpsales@pearsontechgroup.com. For sales outside the U.S., please contact International Sales at international@pearson.com.

Company and product names mentioned herein are the trademarks or registered trademarks of their respective owners.

Printed in the United States of America

Third Printing January 2011

ISBN-10: 0-13-701023-0
ISBN-13: 978-0-13-701023-3

Pearson Education LTD.
Pearson Education Australia PTY, Limited
Pearson Education Singapore, Pte. Ltd.
Pearson Education North Asia, Ltd.
Pearson Education Canada, Ltd.
Pearson Educación de Mexico, S.A. de C.V.
Pearson Education—Japan
Pearson Education Malaysia, Pte. Ltd.

Library of Congress Cataloging-in-Publication Data
Domash, Harry.
 Fire your stock analyst! : analyzing stocks on your own / Harry Domash.
  p. cm.
 Includes index.
 ISBN-13: 978-0-13-701023-3 (pbk. : alk. paper)
 ISBN-10: 0-13-701023-0 (pbk. : alk. paper) 1. Investment analysis. I. Title.
 HG4529.D66 2009
 332.63'2042—dc22
                                    2009029538

To my loving wife Norma, who has read every word of this book more than once.

Contents

Acknowledgments

Guru Acknowledgments

I want to thank each of the following professionals for sharing their time and insights with me. The strategies described in this book were inspired by their comments and strategies. As you read the book, you'll recognize their ideas in every chapter. Our conversations were quite lengthy, and each could fill a chapter. The following is a very condensed abstract. These are in no way a complete representation of their strategies; they're merely interesting tidbits that came out of the conversations.

John Buckingham

Al Frank Asset Management
Laguna Beach, California

John Buckingham is president and chief portfolio manager of money manager Al Frank Asset Management and editor of the *Prudent Speculator* newsletter. Buckingham follows classic investment strategies, buying underpriced firms with long-term track records and holding them as long as it takes. Buckingham views everything in terms of cycles and likens value investing to farming in that "You plant the seeds and then wait for them to blossom." Buckingham relies on a firm's historical performance as a guide to the future. He prefers firms with plenty of cash in the bank, strong cash flow, and low debt. Buckingham favors the price/sales ratio to measure value.

Jim Chanos

Kynikos Associates
New York, New York

Jim Chanos is the famous short seller who was the first to blow the whistle on Enron in January 2001. Short sellers are ardent fundamental analysts, and Chanos ranks among the best. Chanos expends most of his efforts analyzing the balance sheet instead of the income statement. He compares capital expenditures to depreciation charges to see if a company is adequately replenishing its assets. He sees receivables and/or inventories growing faster than sales as a red flag. Chanos considers the frequent occurrence of nonrecurring charges an indicator of poor management quality.

Michelle Clayman

New Amsterdam Partners
New York, New York

Michelle Clayman founded and runs private money management firm New Amsterdam Partners. Clayman has a strong quantitative bent. She derives her analysis criteria by studying historical data. Clayman considers multiple instances of nonrecurring charges, and receivables or inventories increasing faster than sales, as red flags. She requires high return on equity of her candidates.

Jim Collins

Insight Capital Management
Walnut Creek, California

Jim Collins runs investment management firm Insight Capital Management and publishes *OTC Insight*, a top-rated investment newsletter. He employs a quantitative screen comparing stock performance to volatility to define an initial list of candidates, and then he picks the fundamentally strongest from that group. Collins emphasized that sales, not earnings, are the best measure of growth. He looks to the stock charts—specifically, weakening relative strength—for his sell signals. He also considers high valuations compared to the company's own historical values a red flag.

David Edwards

Heron Capital Management
New York, New York

David Edwards is president and primary portfolio manager of private money management firm Heron Capital Management. Edwards, a growth investor, relies mostly on fundamental analysis, but he also watches the price charts to help with the timing of his buy and sell decisions. He emphasized the importance of picking the leading companies in growing market sectors, and his thoughts on how to do that inspired much of what you'll find in Analysis Tool #4, Industry Analysis. Edwards looks to a firm's own historical ratios to establish valuation, rather than to the overall market or its industry. He prefers firms with strong operating cash flow and high return on equity. He believes that for proper diversification, portfolios should contain at least 32 stocks, with no more than 25 percent in any one sector. Edwards follows a strict selling discipline, and my "When to Sell" sections reflect many of his ideas.

Nicholas D. Gerber

Ameristock Funds
Moraga, California

Nicholas Gerber is manager and founder of the Ameristock Fund. Gerber is primarily a large-cap investor with a bent toward value. Gerber introduced two important concepts to me. One, the Porter Five Factor Model, was the inspiration for Analysis Tool #5, Business Plan Analysis. His concept of gauging the growth rate inferred by a stock's valuation inspired the implied growth analysis strategy featured in Analysis Tool #2, Valuation. Gerber uses return on equity to measure profitability, but he double-checks it by requiring book value to grow at the same rate.

Louis Navellier

Navellier &Associates
Reno, Nevada

Louis Navellier, founder and president of the firm bearing his name, publishes several newsletters, runs mutual funds, and manages money. Navellier selects stocks by first running a screen that compares stock performance to volatility, and then he picks the fundamentally strongest from that list. Navellier bases his fundamental analysis on a computer-run analysis of his database to determine the factors that are the best stock selectors in the current market. He shared his recent research with me, and that information helped form the strategies described in this book.

Paul Rabbitt

Rabbitt Analytics
La Quinta, California

Paul Rabbitt is president of stock analysis firm Rabbitt Analytics. Rabbitt uses a computerized database to rank companies, giving them what he terms a Q-Rank. The highest scoring Q-Rank companies show strong relative strength, recent positive earnings surprises, and strong and accelerating earnings growth. Rabbitt was one of the only market experts I interviewed who doesn't use return on equity as a selection criterion. In fact, Rabbitt mentioned that he had recently removed ROE from his criteria list because he found that it didn't help.

Peter Schliemann

Rutabaga Capital Management
Boston, Massachusetts

Peter Schliemann founded private money manager Rutabaga Capital Management. A value manager, Schliemann looks for unloved, under-followed companies in run-of-the-mill businesses that are going through a rough patch. Schliemann believes in the concept of regression to the mean, and he seeks out companies with below-normal profit margins. He focuses on return on capital as a profitability measure, and he seeks out firms with the biggest difference between ROC and cost of capital. Schliemann looks for positive cash flow and avoids companies that are growing by acquisition. He prefers firms where insiders are buying the company's stock with their own money. Schliemann compares a stock to its own history to gauge when it's overvalued or undervalued. He prefers low-expecta-tion stocks, meaning that they have low institutional ownership, few analysts covering the stock, and even fewer buy recommendations. He sees rising receivables, increasing provisions for bad debt, deteri-orating cash flow, and increased borrowings as sell signals.

Susan Schottenfeld

Formerly of TCW Investment Management Company
Los Angeles, California

Susan Schottenfeld, former comanager of the TCW Galileo Value Opportunities Fund, introduced me to the concept of "looking through the valley to the next peak." It's the foundation of value investing—at least the interpretation I've adopted for this book. Schottenfeld sought out companies selling at the low end of their his-torical P/E range based on normalized earnings. She attempted to discover if the company is different now than it was two years ago; that is, is the problem temporary? She looked for catalysts such as new management, better capacity utilization, and divesture of bad units, and she preferred candidates with strong free cash flow. She sold when a firm's stock price reached fair value, or if she noticed a big jump in receivables, inventories, or accounts payables. She would also sell if a competitor was having trouble or if she noted significant insider selling.

Kenneth Shea

Bloomberg
New York, New York

Kenneth Shea was director of equity research at Standard & Poor's when I interviewed him. Shea, mostly growth-stock-oriented, believes that you have to apply different rules depending on where a firm is in its cycle. For instance, although he believes in the impor-tance of free cash flow, he doesn't apply that requirement to fast growers. Shea also considers it important to understand a candidate's business model. He considers management quality an important factor and is wary of companies growing by acquisition. Shea looks for companies with low margins that can improve. He sees slowing revenue growth, as well as big nonrecurring charges, as red flags.

Nancy Tengler

Formerly with Fremont Funds
San Francisco, California

When I interviewed her, Nancy Tengler was president and chief executive officer of Fremont Investment Advisors and co-portfolio manager of Fremont's New Era Value Fund. Although she's a value manager, Tengler didn't mind taking some pages out of the growth manager's playbook. For instance, she preferred stocks with analyst coverage and strong operating margins. Tengler's favored valuation ratio was price/sales ratio, not by itself, but compared to the S&P's price/sales ratio, which she calls the relative price/sales ratio. She compared her relative price/sales ratio to historical values and used it as her primary buy/sell signal. Tengler tracked capital spending to ensure that a company is replenishing its assets. Tengler's somewhat offhand comment that "When value investors sell, they sell to growth investors" gave me tremendous insight into the relationship between the value and growth styles.

John C. Thompson

Thompson Investment Management
Madison, Wisconsin

When I interviewed him, John C. Thompson comanaged the Thompson Plumb Growth Fund. Thompson believes that every company has some years that are better than others, and he looks for firms currently growing slower than their historic rate. Thompson introduced me to the concept of earnings leverage, meaning that a small increase in revenues can lead to a big improvement in profits when a company is operating close to its breakeven point. Thompson looks for firms with no debt and lots of cash. He's a big believer in what he terms free cash flow, but he defines cash flow as excluding changes in working capital, along the lines of EBITDA. Thompson places great importance on understanding a firm's business model.

Thatcher S. Thompson

Gonzaga University
Spokane, Washington

When I interviewed him, Thatcher Thompson was a Merrill Lynch analyst specializing in the business services sector. Factors he considered important were revenue visibility, each company's position vis-à-vis the competition, sales growth and earnings growth, margins, cash flow versus net income, and low debt. Thompson's red flags included negative earnings surprises and/or reduction in guidance, departure of the CFO, growth by acquisition combined with declining margins, and declining cash flow combined with rising receivables.

Geraldine Weiss

Investment Quality Trends
La Jolla, California

Geraldine Weiss, after publishing her *Investment Quality Trends* newsletter for more than 30 years, was about to retire when I interviewed her. Weiss' strategy hinged on tracking blue-chip stocks' dividend yields. My own research confirmed that hers was a market-beating strategy. In our interview, Weiss stressed the importance of strong institutional sponsorship. In fact, if my notes are correct, she said, "There is never too much institutional ownership."

Academic Acknowledgments

This section is a brief review of academic research that contributed to the strategies described in this book. In the intervening years since I compiled the results of these studies in 2002, many additional studies have been published that drew similar conclusions. I'm unaware of any recent research that refutes the findings outlined here:

- "Earnings Quality and Stock Returns: The Evidence from Accruals," Konan Chan, Louis K. C. Chan, Narasimhan Jegadeesh, and Josef Lakonishok. Working paper, January 2001.

Accruals result from increases in inventory and accounts receivable levels and from decreases in accounts payables. This study found that firms showing an increase in earnings accompanied by a large increase in accruals underperform in the three years following the high-accrual year compared to the previous three years. The study found changes in inventory to be the most important accrual factor for predicting future returns.

The study noted that since accrual increases are accompanied by corresponding cash flow decreases, the increase in accruals could be detected by comparing cash flow to earnings. That is, earnings increase, but cash flow doesn't.

- "Value Investing: The Use of Historical Financial Statement Information to Separate Winners from Losers," Joseph D. Piotroski, *Journal of Accounting Research*, Vol. 38, No. 3, Supplement 2000.

  Piotroski found that applying simple financial health tests using financial statement data to eliminate weak companies can significantly improve the performance of value portfolios.

- "Earnings Surprises, Growth Expectations, and Stock Returns, or Don't Let an Earnings Torpedo Sink Your Portfolio," Douglas J. Skinner and Richard G. Sloan. Working paper, April 2001.

  This paper found that growth stocks exhibit a much larger negative response to negative earnings surprises than value stocks. The study found that "it is the disappointment per se and not its magnitude that is important to stock market participants." The authors say, "When earnings news is positive, growth stocks outperform value stocks, but that when growth stocks disappoint, they underperform value stocks by substantially more than they outperform when the news is good."

- "Characteristics of Price Informative Analyst Forecasts," Cristi A. Gleason and Charles M. C. Lee. Working paper, September 23, 2000.

  This paper found that stocks with analyst forecast revisions move in the direction of the revisions, but only if, in the case of positive changes, the revised forecasts are also above the consensus forecast. The study found that the effect also worked the opposite; that is, negative forecast revisions sink the stock price if the revised forecasts are below the consensus. The study found that the "magnitude of the revision is relatively unimportant."

- "Cash Flow Is King: Cognitive Errors by Investors," Todd Houge and Tim Loughran, *Journal of Psychology and Financial Markets*, Vol. 1, No. 3 and No. 4, 2000.

  This article found that high-cash-flow firms significantly outperform low-cash-flow firms.

Special Acknowledgment

I would like to thank Standard & Poor's Institutional Market Services unit, particularly J. P. Tremblay, Director, Investment Products, and analyst Jerome Blanchette for providing me with historical data derived from S&P's COMPUSTAT database. S&P's data very much facilitated my research.

About the Author

Harry Domash is best known for his investing tutorial columns that have appeared regularly in print publications such as *Business 2.0 Magazine*, the *San Francisco Chronicle* and other newspapers, and on numerous websites including MSN Money and Morningstar.

He publishes DividendDetective.com, a site specializing in high-dividend investing, and WinningInvesting.com, a free site featuring "how to" investing tutorials and other resources. Domash conducts fundamental analysis workshops and is a frequent speaker at Money Show investing seminars in Las Vegas, San Francisco, and at the American Association of Individual Investors' meetings. His books include *The Everything Online Investing Book: How to Use the Internet to Analyze Stocks and Mutual Funds*.

Introduction

This is a book about analyzing stocks.

It is not a get-rich-quick kind of book. I have no magic formulas to tell you about. I wrote it for people who know that making money in the stock market takes more than running a screen or watching CNBC. This book is for investors willing to put in the time and effort it takes to find and research profitable stock investments.

The process of writing this book turned out to be a huge educational experience for me. I thought I knew something about the subject when I started. After all, I'd been teaching it, writing about it, and doing it for years.

I had pored over scores of investing how-to books by famous and not-so-famous gurus and studied their teachings. I meticulously researched how I would have fared if I had followed their strategies. Based on their work, I synthesized and tested my own strategies.

In the process of researching this book, I interviewed 15 professional money managers and market analysts. I had never met any of them when I started. I found some because they managed best-in-class mutual funds with solid long-term market-beating performance records. Others were market analysts or private money managers practicing innovative strategies I'd heard about from other professionals or through their own writings. About half of those I contacted graciously agreed to talk to me.

In truth, I may have misled them. They probably thought I was writing one of those books that feature a single guru per chapter, a sort of mini-biography describing their childhood, working style, office environment, and investing methods.

I didn't do any of that. I focused our conversations on just three areas: how they identify investment candidates, how they analyze them, and how they decide when to sell.

I had interviewed money managers before, but not at that level, and not in this context. It was an on-the-job learning experience, and I flubbed the first couple, in terms of asking the right questions. But after a while, I got the hang of it.

Interviewing a money manager is a lot different from reading a book he's written or hearing him speak. For starters, you don't have to go over the same ground if you've already read his works or heard descriptions of his methods. Instead, you can zero in on the details, asking questions such as: How do you define overvalued? How do you identify good management? How do you pinpoint an industry's strongest player? What are your sell signals?

Often the conversations took me to unexpected places. For instance, I was unaware of Porter's Five Forces Model before Nicholas Gerber gently brought it to my attention. (By the time Ken Shea mentioned it a week or so later, I responded as though it were old news.) The Porter model inspired the business plan evaluation strategy that became Analysis Tool #5.

Some interviews led me to academic research that I'd always assumed was just too, well, academic to be of interest. That's how I discovered the work of University of Chicago Business School professor Joseph Piotroski, whose research inspired the fiscal health exam featured in Chapter 10.

Perhaps my biggest surprise concerned value investing. I'd read books that were packed with data proving that low P/E stocks outperform glamour stocks, but I could never make it work in practice. The low P/E stocks just kept getting cheaper after I bought them. After interviewing several money managers, it hit me that what they did bore little resemblance to what I'd read about value investing. They weren't buying low P/E stocks. They were buying successful companies that had stumbled! There's a world of difference between those two approaches.

The wealth of information that these market experts and researchers so kindly shared with me forms the basis of what follows. But being an ungrateful sort, I didn't give them their deserved recognition by describing each of their strategies separately. Rather, I distilled them into the combined analysis tools and strategies that make up this book.

What's in This Book

I've read many investing books filled with great concepts and strategies that left me feeling unfulfilled, because they didn't tell me how to put those wonderful ideas into practice. This book describes practical step-by-step strategies for finding, researching, and evaluating investment candidates. Equally important, it also tells you when to sell.

I describe two step-by-step strategies—one for growth stocks, and the other for value investors. Some experts advise that the two are, in fact, similar strategies. While it's true that you can have a value-priced growth stock, the two analysis processes are very different. When value investors are selling, growth investors are buying. So it's unlikely that the value and growth investors would own the same stock at the same time. While the two strategies are different, they draw on a common set of analysis tools.

What's Different?

This book isn't a rehash of conventional wisdom and familiar strategies. The methods described make use of information readily available to anyone connected to the Internet, but in new ways, including the following.

How to Gauge the Risk of Owning a Specific Stock

In the past, investors relied mostly on past price share performance (beta) to determine the risk of owning a stock. But in the end, stocks move in response to changes in a company's earnings prospects. A price chart shows you history; analyzing fundamentals can help you see the future. You'll discover how to use those fundamentals to evaluate the risks specific to each stock.

Analyzing the Analysts

Recent events demonstrate that you can't depend on analysts' recommendations to make money in the market. But there's still much to be learned from their ratings and forecasts.

What a Stock's Valuation Tells You

Knowing the expectations implied in a stock's valuation tells you much about the rewards versus risks of owning the stock.

How to Set Target Prices

This is something that the pros always do, but nobody ever told you how.

Industry Analysis

Has your candidate picked a market worth pursuing? If so, are you riding the winning horse?

Business Plan Analysis

Is your candidate more like Wal-Mart or Kmart? Analyzing its business plan will help you find out.

Financial Fitness Evaluator

Bankruptcies are bad news for stockholders, but nobody ever told you how to find out if your stock is a bankruptcy candidate.

How to Use Sale Forecasts

Few investors pay attention to analysts' sales forecasts, or even know that they are available. You'll find out how to use them to identify companies likely to come up short at report time.

Analyze Profitability

Profitability is more than earnings per share. You'll see how to find out if your candidate is really making money.

Detect Accounting Shenanigans

Some executives will do whatever it takes to meet earnings forecasts. You'll read about how to find out if they're cooking the books to do it.

When to Sell

You'll learn specific rules for selling, depending on whether you're a growth or value investor.

Notes on Examples

Many examples compare annual operating characteristics of firms that have different fiscal year-end dates. For the sake of clarity, I used the closest calendar year for the comparisons. For instance, if one company's fiscal year ended November 30, 2007, and another on January 31, 2008, I labeled the annual data for both as calendar year 2007. So while the figures shown may be technically inaccurate, they're close enough to support the point made by the examples.

Accounting Shortcuts

Certain accounting formulas such as return on assets call for determining the average asset totals over the course of a year. Instead, I use the year-end figures because you can pick them directly off the balance sheet instead of having to calculate them. Consistently applying such shortcuts simplifies the calculations and doesn't materially affect your results.

Frequently Mentioned Websites

The following websites are the primary resources necessary to implement the analyses described in this book. Most are referenced throughout the book, so I've listed their web addresses (URLs) here rather than everywhere they appear.

The addresses of additional websites required only for specific analysis strategies are included where they're referenced.

- **Hoover's (www.hoovers.com)**—A good source of easy-to-understand company descriptions and, best of all, a usually accurate list of a firm's top three competitors.

- **Morningstar (www.morningstar.com)**—Morningstar's Five-Year Restated report saves you the trouble of computing the trailing 12 months of operating cash flow, a data item required in the Busted Cash Burner analysis, discussed in Chapter 10. Morningstar's Stock Valuation report listing historical price/earnings, price/sale, price/book, and price/cash flow ratios for the trailing 12 months as well as each of the past 10 years is also unique.

- **MSN Money (http://moneycentral.msn.com)**—One of only two websites I've found that provides detailed financial statement data in a user-friendly format. MSN Money's 10-Year Financial Summary reports are the mainstay of the target price strategy, discussed in Chapter 6.

- **Reuters (www.reuters.com/finance/stocks)**—A good resource for viewing detailed financial statements. Reuters' Ratio report enables you to compare a company's valuation ratios, performance measures, and much more to its market sector, industry, and all the firms making up the S&P 500 Index. Reuters is one of only two websites (Yahoo! is the other) that display analysts' sales (revenue) forecasts for most stocks.

- **Smart Money (www.smartmoney.com)**—The only website I've found that displays quarterly financial statements going back 15 quarters and annual statements going back 10 years. Most websites show only financial statements going back five quarters and five years. Smart Money is one of only a few websites that list EBITDA as a separate line item on its income statements, an item needed to asses financial strength (see Chapter 10).

- **Yahoo! (http://quote.yahoo.com)**—Along with Reuters, one of only two websites that show you analysts' sales (revenue) forecasts. Yahoo!'s Key Statistics report includes most of the data you need to do the Quick Prequalify analysis described in Chapters 1 and 15.

Part I

Getting Started

1

The Analysis Process

Experts tell us that investment success requires a disciplined approach to finding, researching, and analyzing potential investments. This chapter describes one such approach, and the ensuing chapters fill in the details. It's based on sound principles that are practiced by market-beating money managers. It's certainly not the only way, and it may not be the best way. But it's a place to start, and following it will make you a better investor. After you've mastered these strategies, you can modify them to suit your needs.

The process involves identifying potential candidates, weeding out the obvious misfits, researching and analyzing the survivors, picking the best prospects, and, equally important, applying a clear-cut set of selling rules.

Identifying Potential Candidates

Finding stocks to analyze can be as easy as visiting the gym, talking to your neighbors, picking up a magazine, surfing the Internet, or turning on the TV. You'll find no shortage of tips. You'll welcome all such advice once you've gained confidence in your analysis skills, because you'll be able to weed out bad ideas quickly.

As your experience grows, you'll get a feel for how to identify strong candidates. You'll find yourself increasingly taking advantage of screening to uncover investment ideas. *Screening* is a technique for scanning the entire market for stocks meeting your requirements. It's

3

a powerful tool, but to use it effectively, first you have to understand how to identify the best candidates. That will come with time. In the meantime, I've provided a few sample screens in Chapter 3 to get you started.

Treat all names you get, whether from your own screens, friends, TV gurus, or even Warren Buffett, as tips to analyze using the techniques you are about to learn.

Concentrate on the Strongest Candidates

Our analysis techniques utilize a survival-of-the-fittest strategy, which entails weeding out the weakest candidates at every step of the analysis. This strategy works best if you start with a large group of stocks—say, 10 to 20—instead of just a few. Researching stocks takes time and effort. Eliminating weak contenders as soon as you discover them enables you to focus your research on the strongest candidates. Be ruthless. There is no point in wasting time researching stupid ideas.

Quick Prequalify

Use the quick prequalify test to rule out the obvious misfits. These may be stocks that would be bad news for any investor. Perhaps they're firms with businesses based more on hype than reality, with little or no sales or earnings. Or they could be stocks that simply don't fit your investing style. For instance, perhaps they're worthwhile value candidates, but you're a growth investor.

Here's what's included in the quick prequalify tests:

- **Company and industry overview**: Learn about the company's business and industry. It may be in a market sector that you favor or one that you want to avoid. For instance, some pundits say that demand for crude oil will exceed supply for the foreseeable future, driving up all energy prices. Others disagree. So your take on that topic would influence how you view deepwater drilling companies and energy stocks in general.

- **Market capitalization** defines a company's market value. It's how much you'd have to pay to buy all the shares. The biggest firms are designated large-caps, and progressively smaller firms are termed mid-caps, small-caps, and micro-caps.

  There is no good or bad market capitalization, but each size has its own potential risks and rewards. Generally, larger companies are safer investments, but smaller firms offer more growth potential. That said, even these generalities vary with market conditions.

  You may decide that a particular company size range best suits your needs or, conversely, that you're open to all possibilities. Whatever you decide, in this step, rule out the candidates that don't fit your requirements.

- **Valuation ratios** such as price to earnings (P/E) or price to sales (P/S) tell you how market participants view a stock. High valuations reflect in-favor stocks with strong growth expectations. Thus, they appeal to growth investors. Conversely, value players look for stocks with low valuation ratios, indicating that most market players (growth investors) view them as losers.

  Any given candidate will fit into either the growth or value category, but not both. The valuation ratios give you a quick read as to whether you have a value or growth candidate on your hands.

- **Trading volume** is the average number of shares traded daily. Low-trading-volume stocks are a bad idea because they're subject to price manipulation. Further, mutual funds and other big players can't buy them. Here's where you'll toss these bad ideas.

- **Float**: Corporate insiders such as key executives and board members are restricted as to when and how often they can buy and sell their company's shares. So, insider-owned shares are considered unavailable for trading. The float is the number of outstanding shares that insiders don't own, and thus are available for daily trading.

  Acceptable float values depend on your investing style. Large firms typically have floats running from a few hundred million shares into the billions. However, investors looking for stocks with maximum growth potential often seek out stocks with much smaller floats, typically below 25 million shares. With relatively few shares available, small float stocks could take off like a rocket when the company reports good news and the demand for shares overwhelms the available supply.

- **Cash flow**: While reported earnings reflect myriad accounting decisions, cash flow is the cash that actually flows into, or out of, a company's bank accounts from its operations. Because it's based on actual bank balances, cash flow is the best measure of profits.

  Except for the fastest growers, viable growth candidates should be reporting positive cash flow, meaning that cash is flowing in, not out. Thus, this is the step where growth investors would rule out cash burners. On the other hand, value investors would take a longer view and overlook negative cash flow triggered by short-term problems.

- **Historical sales and earnings growth**: Whether you're seeking out-of-favor value prospects or hot growth candidates, your best prospects are firms with a long history of solid sales and earnings growth. In this step, you'll dispose of stocks that flunk this basic requirement.

- **Check the buzz**: There's no point wasting time researching a stock if its main product has just been rendered obsolete by the competition. This is where you catch up on the buzz surrounding your candidate. If you're looking for growth stocks, negative buzz is bad news and disqualifies them. For value prospects, negative buzz reflects the market's disenchantment with the stock, thus making it a better value candidate.

You will eliminate many of your bad ideas during this quick prequalify check. Once you get the hang of it, you'll be able to run each stock through this test in less than five minutes. Take your survivors on to the detailed analysis.

Detailed Analysis

Part II of this book, containing Chapters 4 through 14, describes 11 different stock analysis tools that can be applied to both the value and growth investing styles. Chapter 16 describes how to apply these tools to analyze value candidates. Chapter 17 does the same thing for growth candidates.

The value and growth analysis strategies both consist of 11 steps, each step using the corresponding analysis tool. For instance, Step 7 involves analyzing a candidate's financial health and employs Tool #7, Analyze Financial Fitness.

You'll get the best results by familiarizing yourself with each of the 11 tools described in Part II before attempting to analyze value and/or growth candidates.

Eliminate a candidate as soon as it fails any step. For example, don't carry a candidate to Step 2 if it fails Step 1.

Step 1: Analyze Analysts' Data

Brokerages and other firms employ stock analysts to evaluate and rate stocks. Start your detailed analysis by reviewing analysts' buy/sell recommendations and earnings and revenue forecasts to determine the market's enthusiasm for your candidate. The best value candidates are stocks that analysts don't like. Conversely, growth investors need to see some, but not too much, enthusiasm for their candidates. The Sentiment Index, described in Chapter 4, is a useful tool for gauging analysts' enthusiasm.

Analysts' earnings growth forecasts are another measure of a stock's suitability as a growth or value candidate. Strong forecast earnings growth disqualifies value candidates but identifies good growth prospects.

Step 2: Valuation

Valuation is an important issue for both growth and value investors, but for different reasons. If you're looking for growth, checking valuation tells you whether you've arrived too late at the party. For value candidates, valuation analysis tells you whether the upside potential justifies the risk.

Step 3: Establish Target Prices

Value investors typically set target prices to establish buy and sell points for qualified stocks. For instance, a stock may appear to be an attractive candidate, but a target price analysis might find that its current share price is too high to offer the needed risk/reward ratio. If so, the value investor might wait for the stock to come down in price before buying. It isn't bought if it doesn't reach the required buy price. Once purchased, the stock is sold when it reaches its calculated sell price range.

Although setting buy and sell targets is a linchpin of the value strategy, growth investors could benefit by going through the same analysis. Tool #3, Establish Target Prices, makes it easy.

Step 4: Industry Analysis

For growth investors, companies operating in fast-growing market sectors make the best candidates. By contrast, value investors find the best prospects in slower-growing markets. In this step, you analyze your candidate's industry growth prospects and related factors. If you're looking for growth candidates, picking an attractive industry is all for naught if you pick the wrong player. Consequently, the industry analysis also describes how to pick the strongest player in an industry.

Step 5: Business Plan Analysis

Wal-Mart dominates the retail industry, while former champ Kmart has fallen by the wayside. The difference is in the business models. In this step, you determine if your candidate is more like a Wal-Mart or a Kmart.

Step 6: Evaluate Management Quality

Many money managers consider gauging management quality an important part of the analysis process. You don't have time to visit candidates' plants and schmooze with key executives, and you don't have to. You can evaluate management quality from the comfort of your own home by reviewing the relevant experience of key executives and directors, measuring the firm's accounting quality, and completing other easily accomplished checks.

Step 7: Analyze Financial Fitness

You lose big if one of your stocks files for bankruptcy. But it doesn't have to go bankrupt to ruin your day. Just the rumors that it might are enough to sink its share price. Stock analysts typically don't check a firm's financial strength before advising buying. That's why so many advised buying Fannie Mae, Freddie Mac, Lehman Brothers, and other recent bankruptcies just months before they failed.

You don't have to be a victim. You can measure any public corporation's financial health using the strategies described in this step.

Step 8: Profitability and Growth Analysis

In the long run, stock prices follow earnings. In this step, you analyze sales and profitability trends to determine whether your stock's earnings are more likely to head up or down from here. You also find out if your candidate is really profitable or just gives the appearance of making money.

Step 9: Detect Red Flags

You lose big when your stock reports disappointing results or management cuts growth forecasts. Those disasters usually don't come without warning, however. In this step, you check for red flags signaling future disappointments so that you can act ahead of the news.

Step 10: Ownership Considerations

It may not be fair, but it's a fact of life that mutual funds and other institutional buyers have access to better information than individual investors. Thus, it makes sense to see what the big players think of your stock before you buy.

Insiders are directors, key officers, and large investors. While it's good when key officers and directors hold big positions in the company, too much insider ownership signals danger.

This is where you sort out institutional and insider ownership data to determine if it's favorable or unfavorable.

Step 11: Price Charts

It's against the law, but sometimes investors who are privy to market-moving news about a company's prospects act on that information before the news gets out. When that happens, the stock's price action might be your first clue that something is going on.

In this step, you learn how to find out whether the stock chart is signaling that it's okay to buy.

Analysis Scorecards

Chapter 18 includes separate scorecards for growth and value analysis candidates. Make copies and fill out the appropriate scorecard when you analyze a stock. You'll be amazed how just filling out a scorecard will improve your results.

When to Sell

For many, determining when to sell is more difficult than deciding what to buy. When things go wrong, it's easy to procrastinate on selling while you wait to see if your stock moves back up tomorrow.

Establishing a strict sell discipline is an effective antidote for seller's procrastination. However, in many instances, a condition triggering a sell signal for growth stocks wouldn't apply to value stocks. For example, a cut in earnings forecasts triggers an automatic sell for growth investors, but it wouldn't faze a value player. Conversely, a strong price chart would be good news for growth investors but might trigger a value stock sell signal.

Both the value and growth analysis chapters include sell rules specific to each style with no wiggle room.

Summary

Following an organized approach to finding, researching, buying, and selling stocks will make you a better investor. Now that you know where we're heading, read on to get started.

2

Evaluating Risk

Risk is the probability of losing money. All stocks are risky compared to government-insured savings accounts, but some stocks are much riskier than others. Yet investors rarely evaluate the inherent risks when contemplating buying a stock. But it makes sense to do so. Here's why.

Suppose that you are considering two stocks, and your analysis shows that both could double in price over the next two years. But Company A's stock is twice as risky as Company B's. Knowing that, the choice between Company A and Company B becomes obvious.

Portfolio Risk

You can reduce your overall risk by diversifying your investments over a variety of stocks in diverse industries.

The airline and oil industries provide a classic example. Increasing oil prices translate to high profits for the oil industry, but the resulting increases in fuel costs depress airline profits and hence airline stock prices. Conversely, airlines tend to do better when fuel prices drop and the oil industry is suffering.

Opinions vary on the number of different holdings required for adequate diversification. Some say that you can achieve adequate diversification with as few as 12 stocks, while others say as many as 40 or 50 different holdings are required. Diversify as much as possible, and, above all, avoid investing more than 25 percent of your funds in any one sector, such as energy, healthcare, or financial.

Does Low Valuation Equal Low Risk?

Several academic studies found that portfolios made up of low-valuation stocks—say, those with low P/E ratios—outperformed higher-valuation portfolios. However, in many of those studies, just a few strong stocks skewed the results. In fact, most of the stocks in those portfolios lost money.

In my experience, it depends on market conditions. Sometimes growth stocks outperform, and in other markets, value stocks do best. In either case, you can't assume that lower-valued stocks are less risky than pricier stocks.

Risk Factors

When you evaluate individual stocks, your risk hinges on these three issues:

- Overall market risk
- Industry risk
- Risks specific to your stocks

We'll examine overall market and industry risks and then move on to evaluate the risks specific to individual stocks.

Market Risk

Even if you're a great stock picker, it's tough making money holding stocks in a bear, or downtrending, market. On the other hand, you can make lots of mistakes and still rake in profits in a strong market. That's where the market expression "Don't mistake a bull market for brains" came from. Consequently, overall market risk is an important factor in the risk equation.

Of course, predicting future stock market direction requires knowing which way the overall economy is heading, as well as interest rates, inflation, and a host of other factors. Economists spend their careers trying to discover the answers to these questions, usually without much success.

If you want to try your hand at predicting the economy, Appendix B lists 14 web resources that will help you do so.

Otherwise, you can get a handle on market risk by looking at two easily determined factors: Is the market currently undervalued or overvalued? and Is the market currently moving up or moving down?

Market Valuation

Several studies have found that the difference between the market's valuation and prevailing interest rates can be a good market risk indicator. It's an inverse relationship. In other words, low prevailing interest rates support higher market valuations.

Most analysts use the S&P 500 Index as a proxy for the entire market and use the S&P's price to earnings (P/E) ratio to gauge valuation. The S&P 500's P/E ratio is the market-weighted average P/E of the stocks making up the index. Market-weighted means the bigger the firm in terms of market capitalization, the more weight that is given to its P/E in the calculation.

The easiest way to gauge valuation is to invert the S&P's P/E, which gives you earnings yield. For instance, the yield is 5 percent if the P/E is 20 (1/20 = 0.05, or 5%). Then compare the market yield to prevailing interest rates, typically the three-month U.S. Treasury bill rate.

Usually the market yield is higher than the T-bill rate. What's important is the spread (difference) between the two rates. The market gets dangerous when the market yield is close to or drops below the T-bill rate (the spread is low or negative).

Table 2-1 compares market yields, the three-month T-bill rate, and the spread between the two as of December 31, going back to 1984. The table also shows the following year's S&P 500 index returns.

For example, Table 2-1 shows that as of December 1994, the market yield was 1.0 percent higher than the T-bill rate, and the S&P 500 moved up 34 percent in the next 12 months.

As is the case with most market indicators, comparing the market earnings yield to the T-bill rates doesn't always work, but it's clear that negative spreads signal higher risk than positive spreads. That makes sense, because negative spreads result from low market yields, which correspond to high market valuations (high P/Es).

TABLE 2-1   Market Yields, T-Bill Interest Rates, the Spread Between the Two, and the Following Year's S&P 500 Index Return

Date	Market Yield (E/P)	Three-Month T-Bill	Spread	Following Year's S&P Return
12/08	5.0%	0.1%	4.9%	
12/07	4.5%	3.4%	1.1%	–38%
12/06	5.7%	5.0%	0.7%	4%
12/05	5.6%	4.1%	1.5%	14%
12/04	4.8%	2.2%	2.6%	3%
12/03	4.4%	1.0%	3.4%	9%
12/02	3.1%	1.2%	1.9%	26%
12/01	2.2%	1.7%	0.5%	–23%
12/00	3.8%	5.9%	–2.1%	–13%
12/99	3.3%	5.3%	–2.0%	–10%
12/98	3.1%	4.5%	–1.4%	20%
12/97	4.1%	5.4%	–1.3%	27%
12/96	5.2%	5.2%	0.0%	31%
12/95	5.5%	5.1%	0.4%	20%
12/94	6.7%	5.7%	1.0%	34%
12/93	4.7%	3.1%	1.6%	–2%
12/92	4.4%	3.2%	1.2%	7%
12/91	3.8%	4.0%	–0.2%	5%
12/90	6.5%	6.6%	–0.1%	26%
12/89	6.5%	7.8%	–1.3%	–7%
12/88	8.6%	8.4%	0.2%	27%
12/87	7.1%	5.9%	1.2%	13%
12/86	6.0%	5.8%	0.2%	2%
12/85	6.9%	7.3%	–0.4%	15%
12/84	10.0%	8.1%	1.9%	26%

Market Direction

Sizing up the current market direction gives you a heads-up as to whether it makes sense to invest new money or stay on the sidelines. A strong uptrend gives you a green light to add to positions, while a strong downtrend advises caution.

Since many investors rely on the S&P 500 to represent the market, the easiest way to gauge market direction is to compare the index to its 200-day moving average (MA), as shown in Figure 2-1. If the S&P is above its 200-day MA, it's probably in an uptrend, and vice versa. The distance between the index and its moving average reflects the trend strength. The trend is strong if the index is far above or below its moving average. It indicates a trendless or consolidating market if the index is hovering near, or crisscrossing, its moving average.

Figure 2-1   Using MSN Money to display a chart of the S&P 500 Index and its 200-day moving average. Consider the market in an uptrend when the index is above its moving average.

The S&P 500 Index reflects the action of large-cap stocks in a wide variety of industries. Other indexes may provide better indications, depending on the particular market sector you're considering. For instance, the NASDAQ reflects the action of tech stocks, and the Russell 2000 index better shows how small-caps are faring.

A variety of other indexes are available to show the action of mid-caps, value or growth stocks, or individual industries.

StockCharts.com (www.stockcharts.com) is a good place to find these indexes. Click Market Summary (Free Charts) to see the complete list.

It's best to avoid buying stocks in a downtrending market unless they belong to an industry sector showing strength despite the market.

Spotting Strong Industries in a Weak Market

No matter how weak the market, you can usually find stocks in some industries that are bucking the trend. For instance, when I wrote this section in March 2009, the markets were in a funk. General Motors was facing bankruptcy, and major banks were teetering. Yet, at the same time, stocks in gold mining and the oil and gas exploration and production industries, and stocks in emerging markets, such as Brazil and China, were racking up gains.

I didn't have to spend hours digging out that information. I found everything I just described and more by taking advantage of features of exchange-traded fund (ETF) reports that are readily available at no charge on Morningstar and MSN Money. You can use these reports to pick up on major market trends in the beginning stages.

As you may know, ETFs are similar to index mutual funds in that they replicate the returns of predefined stock indexes. However, unlike mutual funds, ETFs trade just like stocks. You can buy or sell them at any time during market hours.

Interest in ETFs has soared in recent years, and the ETF industry has responded by creating new funds to track just about every conceivable index. You can find ETFs that track value stocks, Russian stocks, oil prices, insurance companies, healthcare stocks—you name it. In fact, it's hard to imagine an industry or market segment that isn't represented by one or more ETFs.

You can download reports from both Morningstar and MSN Money that list all ETFs, including their total returns (price appreciation plus dividends) for periods ranging from one week (MSN Money only) to five years. Here's the best part. By clicking the corresponding column header, you can sort the entire list by any of the provided return time frames. For instance, if you click four-week returns (4-Wks), you see the entire ETF list sorted with the last four weeks' top-returning funds listed at the top and the biggest losers at the bottom, as shown in Figure 2-2.

Name	Ticker	Category	Holdings	Morningstar	Last Price*	1-Wk	4-Wks
B2B Internet HOLDRs	BHH	Specialty - Technology	holdings		$0.35	-5.66	29.63
iPath DJ AIG Tin TR Sub-Idx ETN	JJT	Specialty - Natural Resources			$29.50	1.11	27.63
iShares MSCI Thailand Invest Mkt Index	THD	Diversified Emerging Markets	holdings		$29.97	2.32	27.05
Market Vectors Indonesia ETF	IDX	Diversified Emerging Markets	holdings		$37.00	-0.98	24.80
ELEMENTS BG Large Cap ETN	BVL	Growth			$7.50	0.00	22.21
Market Vectors Coal ETF	KOL	Specialty - Natural Resources	holdings		$20.24	-11.42	21.49
Claymore/Clear Global Timber Index	CUT	Specialty - Natural Resources	holdings		$13.06	-8.35	20.81
PowerShares Global Wind Energy	PWND	Specialty - Natural Resources	holdings		$13.65	-6.38	20.16
Rydex S&P Smallcap 600 Pure Value	RZV	Small Company	holdings	★★★★★	$20.75	-13.03	19.25
BearLinx Alerian MLP Select Index ETN	BSR	Specialty - Natural Resources			$28.42	4.50	19.23
ELEMENTS BG Small Cap ETN	BSC	Small Company			$7.67	-2.51	19.15
Ultra Silver ProShares	AGQ	Specialty - Precious Metals	holdings		$44.25	0.02	18.82
Global X/InterBolsa FTSE Colombia 20 ETF	GXG	Growth and Income	holdings		$19.43	-0.36	18.69
PowerShares Global Coal	PKOL	Specialty - Natural Resources	holdings		$17.77	-9.32	18.26
iShares MSCI Turkey Invest Mkt Index	TUR	Diversified Emerging Markets	holdings		$33.16	0.73	17.97

Figure 2-2   A portion of the MSN Money ETF Performance chart sorted by four-week returns

Thus, you can easily spot market trends, whether they involve countries, industries, types of stocks (large-cap growth, small value), commodity prices, or whatever. By comparing returns over shorter and longer time frames, you can see which market segments are rotating into, or out of, favor.

Company-Specific Risks

Company-specific risks relate to a firm's business plan, stock valuation, profitability, accounting practices, growth strategy, and other factors particular to the company, rather than to its industry or the overall market.

Some of the risks listed in the following sections are serious enough to disqualify a candidate from further consideration and are identified as such in the description. Others are less severe and, by themselves, would not disqualify the stock. However, in the end, you'll do best by picking the candidates with the fewest risk factors.

Products on Allocation

Companies selling products into markets where demand exceeds supply can fill only a portion of each customer's order until the firm can ramp up its production. Customers soon figure out that they must order two or three times what they really need to get sufficient product. They often stockpile inventory to make sure that they don't run short. The resulting exaggerated order rate causes analysts, investors, and company officials to overestimate demand.

Eventually production catches up, and customers begin receiving full instead of partial orders. Because they overordered, they find themselves overstocked, and they start canceling orders. This scenario invariably plays out faster than everyone expects. Martek Biosciences provides a good example.

Martek produces nutritional products from microscopic organisms called microalgae. It so happens that microalgae contains certain acids that, when added to infant formula, aid in the development of the eyes and central nervous system. That's a big deal. By mid-2003, Martek had licensed nine infant formula makers to include its patented additive in their products. Martek was producing product at a $100 million or so annual pace, but it couldn't keep up with demand, and it had to put its customers on allocation. This situation continued until early 2005, when production caught up with demand. In April of that year, Martek said it had discovered that its customers had been inflating earlier purchase orders to receive higher allocations. By its July 2005 quarter, Martek's formerly blistering year-over-year quarterly sales growth had morphed into an 18% year-over-year drop.

Litigation

Large corporations are almost always being sued—sometimes by disgruntled employees or customers, sometimes by other corporations over patents or other issues, and sometimes by shareholders upset because they lost money on the stock. These lawsuits are part of the costs of doing business and usually do not affect your analysis. However, sometimes a company is involved in a lawsuit that could materially affect its business prospects or even threaten its survival.

More than 40 corporations were forced into bankruptcy by asbestos lawsuits. Accounting and auditing giant Arthur Anderson was driven out of business by litigation stemming from its involvement in the Enron fiasco. A firm doesn't have to actually lose a lawsuit; just the threat of major litigation can trigger a large share price drop.

Corporations must disclose all significant lawsuits in their quarterly and annual reports. Management, of course, routinely says that all such claims are without merit. Nobody, certainly not company management or stock analysts, can predict the outcome of a lawsuit. Avoid all stocks facing litigation with a potentially costly outcome.

Restates Earnings

A company usually restates earnings when its auditor or the Securities and Exchange Commission (SEC) finds that its earlier reported earnings were too high. Any significant downward earnings restatement is a red flag signaling that the company has been practicing creative accounting to enhance its reported earnings. Circumstances vary, but just because it was caught once doesn't mean management has changed its ways. Avoid firms that have significantly restated earnings downward unless new management is now in charge.

The Sector Outlook Diminishes

Earnings disappointments or reduced guidance from one company in a market sector warns that all companies in the same market face similar problems.

The teen apparel retail sector in late 2008 affords a good illustration. On September 4, Abercrombie & Fitch, a major player, dropped after reporting that August same-store sales (sales at stores open at least one year) had fallen 11 percent from the year-ago figure. Abercrombie's share price dropped 5 percent on the day of the announcement and continued down from there. In fact, the news dropped its share price by 25 percent over the next five days.

Analysts, however, blamed Abercrombie's management for the sales shortfall and continued to recommend buying rival American Eagle Outfitters, which targets the same market. American Eagle's share price didn't budge on Abercrombie's announcement, giving Eagle's shareholders plenty of time to bail out before the firm got around to confessing that its sales were lagging year-ago figures on October 8.

Interest Rate Risk

Interest rate changes, or even the prospect of changes in rates, usually move the market. The market perceives rising interest rates as bad for stocks in general, and such events usually move the market down. Interest-sensitive industries, such as home builders, utilities, and all companies carrying high debt, can be especially hard hit when rates rise. Banks and others in the financial sector suffer when the spread between short- and long-term interest rates narrows.

Conversely, energy, healthcare, and technology stocks often outperform the market in rising interest rate environments.

Interest rate change, actual or prospective, in the direction that works against a particular company's industry sector adds risk but is not necessarily a disqualifying factor.

Company-Specific Risks Described in Subsequent Chapters

The following sections describe company-specific risk factors that are discussed in more detail in Part II.

Financial Health

Company failure is the most disastrous stock ownership risk you face. Shareholders typically lose their entire investment when a company files for bankruptcy. Don't even think about buying a stock without first checking its financial health to make sure that it's not a bankruptcy candidate. Chapter 10 tells you how.

Business Plan/Growth by Acquisition

Some companies are better investment prospects than others because they have superior business plans. They may address markets with little competition, produce products seen as superior by consumers, have better distribution methods, and so on.

You can't assume that a firm has a viable business plan just because it's publicly traded and analysts recommend buying its stock. The dot-com bust illustrated that, given the right circumstances, firms with little chance of success can raise billions of dollars from eager investors, both amateur and professional.

A firm's growth strategy is an especially important factor to consider when analyzing a business plan. Most firms grow by developing new products, opening new stores, and so forth. However, some resort to an acquisition strategy to maintain growth after they've saturated their original markets. Early successes implementing this strategy lead to overconfidence. Eventually the company makes a bad acquisition, its results fall short of expectations, and the shortfall sinks its share price. Because it was issuing shares to pay for the acquisitions, the lower stock price devalues its acquisition currency, further slowing growth, which puts more pressure on the share price.

Chapter 8 describes how to evaluate a business plan, including how to spot companies growing mainly by acquisition. That chapter includes a scorecard for evaluating business plans. Possible scores range from −11 to +11. Candidates with negative scores are riskier than those with positive scores, but a negative score is not by itself a disqualifying factor.

Valuation

The market often bids up profitable companies in exciting indus-tries to unrealistic valuations, making them risky investments despite their strong prospects. Eventually most firms trade at prices reflect-ing their long-term growth prospects. You can determine the annual earnings growth rate implied by a stock's current valuation using the methods described in Chapter 5. Few firms grow earnings as much as 40 percent annually for sustained periods, and most don't achieve anywhere near that rate. Consider stocks with implied earnings growth of 30 percent or higher as risky bets, but high valuation by itself is not necessarily a disqualifying factor.

Faltering Growth/Creative Accounting

Young companies exploiting emerging market opportunities often experience explosive growth in their early years. The market expects that growth to continue indefinitely and prices the firm's shares accordingly. Those early growth rates are unsustainable, and company management sometimes resorts to accounting shenanigans to maintain the illusion of growth when real growth slows. Eventually the house of cards collapses, earnings fall short of expectations, and the stock price crumbles. Chapter 12 describes how to spot red flags signaling slowing growth and the accounting shenanigans that fre-quently mask faltering growth. Avoid stocks showing any red flags.

High Expectations

Unmet expectations lead to disappointment, and the market reacts by hammering the offending company's stock price. The higher the expectations, the greater the chance of disappointment. Conse-quently, high expectations equate to high risk. Chapter 4 describes how to calculate a Sentiment Index score based on analysts' buy/sell recommendations. Sentiment Index values of 9 or higher indicate risk, but high Sentiment Index scores alone are not a disqualifying factor.

Summary

Professionals always evaluate the risks intrinsic to a prospective stock purchase, and you should too. Be wary of investing in overvalued markets or in downtrending markets or sectors. There are thousands to choose from, so disqualify stocks with risk in the areas of product allocation, litigation, earnings restatement, sector outlook, financial health, and creative accounting. The existence of any of the less serious risk factors makes a stock less desirable. In terms of risk, "less is more."

3

Screening

Stock screeners are programs, usually accessed through websites, that allow you to search the entire market for stocks meeting your specific requirements. Screening is the most efficient way to find stock candidates, because you can tailor your screens to filter out undesirable stocks, permitting you to focus your research on worthwhile candidates. Screening is an art that requires practice to get it right. When you first try a new screen, it will turn up too many or too few candidates. When you get the right number—say, 20 or so—you'll find that you don't like most of them. Eventually you'll devise a set of screening parameters that gives you a manageable list of candidates worth researching.

While many financial websites offer screening programs, a surprising number are poorly designed, apparently by people who have never bought a stock. Often, the screening parameters don't make sense. For instance, who would want to screen for stocks that earned exactly $3.50 per share last year? In other instances, the screening parameters simply don't work.

I've found four free screening programs that are mostly reliable, although even some of these have quirks you need to know about. I've listed the four screeners in order of ease of use, with the simplest listed first:

- Morningstar
- Google
- Zacks
- Portfolio123

Morningstar

Morningstar's free Stock Screener offers only 18 screening criteria. However, that number is misleading. Morningstar allows you to search for stocks based on its proprietary "stock grades." Morningstar grades stocks from A to F in three categories: growth, profitability, and financial health. Morningstar combines a number of separate fundamental factors to compute each grade. Thus, it would probably take 20 or 30 separate screening parameters to replicate what you get by using the three grades.

Also unique to Morningstar, you can search for stocks based on eight different categories (stock type), such as "distressed," "speculative growth," and "high yield." Furthermore, you can choose to narrow your search to one of nine different "equity styles," such as "large value," "mid-growth," and "small core."

You can find Morningstar's Stock Screener from its homepage (www.morningstar.com) by going to the Tools section and selecting Stocks and then Stock Screener.

Google

Google's Stock Screener offers more than 50 screening parameters in seven different categories. Even so, it's still very simple to operate. That said, the rocket scientists who designed Google's program probably don't invest in stocks much.

For instance, the Price category includes search parameters, such as "200d avg price," more commonly known as the "200-day moving average." Unfortunately, all you can do is screen for stocks with 200-day MAs between minimum and maximum values that you specify. You can't screen for stocks trading above or below their moving average (MA), which is how you use such parameters.

Those complaints aside, Google's screener is a good bridge between Morningstar's ultra-simple Stock Screener and the more powerful Zacks and Portfolio123 screeners. From Google Finance (http://finance.google.com), click the "stock screener" link next to the Get Quotes button.

Zacks

Zacks Investment Research specializes in analyzing how changes in analysts' buy/sell ratings and earnings forecasts move share prices. Its Custom Stock Screen provides more than 125 screening parameters. More than 50 of them involve analyst buy/sell ratings and earnings forecasts. Despite its power, the Zacks screener is still relatively user-friendly.

Select Screening from Zacks' homepage (www.zacks.com), and then select Custom Stock Screener (Screening Tools) to get to the screener. Once there, click a Category to see the search parameter choices available for that group.

Portfolio123

Portfolio123 (www.portfolio123.com) offers, arguably, the most powerful free web screener available. It may take you some time to learn how to use it, but it's worth the effort.

Once you've figured it out, Portfolio123's screener will become your best stock market friend. It's the only free screener that allows you to compare data values. For instance, you could search for stocks with debt/equity ratios below the industry average, or for stocks with gross margins higher than their five-year industry average. Unlike the other screeners, you can save your Portfolio123 screens, an important feature that spares you the time and effort of entering your search parameters every time that you want to rerun a screen. It's easy to modify existing screens or add new ones.

For a $29 or $49 monthly fee, depending on which options you select, Portfolio123 offers backtesting, which gives you a way of trying your stock-picking ideas without risking real money. For example, say you've decided that the key to success is finding stocks with P/E ratios between 25 and 30 that grew sales at least 25 percent over the past year. You could use Portfolio123's backtesting feature to find stocks that would have met your criteria had you run the screen at some point in the past—say, two years ago. Portfolio123 tells you how you would have fared had you bought those stocks two years ago.

You'll probably devise your own screens after you've read this book. But here are a few sample screens to get you started and demonstrate how the screening programs work.

Google Growth Screen

This screen seeks out cash-rich, debt-free, profitable, and reasonably priced stocks that are in favor with the smart money.

From Google Finance (http://finance.google.com), click the "stock screener" link next to the Get Quotes button. When you get there, Google displays a default screening program using four of the 60 or so available criteria (selection choices). Start by deleting all but the Market-Cap criterion (click the X to the right of each criterion you want to delete).

Company Size: Market Capitalization

Specify a $1 billion minimum market cap.

Smaller companies are usually riskier than larger companies. They typically offer less diverse product lines, weaker balance sheets, and less experience dealing with economic downturns. Thus, you can reduce your risk by avoiding very small firms. Most investors use market capitalization, which is how much you'd have to shell out to buy all of a firm's shares, to measure company size.

Firms with market caps below $2 billion are termed small-caps, and those above $8 billion are large-caps. Those in between are mid-caps. I set my minimum market cap at $1 billion. Try reducing your minimum to $500 million (500M) if you want to see more stocks, or increasing it to $5 billion if you want to cut your risk.

Valuation: Price/Sales Ratio

Specify a minimum P/S ratio of 2 and a maximum of 7.

The price/sales ratio is similar to the more familiar price/earnings (P/E) ratio, except that it compares the current share price to the last 12 months' per-share sales instead of per-share earnings.

The screen avoids stocks with P/S ratios below 2 because those stocks are more likely value candidates than growth stocks. On the downside, setting that minimum rules out supermarket chains and other low-profit-margin businesses. The way the math works, stocks with low profit margins also have low P/S ratios. Change your minimum P/S requirement to 1 if you want to see such stocks.

Price/sales ratios can run as high as 10, and sometimes much higher for in-favor growth stocks. Specifying a maximum 7 P/S avoids overpriced stocks. Since I arbitrarily picked that number, try increasing it to 8 or 9 if you want to see more stocks, or cut it to 5 or 6 if you want to cut your risk.

Cash-Rich: Current Ratio

Specify a 2.5 minimum.

Given the recently fragile credit markets, the slightest hint of a cash shortage can sink a stock. Thus, it's important to reduce the odds of that happening to your stocks. Using the current ratio to check a firm's cash position is the first of two selection criteria I use to achieve that goal.

The current ratio compares current assets such as cash, inventories, and accounts receivables to short-term debt such as payroll expenses and other current bills. A ratio of 1 means that current assets equal liabilities, while a 2 ratio means that current assets are double current liabilities. Setting the minimum allowable current ratio at 2.5 ensures that passing firms have plenty of cash. Although I arbitrarily picked that number, I don't see much advantage in upping that minimum, and I certainly wouldn't lower it.

Add the current ratio requirement to the screen by selecting Add Criteria, and then Financial Ratios, and finally Current Ratio.

No Debt: Total Debt/Equity Ratio

Specify a 0.1 maximum (most recent quarter).

Refinancing debt is still problematic for all but the top credit-rated corporations. You can avoid such issues by limiting your picks to stocks carrying no long-term debt. To do that, you can use the total debt-to-equity ratio, which compares the total of short- and long-term debt to shareholders' equity (book value).

While it's tempting to specify a 0 ratio, I set my maximum at 0.1 to avoid ruling out firms carrying incidental debt items, such as lease obligations on their balance sheets.

Profitable: Return on Equity

Specify a 20% minimum (TTM).

Unless you're looking for beaten-down value stocks, your best candidates are always profitable firms as opposed to money losers. Return on equity (ROE) measures profitability by comparing net income to shareholders' equity (book value). Most money managers that I know require a minimum 15 percent ROE. However, here I require a minimum 20 percent ROE to focus on the most profitable candidates. Try cutting your minimum to 15 percent if you want to see more stocks.

Follow the Money: Institutional Ownership

Specify 40% minimum institutional ownership.

Institutional buyers such as mutual funds and pension plans are more wired into the market than individual investors. If they don't own a stock, you shouldn't either. "Institutional ownership" is the percentage of a firm's shares held by those big players. The best growth candidates are stocks that are in favor with the smart money. Institutional ownership ranges from 40 to 95 percent for in-favor stocks.

Growth Rules: Five-Year Revenue Growth

Specify 10% minimum five-year revenue growth.

Growth stocks, by definition, should be growing sales and earnings at least 15 percent annually, and more is better. However, the 2008–2009 economic setback tripped up even the best growth stocks. Given the volatile environment, revenues are a steadier growth gauge than earnings. I take a long view by using the five-year figure. Usually, you want to see at least 15 percent average annual revenue growth. But, considering the tough economy, I required only 10 percent.

Results

Ideally, this screen should turn up 15 or 20 strong growth candidates. If it doesn't, modify the parameter values as suggested to increase or decrease the number of hits.

Zacks Growth/Momentum Screen

Momentum investors, such as hedge fund managers, search for growth stocks that are already outperforming the market. But that's not enough. The underlying companies must be profitable and have already racked up strong growth. There's even more. Momentum strategies require pinpointing the stocks in this already-hot group that are getting hotter. That is, earnings forecasts are increasing.

Find the Custom Stock Screener by selecting Screening on the Zacks homepage (www.zacks.com). Select a parameter category, and fill in the required information for the parameters you want to use (leave the others blank). To help you find the screening parameters, I've listed the corresponding category name in parentheses in the following sections.

After you specify a search parameter, be sure to click Add to add it to your screen. (Parameters listed without an Add button are unavailable on the free screener.) Zacks displays your selected search criteria near the top and indicates how many stocks meet your current screen requirements.

Small, But Not Too Small: Market Capitalization

Specify a $250 million minimum

(>=) market cap (Size & Share Volume).

Usually, you'll find the best momentum prospects among smaller stocks, but don't go overboard on that score. Very small firms are less able to withstand changing market and economic conditions. Most analysts use market capitalization (the recent share price multiplied by the number of shares outstanding) to measure company size.

Stocks with market caps below $2 billion are termed small-caps. Market caps above $8 billion are large-caps, and those in between are mid-caps. I arbitrarily set my minimum market cap at $250 million. Try cutting that limit to $200 million, or even $150 million, if you want to see more stocks. Raise it to $500 million if you want to cut your risk.

Follow the Money: Institutional Ownership

Specify a 40% minimum (>=) held by institutions (Ownership).

Institutions are mutual funds, pension plans, and other big investors. By virtue of the huge trading commissions they generate, institutional investors have access to inside information we'll never see. Thus, if they don't own a stock, you shouldn't either. Institutional ownership is the percentage of a firm's stock held by those big players. It runs from 40 percent to 95 percent for in-favor growth stocks. Specify 40 percent minimum institutional ownership.

Analyst Buy/Sell Ratings: Current Broker Recommendation

Specify a maximum (<=) 3.0 (Broker Rating).

Stock analysts publish buy/sell recommendations on the stocks they follow. Zacks compiles the analysts' advice into strong buy (1), buy (2), hold (3), sell (4), and strong sell (5) categories. It assigns the value shown in parentheses to each category. For instance, if all analysts were at strong sell, the consensus rating would be 5. Since, if anything, analysts tend to be overoptimistic, it pays to avoid stocks that they are advising selling. Specify "hold" or better, which equates to a maximum rating of 3.

Expected Earnings Growth: Long-Term Growth Consensus Estimate

Specify a minimum (>=) 15% (EPS Growth).

Analysts also publish estimates for long-term (three to five years) average annual earnings growth for stocks they follow. I require a

minimum 15 percent. Consider increasing that minimum to 20 percent, or even 25 percent, if you want to limit your search to only the
hottest prospects.

Profitable: Return on Equity

> Specify a minimum (>=) 15% (Return on Investment).

In any market, you'll always do best by sticking with profitable
companies. Return on equity (income divided by book value) is the
most widely used profitability measure. For profitable companies,
values typically range from 5 percent to 25 percent, where higher is
better. Most money managers require at least 15 percent ROE, so
specify a minimum 15 percent current ROE.

No Debt: Debt/Equity Ratio

> Specify a maximum (<=) 0.1% (Liquidity & Coverage).

In this market, the last thing you need is a high-debt stock. The
debt/equity ratio, which compares long-term debt to book value, is a
popular debt measure. A 0 D/E signals no debt, and the higher the
ratio, the higher the debt. Specify a maximum 0.1 debt/equity ratio,
which is just high enough to avoid precluding companies with minor
incidental debt.

Earnings Estimate Trend: % Change F1 Estimate (4 Weeks)

> Specify a minimum (>=) 5% (EPS Estimate Revisions).

Research done by Zacks and many others has found that changes
in analyst earnings estimates move share prices. Stocks tend to move
up after estimates increase, and vice versa. Furthermore, once earnings estimates have moved, they tend to move further in the same
direction. Thus, stocks with recent positive earnings estimate changes
have better price appreciation potential than those that don't. Zacks'
"% Change F1 Estimate (4 weeks)" parameter tracks the last four
weeks' percentage change in current-year consensus earnings forecasts.

Strong Price Chart: Relative Price

Specify a minimum (>=) 1.5 (Price & Price Changes).

Contrary to the familiar "buy low, sell high" mantra, stocks that have already outperformed the market are more likely to continue their winning ways than other stocks. Conversely, stocks that have underperformed will probably continue to disappoint shareholders.

Zacks' Relative Price Change parameter compares the year-to-date price change of each stock to the S&P 500. A relative price of 1 means that a stock has performed equal to the S&P, while an RP of 2 means that the stock has doubled the S&P's price appreciation. My 1.5 minimum requirement means that passing stocks must have moved up at least 50 percent more than the index. Since RP measures year-to-date price action, the same values will give you different results in January than in December.

Portfolio123 Down & Out Value Stock Finder

This screen uses Portfolio123's unique capabilities to find companies with strong historical sales growth and profitability histories that have recently stumbled.

Although registration is free, you must be a Portfolio123 member to use the screener. After you've registered (select the free member option), click the Screener tab, and then click New to set up a new screen. Here's a brief rundown on how to use the screener.

Portfolio123 calls each screening term a "rule." For instance, if you wanted to limit your results to stocks trading for more than $10 per share, you could set up your first rule as follows:

price > 10

If you're rusty on algebraic terminology, the > symbol means "greater than." The >= symbol means "greater than or equal to," and the <= symbol means "less than or equal to." Finally, the symbol * means "multiply."

Thus, if you wanted to confine your list to stocks with market caps of $900 million or lower, your rule would look like this:

MktCap <= 900

Portfolio123 lists its screening parameters in the Rule Reference section near the bottom of the page. Select Stock Factor to see all available individual stock screening criteria. Click a category name such as Price & Volume to see the available parameters in that category. Then click a specific factor, such as Beta, to see Portfolio123's definition for that factor. For instance, the definition for MktCap is "Market Capitalization ($ millions)." Double-click the factor name to insert it into a screening rule. Figure 3-1 shows the screening rules for the Down & Out Value Stock Finder.

Save	Save As...	Revert	Copy to Universe...	Report ⑦	Screen Factors ▾
⊙ ⚒ ⇨ ▲ ▼	ROA%5YAvg>=10
⊙ ⚒ ⇨ ▲ ▼	ROA%TTM <=0.7* ROA%5YAvg
⊙ ⚒ ⇨ ▲ ▼	Pr2SalesTTM<=1.5
⊙ ⚒ ⇨ ▲ ▼	DbtLT2EqQ <=0.5
⊙ ⚒ ⇨ ▲ ▼	QuickRatioQ>=1.1
⊙ ⚒ ⇨ ▲ ▼	AvgVol (60) >=50000
⊙ ⚒ ⇨ ▲ ▼	SalesTTM>=50
⊙ ⚒ ⇨ ▲ ▼	Sales5YCGr%>=10
⊙ ⚒ ⇨ ▲ ▼	Sales%ChgPYQ<=0.5* Sales5YCGr%
⊙ ⚒ ⇨ ▲ ▼	AvgRec>=3

Figure 3-1   Portfolio123 Screening Rules for the Down & Out Value Stock Finder

After you've set up one or more rules, click Totals to see how many stocks meet your screening requirements.

The following sections describe the details of setting up the Down & Out Value Stock Finder screen.

Strong Long-Term Profitability: Return on Assets: Five-Year Average

ROA%5YAvg >= 10

Return on assets (ROA; net income divided by total assets) is a profitability measure. The higher the ROA, the more profitable the company. The average ROA for all stocks is in the 7 to 8 range. This term requires a minimum value of 10 for five-year average ROA, limiting the list to stocks recording above-average long-term profitability.

Try increasing the minimum to 15 if you want to see only candidates with stronger profitability numbers.

Depressed Current Profitability: Return on Assets

$$ROA\%TTM <= 0.7 * ROA\%5YAvg$$

This term finds companies with currently depressed ROAs compared to their historical average, a desirable trait for value candidates.

Specifically, it requires that the current (trailing 12 months) ROA must be no higher than 70 percent of the average ROA over the past five years. Try cutting the multiplier to 0.5 if you want to limit the field to stocks with recent profitability ratios of only half of their long-term average.

Value Priced: Price/Sales Ratio

$$Pr2SalesTTM <= 1.5$$

Price/sales is a valuation ratio similar to the P/E ratio, except that it compares the current share price to the last 12 months' per-share sales instead of per-share earnings. P/S ratios below 1.5 typically define value-priced stocks, while higher ratios identify growth stocks. This term sets the maximum P/S ratio for passing stocks at 1.5. Try cutting the maximum to 1.0 if you want to limit the field to deep-value stocks.

Say No to High Debt: Debt/Equity Ratio

$$DbtLT2EqQ <= 0.5$$

The debt/equity ratio compares long-term debt to shareholders' equity (book value). Zero ratios signal no debt, and the higher the ratio, the higher the debt. Most value candidates are established companies that have accumulated some debt. Setting a 0.5 maximum D/E rules out debt-heavy companies.

Sufficient Cash: Quick Ratio

QuickRatioQ >= 1.1

The quick ratio compares the total of cash and accounts receivables to current liabilities. The ratio is 1.0 when cash and receivables equal current liabilities. The ratio would be 2.0 if cash plus receivables were double current liabilities. Requiring a minimum 1.1 ratio rules out firms facing a short-term cash crunch. Try raising the minimum to 2.0 if you want to see only cash-rich companies.

Actively Traded: Average Daily Volume Last Quarter

AvgVol (60) >= 50000

The average daily trading volume reflects the number of shares traded daily. This term limits the field to stocks trading at least 50,000 shares daily, on average, over the past 60 days. Requiring a 50,000 daily volume precludes lightly traded stocks, which are subject to price manipulation and other problems.

Real Sales: 12-Month Revenue

SalesTTM >= 50

Most publicly traded corporations rack up sales exceeding $100 million annually. This term requires a minimum of $50 million in sales over the past 12 months, ruling out firms without meaningful sales.

Long-Term Grower: Five-Year Revenue Growth

Sales5YCGr% >= 10

Companies can't grow without growing sales. This term requires that passing stocks must have recorded at least 10 percent average annual sales growth over the past five years. This requirement, combined with the next test, ensures that although they are currently down and out, qualifying firms have a reasonably strong historical sales growth history.

Sales Growth Slowdown: Revenue Growth Quarter Versus Quarter

Sales%ChgPYQ <= 0.5 * Sales5YCGr%

Limits passing stocks' recent quarter's year-over-year sales growth (Sales%ChgPYQ) to 50 percent of their five-year average annual growth rate (Sales5YCGr%). This requirement identifies companies with recent sales growth below long-term trends, a hallmark of promising value stock candidates.

Out of Favor: Analyst Buy/Sell Mean Rating

AvgRec >= 3

Services such as Reuters compile analyst ratings for each stock into five categories and assign the numeric value shown in parentheses to each category: strong buy (1), moderate buy (2), hold (3), moderate sell (4), and strong sell (5).

The best value candidates are out of favor with most market players, including analysts. This term requires that the consensus analyst rating must be hold (3) or worse. Try changing the minimum rating value to 3.5 if you want to limit the field to only the most out-of-favor stocks.

Portfolio123 Growth Stock Screen

This screen uses Portfolio123's screener to find strong earnings growth stocks that are already outperforming the market. Not long-term buy-and-hold candidates, these stocks are only suitable for a strong market.

Not Too Small: Market Capitalization

MktCap >= 400

All else equal, smaller companies are riskier bets than larger stocks. Market capitalization, which is how much you'd have to shell out to buy all of a company's shares, is the best way to measure company size. Some risk-averse investors won't go below $1 to $2 billion in market cap. However, many promising growth candidates can be found in the $500 million to $1 billion range. This term rules out stocks with market caps below $400 million. Try raising the minimum to $1 billion if you want to reduce your risk.

Low Debt: Total Debt to Equity

DbtTot2EqQ <= 0.1

The best growth candidates carry little or no debt and are loaded with cash. The total debt/equity ratio compares the total of short- and long-term debt to shareholders' equity (book value). A 0 D/E signals no debt, and the higher the ratio, the higher the debt. Typically, firms with D/E ratios above 0.5 are considered high debt. This term limits the field to firms with a maximum 0.1 D/E ratio. Try raising your maximum D/E to 0.2 if you want to see more stocks.

Loaded with Cash: Quick Ratio

QuickRatioQ >= 2

The quick ratio compares current assets readily converted to cash (cash plus accounts receivables) to current liabilities. A quick ratio of 1 means that current cash equals current liabilities. This term requires a minimum 2 quick ratio, which means that cash plus receivables must be double current liabilities.

Profitable: Five-Year Average Return on Assets

ROA%5YAvg >= 10

Profitability measures shareholders' return on investment. Whether you're looking for growth or value stocks, you'll always do best by sticking with the most profitable companies. ROA compares net income to total assets. The higher the ROA, the more profitable the company. This term requires a minimum 10 ROA, which rules out low-profitability stocks. I use the five-year average ROA because the recent economic slump tripped up even normally profitable companies.

In Favor: Analyst Buy/Sell Rating

AvgRec <= 2

Services such as Reuters compile analyst ratings for each stock into five categories and assign the numeric value shown in parentheses to each category: strong buy (1), moderate buy (2), hold (3), moderate sell (4), and strong sell (5).

The best growth candidates are in favor with most market players, and analyst buy/sell ratings are the best gauge of a stock's popularity. This term requires that passing stocks must be rated at moderate buy (2) or better by most analysts.

Good Growth Prospects: Forecast Long-Term Growth

LTGrthRtMean >= 15

Given enough time, share prices more or less track earnings growth. So, all else equal, stocks with the strongest earnings growth usually do the best. Many analysts forecast long-term (five-year) average annual earnings growth for stocks they cover. This term requires that analysts must be forecasting at least 15 percent average annual long-term earnings growth for passing stocks. Consider raising that to 20 percent if you want to limit your list to the hottest candidates.

Not Too Cheap: Recent Price

price >= 15

Stocks changing hands at low trading prices usually got that way because most market players see problems ahead. Whether they are right or not, cheap stocks are riskier than more expensive stocks.

For that reason, many growth stock money managers avoid stocks trading below $15. This test requires that passing stocks meet that criterion.

Strong Long-Term Price Chart

price >= 1.20 * SMA(200)

Valid growth candidates should be in strong uptrends. You can judge whether a stock is trending up or down by comparing its current share price to its moving average (average closing price over a specified number of trading days). Stocks trading above their moving averages are said to be in an uptrend, and those trading below their MAs are in a downtrend. The distance that a stock is trading above or below its moving average reflects the trend strength.

The 200-day moving average works well for measuring long-term trends. This term requires that a passing stock must be trading at least 20 percent above its 200-day MA, signaling a strong uptrend. Try cutting that requirement to 15 percent above the 200-day MA if you want to see more stocks, but don't go below that figure.

Strong Medium-Term Price Chart

$$price >= 1.05 * SMA(50)$$

The 200-day test ensures that passing stocks are in long-term uptrends. This test uses the 50-day moving average to isolate stocks that are in medium-term uptrends as well.

Because the 50-day MA tracks the share price closer than the 200-day MA, this test only requires that a stock be trading 5 percent above its 50-day average. In terms of trend strength, this is equivalent to trading 20 percent above its 200-day average. Try cutting the margin to as low as 1 percent above the 50-day MA if you want to see more stocks.

Zacks' Bulletproof Stocks

Whether or not your stock actually files for bankruptcy, just the rumors will be enough to drive the share price into the ground. This screen uses the Zacks' Stock Screener to find stocks that are unlikely to be bankruptcy candidates anytime soon.

Unless they're filing for bankruptcy to avoid big lawsuits, companies fail for only one reason: They've run out of cash. Avoiding bankruptcy candidates comes down to developing a set of requirements that cash-starved companies can't possibly meet. That's the goal of this screen. I call the survivors "bulletproof stocks." Here are the bulletproof stock qualifications:

- Maximum 0.1 debt/equity ratio
- Minimum 2.0 quick ratio
- Positive operating cash flow
- Positive net income
- Current share price at least $5
- Annual sales at least $50 million

The debt/equity and quick ratios limit the field to cash-rich firms with virtually no debt—at least as of the end of their last reporting period.

The positive operating cash flow requirement, in theory, eliminates cash burners. But it's not foolproof. Insisting on positive net income helps ensure that the company is, in fact, profitable.

Stocks usually trade below $5 per share when most market players see serious fundamental problems. Limiting the field to stocks trading above that level helps ensure that the firm's fundamental outlook hasn't seriously deteriorated since it published the debt, cash, and cash flow numbers that form the basis of this analysis.

The $50 million annual sales requirement rules out companies that look good on paper but, in reality, have no substantial business.

You can find the Custom Stock Screener by selecting Screening on the Zacks homepage (www.zacks.com). To help you find the screening parameters, I've listed the corresponding category name in parentheses in the following sections.

Debt/Equity Ratio

debt/equity ratio <= 0.1 (Liquidity & Coverage)

The debt/equity ratio compares long-term debt to shareholders' equity (book value). Zero values reflect no long-term debt, and the higher the ratio, the higher the debt. Setting the maximum allowable D/E at 0.1 instead of 0 allows companies with incidental debt items such as long-term leases to pass the test.

Quick Ratio

quick ratio >= 2.0 (Liquidity & Coverage)

The quick ratio compares the total of cash on hand plus accounts receivables to current liabilities. Specifying a minimum 2.0 ratio means that cash plus receivables must be at least double current liabilities.

Operating Cash Flow

cash flow (millions) >= 0.001 (Income Statement & Growth)

Operating cash flow is the actual cash that flowed into or out of a firm's bank account. Unlike reported earnings, which are subject to myriad accounting decisions, it's hard to fudge the cash flow numbers. All we're looking for here is that cash flowed in, not out. We don't care about the numbers.

Net Income

net income (millions) >= 0.001 (Income Statement & Growth)

In theory, the positive operating cash flow requirement should be sufficient to ensure that passing stocks are profitable, on a cash basis. But you can't underestimate the creativity of motivated accountants. Checking for positive net income helps ensure that the firm is profitable.

Current Price

current price >= 5 (Price & Price Changes)

Cheap stocks are usually cheap for good reason. This check helps rule out stocks that look good based on the most recent quarterly report, but, in fact, are facing serious problems.

Annual Sales

annual sales >= 50 (Income Statement & Growth)

Zacks' annual sales parameter actually totals the sales from the last four reported quarters. Requiring $50 million sales during the last 12 months filters out companies that aren't real businesses.

The screen should turn up at least 300 bulletproof stocks. Zacks doesn't give you a way to print the list directly, so use the "export" function to download the results into an Excel spreadsheet.

The Zen of Screening

It takes some practice to become proficient at screening. When you run your first screens, you'll probably come up with no hits, because you've specified too many parameters and/or made your requirements too tight. When that happens, it's hard to figure out which search parameters are causing the problem.

It's easier to go the other way. That is, start with just a few parameters and relatively loose requirements so that you get too many hits. Then add parameters and tighten requirements one by one until your screen comes up with a reasonable number of candidates to research—say, 15 to 30 stocks.

After you've done some preliminary research, you'll probably be unhappy with many of the stocks in your first group of candidates. If that's the case, modify your screening parameters to disqualify the offending stocks. Repeat the process until your screens produce reasonably sized lists of qualified stocks.

Premade Screens

Some websites offer ready-to-use or premade screens. The advantage of premade screens is you don't have to devise your own search parameters. All you have to do is click and view the results. One problem with premade screens is that you don't have much of a feel for the quality of the screening strategy.

There is an exception. The American Association of Individual Investors (AAII) website (www.aaii.com) offers a large variety of premade screens and tracks their performance over time. AAII, a not-for-profit organization, provides education in the area of stock and mutual fund investing. You have to be a member to access the screening area. Membership is $49 a year and includes a monthly investing magazine that by itself is worth the price. The magazine doesn't tout stocks. It's educational in content and describes stock and mutual fund selection strategies that well-known money managers follow.

When I checked, the AAII website was running 50 or so value, growth, combined growth and value, small-cap, and specialty screens based on the stock-picking strategies of the likes of Benjamin Graham, John Neff, David Dreman, Geraldine Weiss, Warren Buffett, and many more. One AAII screen is based on Joseph Piotroski's value-stock selection criteria that inspired my detailed fiscal fitness exam described in Chapter 10.

AAII runs the screens monthly, so you can see the top stocks picked by each screen as of the end of the past month. AAII also updates each screen's performance figures at the same time and once a year compares the performance of all the screens.

Summary

Screening is the best way to find stock candidates. But coming up with screens that work for you is a process of trial and error. However, like so many things in life, the more you work at it, the better your results.

Consider the results of all screens, whether based on your ideas or the ideas of a guru, as a list of research candidates, not as a buy list.

Part II

Analysis Tools

4

Analysis Tool #1:
Analyze Analysts' Data

Tomorrow, or even next week, your stocks will move up or down, driven more by the winds of the market than fundamentals. But long-term, trading prices usually reflect the market's earnings growth expectations for a stock. All else equal, you make money when expectations rise and lose money when they decline.

And who sets those expectations? Stock analysts.

Sure, analysts have come under fire time and time again for giving bad advice. They told us to buy ridiculously overpriced tech stocks when the market was in bubble territory in 1999 and 2000. In 2001, they urged us to buy Enron shortly before the energy trader collapsed. In 2007 and 2008, analysts were advising buying Fannie Mae, AIG, and oh so many bank stocks even while the credit markets were collapsing.

After all that, analysts' buy/sell ratings and earnings forecasts still mold most investors' expectations for any given stock.

While you're unlikely to make money simply following analysts' buy/sell ratings, plenty of information embedded in those ratings and earnings forecasts can help you make better investing decisions. You just need to know what to look for.

The Sentiment Index described later in this chapter helps you find out whether the stock you've been following would be better viewed as a growth or value candidate. A quick look at earnings growth forecasts and recent earnings surprises tells you a lot about a stock's price appreciation prospects. Finally, you can use revenue forecasts, which most investors ignore, to gauge a firm's real growth prospects.

Who Are the Analysts?

Stock analysts come in two varieties: buy-side and sell-side. Investment bankers, including most full-service brokerages, hire sell-side analysts to write research reports and issue buy/sell ratings and earnings forecasts for stocks they want to follow. Why are they called "sell-side" analysts? Originally, brokerages derived most of their income from commissions on stock sales, and the analyst reports and rating changes encouraged the brokers' customers to trade more. Hence the term sell-side analyst. These days, investment banking accounts for the lion's share of full-service brokerage income, but the sell-side label stuck.

Brokerages employ scores of analysts. Most cover a specific industry such as semiconductor equipment or restaurants. The analysts write research reports on the industry as a whole and on specific companies within the industry. Analysts publish sales and earnings forecasts; buy, hold, and sell recommendations; and target prices for companies they follow. They update those ratings and forecasts whenever one of their companies reports quarterly results, changes guidance (forecasts), or announces other significant news.

Sell-side analysts' ratings and reports are widely distributed. Third parties including Thomson Reuters and Zacks Investment Research tabulate the analyst opinions and publish them in the form of analysts' consensus ratings and forecasts for every covered stock.

Institutional buyers, such as mutual funds, pension plans, and other big players, read the sell-side analysts' reports, but many also employ their own analysts. These "buy-side" analysts do their own research and arrive at their own opinions about a company's prospects. Alas, you and I never see the buy-side analysts' reports.

However, many stockbrokers offer clients access to sell-side analysts' research reports published by one or two investment bankers. Those reports are worth reading if they are available for the stocks you follow.

Analysts usually publish an in-depth report describing the business model, industry, and competitive situation when they first start following a stock. After that, they typically publish short updates after earnings reports and conference calls or when other significant news breaks. The in-depth reports and short updates always include the analysts' current buy/sell recommendation (rating), and earnings and sales forecasts for the current and next quarter and for the current and next fiscal year. Sometimes analysts issue short updates when they change their ratings or forecasts.

Analysts' Ratings

The point of an analyst's report is to advise clients whether to buy or sell a stock. But it's not that simple. Many brokerages use different terminology to express the same opinion.

For instance, Goldman Sachs would put a stock on its Recommended List if it thinks the stock is going up in short order. But Merrill Lynch would simply label it a "buy," JMP Partners would say "strong buy," and Friedman Billings Ramsey would say "outperform." The only way you can be sure of a specific ratings definition is to consult the brokerage's rating explanation, which is usually included near the end of the report.

The terminology is not a problem when you're looking at ratings compiled by Thomsen Reuters or Zacks. They figure out all of that when they sort the ratings into five categories: strong buy, moderate buy, hold, moderate sell, and strong sell.

When you look at the compiled ratings, interpret only strong buy ratings as meaning that the analyst is advising you to buy the stock. Anything short of strong buy means that the analyst is not excited about the stock's prospects and wouldn't add it to his own portfolio.

"Sell" Is a Four-Letter Word

Sell-side analysts are real people like you and me who happen to have very well-paying jobs. You can't blame them for wanting to hold onto those jobs. Their employers, mostly investment bankers, derive much of their profits from helping client companies issue stock, make acquisitions, borrow money, and so forth. How much money is involved? Say an investment banker brings a new company public by underwriting its IPO. The underwriting fee is negotiable, of course, but think 7 percent. So a deal is worth 7 percent of $150 million, or $10.5 million, if the new company issues 10 million shares at a $15 offering price. When one company acquires another, both firms hire investment bankers to advise them on the transaction, incurring fees running into tens of millions of dollars.

With that much money involved, the competition to land these juicy contracts is intense. Naturally, the client—say, a new company going public—picks the investment banker it believes will do the best job, meaning the one who will sell the most shares at the highest price and, equally important, keep the share price up after the IPO. That's important, because company executives own tons of shares they will eventually want to sell. That's where the analyst comes into the picture. A highly regarded analyst's strong buy recommendation can make a big difference in a stock's trading price.

From an investment banker's perspective, most public corporations are potential clients. The top executives running those corporations have plenty of incentives to keep the share price up. They may be on bonus plans tied to the share price, have stock options, or own shares outright.

You can understand why they would take it personally when an analyst's sell rating tanks the share price. But they don't just get mad; they can get even by diverting investment-banking business to another firm. Analysts understand that. Most don't see anything to gain by advising selling a stock. Instead they say hold, neutral, or market perform, and the pros know that means sell.

On occasion, analysts do want to advise selling, but some investment banks don't allow sell ratings. So, the policy of the analyst's employer, not his view of the stock's prospects, determines whether a stock will be rated hold or sell. Bottom line: Interpret hold, sell, and strong sell ratings as sell.

Note

Standard & Poor's analysts are the exception to the "hold means sell" rule. S&P does issue sell ratings, and a hold recommendation means exactly that: Don't sell if you own it, but don't buy it either.

Consensus Ratings

As mentioned, Thomsen Reuters and Zacks compile analysts' individual buy/sell ratings into a single consensus number for each stock. They do that by first assigning each individual rating to one of five categories: strong buy (1), buy (2), hold (3), sell (4), or strong sell (5). Each category has the numeric value shown in parentheses.

The compiler tabulates and averages the individual analyst ratings. For instance, if three analysts all rate a stock strong buy, the total is 3, and the average (the total divided by the number of ratings) is 1. That makes sense, but you need to be careful about how you interpret those numbers.

For instance, the consensus rating for a stock with one strong buy (1) and one hold (3) would be 2 (4/2), equating to a buy, even though neither analyst actually rated the stock a buy. As another example, say that two analysts rate a stock strong buy, and two advise selling. The consensus rating would be hold, even though none of the analysts gave that advice. Table 4-1 illustrates how the ratings are shown on Yahoo!'s Analyst Estimates report.

Despite the shortcomings, compiling consensus ratings this way enables you to get a sense of the ratings trend by comparing older ratings to the current value. For instance, you'd see that analysts are getting more excited about a stock if last month's rating was 2.2 (weak buy) and this month it's 1.8.

Table 4-1   Analysts' Consensus Rating of 2.0 Equates to Buy Even Though None of the Six Analysts Following the Stock Rated It Buy

	Current Month
Strong buy	3
Buy	0
Hold	3
Sell	0
Strong sell	0
Mean	**2.0**

Here's my rule of thumb for interpreting the consensus number:

1.0 to 1.5: Strong buy

1.6 to 2.4: Buy

2.5 to 3.5: Hold

3.6 to 5.0: Sell

Do Strong Buys Outperform Sells?

Since (in theory, at least) analysts spend all day evaluating stocks, making money in the stock market should be as easy as buying "strong buy"-rated stocks. However, little evidence exists to support that assumption.

Research on the subject is inconclusive. Some studies show that hold-rated stocks outperform strong buys, but other studies draw the opposite conclusion. In fact, there's no solid evidence that strong buys even outperform strong sells. Maybe that's because analysts issue many more buys than sells, and analysts can make some really dumb calls.

Think that's an overstatement? Consider residential home mortgage maker American Home Mortgage, which filed for bankruptcy on August 6, 2007, essentially wiping out shareholders.

That was quite a comedown from January 26 of that same year, when AHM's shares were fetching $34, and at least five stock analysts were advising buying the real estate investment trust (REIT).

Just the day before, the home mortgage maker had reported December quarter earnings $0.03 above forecasts. Besides blowing away December quarter estimates, American had captivated analysts with its $5.40 to $5.70 per share earnings forecast for all of 2007, far above the $4.85 analysts had been expecting.

So, on January 26, Deutsch Bank upgraded its rating to "buy" from "hold" and upped its target price by $2 to $34.50. Not to be outdone, RBC Capital reiterated its outperform (buy) rating and hiked its price target to $40 per share.

All of this unfolded against the backdrop of a collapsing residential real estate market. New-home sales were plunging, and on January 25, 2007, the same day that AHM issued its upbeat December quarter report, the news broke that used-home sales fell 8 percent in 2006 versus the year before, the sharpest annual decline since 1989.

Since AHM's business was making mortgage loans secured by single-family homes, you'd think that the health of the residential real estate market would be relevant.

AHM specialized in a special type of mortgage called Alt-A loans. Unlike subprime loans made to borrowers with bad credit, Alt-A loans were supposedly made to borrowers with good credit scores. The catch was that Alt-A borrowers didn't have to document their income, home values, how they obtained the money to make the down payment—anything. As an Alt-A borrower, you could say that you took home $50,000 per month, if that's what it took to qualify for the loan, and not show any check stubs or tax returns to prove it.

All was well as long as homes were selling at ever-increasing prices. Of course, as everybody except the analysts seemed to know, by January 2007, that was no longer the case.

Nevertheless, on January 31, Ryan Beck raised its advice on AHM to "outperform" from "market perform." AHM closed at $35 that day.

To their credit, on February 16, analysts at Bank of America reiterated their negative outlook and advised selling most mortgage lenders, including AHM. B of A seemed like a voice in the wilderness.

Only five days later, on February 21, Friedman Billings Ramsey, commenting on subprime lender NovaStar Financial's disappointing December quarter results and guidance of little or no taxable income until 2011, reiterated its "outperform" rating on AHM. Friedman said AHM was a different story than NovaStar. Despite Friedman's support, AHM shares dropped $1.80 to $30.80.

AHM shares continued drifting down and were changing hands in the $25 range by March 5, 2007, when AHM declared a $1.12 per share quarterly dividend. RBC Capital reiterated its "outperform" rating the next day.

A few days later, on March 14, Lehman Brothers noted that after examining its balance sheet, it had concluded that AHM was in a better position than other mortgage lenders to "manage through this challenging environment."

On April 5, when AHM shares were still changing hands at $25 or so, Bear Stearns, one of the few heroes in this story, cut its rating to "underperform" from "peer perform." Translation: Bear Stearns cut AHM to "sell" from "hold."

Only four days later, on April 9, citing changing market conditions, AHM lowered its March quarter and full-year earnings forecasts by 55 percent and 25 percent, respectively, and said it would cut its next dividend by 38 percent.

On that news, Deutsch Bank, Friedman Billings Ramsey, and Lehman Brothers cut their ratings to "hold," "market perform," and "equal weight," which all translate to "hold," which, of course, means "sell." Citigroup, already at hold, actually did cut its rating to "sell."

With the stock trading at around $22, Citigroup cut its target price to $19, Deutsch cut its target to $24.50, and Lehman cut its target to $20.

Incredibly, on April 11, 2007, with AHM trading at around $22, AG Edwards, citing AHN's safe dividend, upped its rating to "buy" from "hold."

On April 30, with its share price back up to $25 or so, AHM announced March quarter earnings of $0.54 per share, below the year-ago $1.02, but above the $0.46 figure that analysts were expecting.

On May 1, in a public offering, AHM sold 4 million new shares at $23.75. Citigroup, which had set a $19 target price for AHM shares on April 5, handled the offering. Also on May 1, AG Edwards, citing valuation, cut its rating on AHM to "hold." AHM closed at $23.15.

On June 28, AHM said it was establishing additional reserves for delinquent loan repurchases, would likely experience a loss in its June quarter, and withdrew its guidance (forecasts) for 2007. AHM closed at $20.91.

The next day, on June 29, Friedman Billings threw in the towel, cutting its rating to "underperform" and cutting its target to $15. Standard & Poor's, noting that it believed the dividend secure, cut its earnings estimates but kept its "buy" rating (four stars). AHM closed at $18.38 that day.

On July 18, with AHM changing hands at $13 or so, Lehman Brothers, noting that AHM might cut its dividend again, reiterated its "hold" rating.

On July 20, RBC Capital, still rating AHM at "outperform," said it expected the mortgage maker to generate sufficient income to cover a $0.60 per share quarterly dividend. RBC did lower its target price to $20 from $25. AHM closed at $12.80.

On July 30, AHM, citing unprecedented disruptions in the credit markets, said it would delay its next dividend. JMP Securities, Lehman Brothers, and Standard & Poor's cut their ratings to versions of "sell," while RBC Capital cut AHM to "sector perform" from "outperform." AHM closed at $10.47.

On July 31, AHM in essence said it had run out of cash, couldn't pay its current loan obligations, and couldn't borrow more funds. AHM hired advisers to help evaluate its options, which included liquidating its assets. Its share price closed at $1.04.

On August 1, RBC Capital Markets reiterated its "sector perform" rating.

On August 2, AHM fired most of its employees; on August 3, it stopped accepting mortgage applications; and on August 6, it confirmed that it had filed for Chapter 11 bankruptcy.

The moral of the story is you're on your own; you can't rely on analysts to make your buy and sell decisions for you. But don't go away. Important information can be gleaned from analysts' ratings and forecasts.

Number of Analysts

Each analyst following a stock works for a different brokerage or investment banker. One brokerage may employ thousands of stock-brokers, and each of those brokers may have dozens, if not hundreds, of individual clients. Moreover, analysts' research reports circulate to mutual funds and other big buyers. So each analyst's report potentially reaches tens of thousands of investors. The mere issuance of an analyst report creates awareness of the stock in the investment community, regardless of whether the analyst advises buying or selling.

How many analysts follow a stock? Somewhere between 20 and 30 follow most well-known large stocks. For instance, in early 2009, Apple and Google both had 30 analysts, 24 were following Cisco Systems, and 23 were offering buy/sell opinions on Microsoft.

Smaller firms that have already attracted interest will have somewhere between eight and 17 analysts. For instance, flash memory market SanDisk had 16 analysts when I checked. Firms that haven't yet garnered much attention may have coverage from only one, two, or three analysts.

The number of analysts following a stock is usable information, but how you interpret it depends on your investing strategy. For instance, value investors want stocks given up for dead by the growth crowd, who make up the bulk of the market. All else equal, analysts go where the action is and usually drop coverage when a stock goes into the tank. So the lack of analyst coverage signals a potential value candidate.

However, often everything isn't equal. Sometimes analysts continue covering a troubled stock for business reasons. Distressed companies must often raise cash by selling operating divisions and issuing bonds, bank borrowings, and the like. Those sorts of activities generate big fees for investment bankers. The fact than an investment banker stuck with the firm and continued to provide coverage during the dark days might give it an edge in getting that business.

That's why, in March 2009, down-and-outers such as Fifth Third Bancorp and Las Vegas Sands still had coverage by 19 and 17 analysts, respectively. But you can still spot out-of-favor stocks if you take a closer look at the ratings. For instance, here are the ratings distribution for the 17 analysts that were following Las Vegas Sands:

Strong buy: 1

Buy: 1

Hold: 11

Sell: 3

Strong sell: 1

Most of the analysts covering Las Vegas Sands advised selling (holds and sells), and only one was at strong buy. So despite coverage by 17 analysts, you couldn't say that there was much enthusiasm for Las Vegas Sands.

Sentiment Index

The analysts' ratings tell you a lot about the market's expectations for a company. For instance, you'd interpret the information differently if, instead of only one, 16 of the 17 analysts covering Las Vegas Sands were saying "strong buy."

The Sentiment Index gauges the market's enthusiasm or excitement for a stock, at least from the analysts' perspective. It's based on the premise that only strong buy ratings reflect analyst enthusiasm for the stock. Moderate buys signal disinterest, and holds, moderate sells, and strong sells all translate to "sell." Calculate the sentiment score by adding points for strong buy ratings and subtracting points for holds and sells. Ignore moderate buys.

Sentiment Index Calculation

- **Strong buy**: Add up the number of "strong buy" ratings.
- **Buy**: Ignore.
- **Hold, sell, and strong sell**: Subtract a point for each of these ratings.

For example, a stock with three strong buys and no other ratings would score 3. A stock with three strong buys and three buys would also score 3, because the buys aren't counted. A stock with three holds would score –3. A stock with three holds and one strong sell would score –4.

Interpret negative scores as meaning the stock is out of favor. Scores of 8 and above reflect strong enthusiasm.

Here's an example of how the index works in practice. Transocean is the largest provider of deepwater oil and natural gas well-drilling services. In June 2007, crude oil prices were edging up but hadn't yet gone into the stratosphere. Transocean was trading around $105 per share, and with 33 analysts following, it was hardly unknown.

Nevertheless, the market, at least as gauged by the analysts, wasn't overly exuberant about the stock. With 15 strong buy ratings and 10 holds and sells, Transocean's Sentiment score stood at 5. As you'll learn shortly, this is close to the sweet spot for growth stocks.

By December 2007, however, crude oil prices were on the move, and Transocean was changing hands in the $130 to $150 range. By then, its Sentiment score, at 11, did reflect strong enthusiasm. Transocean peaked in the high $140 range in December and then dropped back to $125 in February. By then, its Sentiment score had dropped back to 5.

After that, crude oil prices skyrocketed and then plunged. By then, for Transocean, fundamentals didn't matter. Its share price merely tracked crude oil prices, both up and down.

Here's how to apply the Sentiment Index:

- **Value candidates**: Stocks with negative scores are clearly in the doghouse and are your best bets. Value-priced stocks with scores between 0 and 2 reflect weak sentiment and may also be value candidates.
- **Growth candidates**: Scores significantly below 0 (such as –4) reflect strong negative sentiment, and that doesn't bode well for growth stocks. Sentiment scores of 8 or higher reflect high risk, but that doesn't mean that they won't trade higher.

Scores between –2 and 7 are acceptable, but I've found that growth stocks with lower scores—say, in the 0 to 4 range—have more upside potential than stocks with higher scores.

Analysts' Estimates

Analysts' consensus earnings forecasts are the single most important factor influencing stock prices. Changes in consensus forecasts often trigger major stock price moves. You can find analysts' forecasts on many financial websites, but Yahoo! and Reuters show you more data than other websites, and both display all the information on a single page, making it easier and faster to access.

Earnings Growth Forecasts

Consensus forecasts—the numbers that determine whether a company's stock moves up or down on report day—typically are simple averages of the individual forecasts.

For example, say four analysts publish forecasts for a company. Three expect $1 per share, and the fourth predicts a break-even quarter—that is, no earnings. The average of the four estimates is $0.75, even though no one expects the company to earn $0.75.

Using Yahoo! as an example, it displays consensus earnings per share (EPS) forecasts for the current and next quarter and for the current and next fiscal year (see Table 4-2). Yahoo! lists the number of analysts making estimates, the high and low estimates, and the year-ago EPS for each period. For example, 12 analysts made forecasts ranging from $0.28 to $0.31 per share for the March 2009 quarter. The consensus forecast (average) was $0.30. The company had reported $0.18 per share earnings in the year-ago March 2008 quarter.

Note

Often the year-ago earnings shown on earnings estimate reports don't match the income statement earnings. Analysts typically go along with the reporting company's preference to use pro forma earnings rather than earnings calculated using generally accepted accounting principles (GAAP).

TABLE 4-2   Example of Analysts' Consensus Earnings and Revenue Forecasts

	Current Quarter: March 2009	Next Quarter: June 2009	Current Year: December 2009	Next Year: December 2010
Earnings Estimates				
Average estimate	0.30	0.30	1.09	1.59
Number of analysts	12	12	12	11
Low estimate	0.28	0.27	1.05	1.42
High estimate	0.31	0.38	1.15	1.90
Year-ago EPS	0.18	0.18	0.66	1.09
Revenue Estimates				
Average estimate	$176 million	$158 million	$651 million	$859 million
Number of analysts	2	2	11	7
Low estimate	$176 million	$154 million	$594 million	$735 million
High estimate	$177 million	$162 million	$774 million	$1.4 billion
Year-ago sales	$124 million	$124 million	$462 million	$651 million
Sales growth	41.9%	26.8%	40.9%	31.9%

Considerable information can be gleaned from the earnings estimates data.

Forecast Spread

The difference between the high and low analysts' estimates, 31 cents versus 28 cents, is typical for a current quarter. The June 2009 quarter and both fiscal years' estimates show wider spreads, signaling that those forecasts likely will move closer over time. A wide spread (such as 5 cents or more) close to the announcement date indicates the likelihood of a significant earnings surprise.

EPS Growth

Table 4-2 shows that analysts expected earnings to grow 65 percent year-over-year in its December 2009 fiscal year (1.09 versus 0.66) and another 46 percent the following year (1.59 versus 1.09).

Growth investors should focus on stocks with at least 15 percent forecast year-over-year earnings growth. The strong year-over-year earnings growth forecasts qualify this stock as an attractive growth candidate.

Value stocks will likely have low or nonexistent forecast earnings growth. Consensus growth forecasts exceeding 5 percent signal relatively high expectations and would disqualify this stock as a value candidate.

Forecast EPS Trend

Consensus earnings forecast trends are even more significant than the forecasts themselves.

The forecast trend is the current forecast for a specific period— say, the current fiscal year—compared to forecasts for the same period one, two, or three months ago. A positive forecast trend tells you that analysts are becoming increasingly optimistic about the company's prospects, and a positive earnings surprise is likely. Conversely, a negative trend raises the specter of further forecast reductions and bad news at report time.

Value Candidates

The best value candidates show flat or negative forecast trends. Positive forecast trends signal increasing enthusiasm, which means that it's probably too late for that stock.

Growth Candidates

Stocks with flat (no trend) or positive forecast trends are valid growth candidates. But growth investors should avoid stocks with negative forecast trends.

The EPS trends report shown in Table 4-3 shows consensus estimates going back 90 days for each of the two quarters and fiscal years covered. Pay most attention to the fiscal year numbers, because the quarterly results can fluctuate for a variety of short-term reasons. Ignore $0.01 changes.

TABLE 4-3   EPS Trends Report for a Strong Growth Candidate

	Current Quarter: March 2009	Next Quarter: June 2009	Current Year: December 2009	Next Year: December 2010
EPS Trends				
Current	0.30	0.30	1.09	1.59
7 days ago	0.30	0.28	1.07	1.44
30 days ago	0.30	0.28	1.07	1.44
60 days ago	0.26	0.27	0.99	1.28
90 days ago	0.25	0.24	0.93	1.16

The report shows that analysts had been consistently increasing their estimates, reflecting a strong growth candidate. Most of your growth candidates won't look this good.

Table 4-4 shows the numbers for a more typical growth candidate. The current fiscal year's forecasts barely moved during the preceding three months, and the next fiscal year's forecast moved up only 2 cents. The flat EPS trend signals less enthusiasm than we saw in Table 4-3, but that wouldn't disqualify the stock as a growth candidate.

TABLE 4-4   EPS Trends Report for an Acceptable Growth Candidate

	Current Quarter: March 2009	Next Quarter: June 2009	Current Year: December 2009	Next Year: December 2010
EPS Trends				
Current	0.23	0.25	1.11	1.34
7 days ago	0.23	0.25	1.11	1.34
30 days ago	0.22	0.25	1.10	1.30
60 days ago	0.22	0.25	1.10	1.30
90 days ago	0.23	0.25	1.11	1.32

Table 4-5 tells a gloomier story. The earnings forecasts had been steadily trending down, and both fiscal year forecasts dropped substantially over the 90-day period. The negative forecast trends are red flags warning of further cuts and/or a negative earnings surprise.

These trends, while unacceptable for growth stocks, would get value investors' attention.

TABLE 4-5 Unacceptable EPS Trends Report for a Growth Candidate

	Current Quarter: March 2009	Next Quarter: June 2009	Current Year: December 2009	Next Year: December 2010
EPS Trends				
Current	0.15	0.19	0.90	1.25
7 days ago	0.15	0.19	0.91	1.25
30 days ago	0.11	0.19	0.91	1.25
60 days ago	0.24	0.27	1.17	1.37
90 days ago	0.25	0.27	1.18	1.42

Long-Term Earnings Growth

Many analysts, as a matter of course, estimate a company's long-term (usually five years) average annual earnings growth. Those forecasts are averaged, and the long-term consensus earnings growth estimates are listed on many websites. These long-term growth forecasts are the G in PEG (P/E divided by expected earnings growth), the valuation method favored by many growth investors (see Chapter 5). Although they are widely used, nobody checks the accuracy of analysts' long-term growth forecasts.

For instance, I've never heard of anyone looking up a particular analyst's long-term earnings growth forecast for, say, Google from five years past and then comparing it to what actually happened.

Nevertheless, long-term consensus forecasts work great as an expectations gauge. High average annual growth forecasts reflect high expectations, and vice versa.

Value investors should favor candidates with 10 percent or less expected annual growth. Growth investors, however, should stick with stocks reflecting at least 15 percent long-term growth expectations; 20 to 25 percent is better.

Earnings Surprise

An earnings surprise is the difference between analysts' consensus forecasts and the actual reported earnings. It's a negative surprise when reported earnings come in below forecasts and a positive surprise when earnings beat forecasts.

Surprises are measured in cents, as in "a 2-cent positive surprise." Most companies routinely report 1- or 2-cent positive surprises. Such amounts are not really surprises and don't move prices much.

All else equal, a negative surprise of any amount drives the share price down, often sharply.

Positive surprises of 4 or 5 cents (or more) usually do move up the share price, although not nearly as much as a negative surprise forces it down. A big positive surprise—say, 10 cents—can have a more pronounced effect. Surprisingly, the surprise percentage isn't as important as the number of cents. A 4-cent shortfall, such as when a company reports $4.04 instead of the expected $4.08, is about as significant as if the company reported $0.08 instead of $0.12.

Although the stock price reacts immediately, significant surprises often have a longer-lasting effect, because they force analysts to reevaluate their forecasts. For instance, analysts almost always increase their earnings estimates following a large positive surprise.

Although a stock reacts to the magnitude of the surprise in cents rather than percentage, some pros believe that in the event of a positive surprise, the surprise percentage does foretell future price action. That is, stocks with higher percentage surprises gain more in the ensuing months than stocks with lower percentage surprises.

History Lessons

You can see recent surprise history on many financial websites. Table 4-6 shows the data you need. It includes estimated earnings, actual reported earnings, and the difference (surprise) in cents for each of the last four reported quarters.

TABLE 4-6 Data Needed to Analyze the Surprise History

Earnings History	June 2008	September 2008	December 2008	March 2009
EPS estimate	3.23	3.49	3.70	3.51
EPS actual	3.25	3.54	3.79	3.57
Difference	0.02	0.09	0.09	0.06

The data shows that the sample company, at least over the past year, had been a habitual positive surpriser. Based only on its surprise history, chances are this company will surprise again on the upside when it reports its current quarter's results.

Conversely, a history of negative surprises signals risk that more bad news is on the way.

Value Versus Growth

Research has shown that, in the event of a negative surprise, growth stocks drop more, percentagewise, than value-priced stocks. That makes sense, because by definition, the market has high expectations for growth stocks and low expectations for value stocks.

For a value stock, a negative surprise is really no surprise, because most players already view the company as a loser. Conversely, growth investors expect their picks to surprise on the upside, so a negative surprise is a real surprise.

Research results are mixed on positive surprises. Some studies show that growth stocks outperform value stocks in the event of a positive surprise, while other research shows the opposite result.

Sales Forecasts

Although it may sometimes seem so, analysts just don't pull their earnings forecasts out of thin air. Rather, they set up detailed earnings models, starting with sales forecasts. From those, they deduct estimated costs to arrive at their earnings forecasts.

While many financial websites display earnings forecasts, only two, Yahoo! and Reuters, also show consensus revenue (sales) forecasts. The availability of sales forecasts is an important breakthrough that many investors haven't noticed.

Consensus sales forecasts are especially important when analyzing growth candidates. Without them, you wouldn't know that a firm's recent earnings growth was driven by a large acquisition or another one-time event and won't be repeated. Other times, slowing sales growth estimates are your first clue that once-hot earnings growth is about to slow.

Table 4-7 shows the forecasts, as you would have seen during the September 2008 quarter, for a company with slowing sales growth. The company entered 2008 growing sales at a 25 percent year-over-year clip. That's why the current-year forecast (2008) shows 20 percent growth, even though analysts forecast only 11 to 12 percent for the last two quarters of the year. The 2009 forecast shows that analysts don't expect sales growth to pick up anytime soon.

Chapters 11 and 12 describe in detail how to analyze sales growth forecasts.

TABLE 4-7　Revenue (Sales) Forecasts

	Current Quarter: September 2008	Next Quarter: December 2008	Current Year: December 2008	Next Year: December 2009
Revenue Estimates				
Average estimate	$87 million	$90 million	$323 million	$364 million
Number of analysts	2	1	1	1
Low estimate	$87 million	$90 million	$323 million	$364 million
High estimate	$88 million	$90 million	$323 million	$364 million
Year-ago sales	$79 million	$81 million	$269 million	$323 million
Sales growth	11.0%	11.5%	20.2%	12.6%

Guidance Changes

Before the rules changed, company execs didn't publicly reveal their sales and earnings expectations (guidance). Instead, they would privately advise a few favored analysts whether they expected to meet, beat, or fall short of published forecasts. That's where the term "whisper number" came from.

In October 2000, the SEC's Fair Disclosure rule (Regulation FD) outlawed such shenanigans. Now, management must announce guidance changes via press releases and/or in conference calls open to the public.

Since all analysts get the same news at the same time, consensus forecasts change immediately. Consequently, changes in guidance have the same effect on a stock price as an earnings surprise. However, so far as I know, nobody tracks management guidance changes the way they track surprises.

Oddly, even though they no longer exist, you still hear people talk about whisper numbers, and some websites continue to track them.

Research Reports

While I don't suggest following analysts' buy/sell advice, it's worth your time to read their research reports. Many are filled with essential information about the company's business plan, the problems it's encountering, and the analysts' take on the competition and industry trends. That's valuable information that would take you days to dig up on your own. Moreover, sometimes an analyst reveals information in the write-up that doesn't support his or her buy/sell rating.

While you can purchase analyst reports on various financial websites at $10 to $75 a pop, you can run up a big bill fast. However, many web brokers offer free research reports to their customers. I suggest starting with your broker's offerings, and even consider opening a second account with a different broker to access additional free reports.

Summary

You probably won't make money following analysts' buy/sell advice per se. But there's plenty of moneymaking information imbedded in their ratings and forecasts, if you know what to look for. Also, you can use analysts' advice and forecasts to help you qualify viable value or growth candidates. Furthermore, analysts' research reports can help you understand a company's business and competitive standing. They often yield clues about the analysts' real view of the company's business prospects.

5

Analysis Tool #2: Valuation

How much is a stock worth?

If we knew, making money in the stock market would be a snap. All we would have to do is buy undervalued stocks and then sit back and wait for them to move up to their "correct value." Of course, it's not that easy. Unless they pay significant dividends, stocks are like baseball cards. They have no value other than what another investor is willing to pay.

That said, countless stock valuation schemes are in use. Many originated when investors did buy stocks mainly for the dividends. Then, it made sense to value stocks based on the present value of their future payouts. While many investors still buy stocks for the dividends, that's a separate topic. For growth and value stock investing, capital appreciation is the goal, and dividends, although welcome, usually don't affect valuations much.

You'd think that, given that shift, analysts would have found new ways of valuing stocks. Some have, but many others still use the same formulas, simply replacing dividends with expected future earnings or cash flows. That's great in theory, but in real life, who will buy your shares at an arbitrary price calculated by those methods?

There is no such thing as a "correct price," because the greed, excitement, fears, expectations, and enthusiasm that determine today's trading price are impossible to quantify. What you *can* do is evaluate the reasonableness of the expectations reflected in the current stock price. This chapter describes two ways to do that:

- Implied growth
- Growth at a reasonable price (GARP)

The first, determining the earnings growth rate implied by a stock's current trading price, although employed by many professionals, is unknown to most individual investors.

The second, growth at a reasonable price, applies only to growth stocks and is arguably the valuation formula of choice for individual investors and pros alike. Unfortunately, GARP relies on analysts' forecasts. This goes a long way toward explaining why so many got it so wrong during the tech bubble days, the China stock bubble days, the oil stock bubble days, the solar stock bubble days, and on and on.

After reading this chapter, hopefully you'll check the implied growth before you chase the next rocket. However, implied growth conveys only what is true today. You'll have to calculate target prices (see Chapter 6) to find out what happens next.

Implied Growth

Benjamin Graham, sometimes called the father of value investing, proposed a practical and easily calculated formula for estimating the "intrinsic value" of a growth stock in his pioneering treatise on fundamental analysis, "Security Analysis." It was cowritten with David Dodd and published in 1934. Don't be put off by the algebraic formulas. I included them to impress you and justify the result. In the end, all you'll have to do is look up implied growth in Table 5-1. Graham and Dodd defined intrinsic value as follows:

$$\text{intrinsic value} = \text{EPS} \times [8.5 + (2 \times \text{forecast annual earnings growth \%})]$$

where EPS is the last 12 months' earnings per share.

Put into words, Graham said that a company's intrinsic value is its latest 12 months' earnings multiplied by a factor equal to 8.5 plus twice its projected annual earnings growth rate.

Later, Graham modified the formula to account for the notion that stock valuations vary inversely with prevailing interest rates. That is, stocks tend to trade at higher valuations when interest rates are low, and vice versa (see Chapter 2). Graham used AAA (highest quality) corporate bond rates as a proxy for prevailing interest rates. The AAA corporate bond rates were around 4.4 percent when he first devised the formula, so the revised version looks like this:

$$\text{intrinsic value} = \text{EPS} \times (4.4 / \text{AAA}) \times$$
$$[8.5 + (2 \times \text{forecast annual earnings growth } \%)]$$

where AAA is the current yield of AAA-rated corporate bonds.

For example, if a company's latest earnings were $1 per share, the bond yield was 5.5 percent, and analysts forecast 20 percent average annual earnings growth over the next five years, the intrinsic value would be

$$\text{intrinsic value} = \$1.00 \times (4.4 / 5.5) \times [8.5 + (2 \times 20)] = \$38.80$$

The intrinsic value is $38.80, based on March 2009's 5.5 percent corporate bond yield.

Graham's intrinsic value hinges on analysts' long-term earnings growth forecasts, which, as pointed out in Chapter 4, are probably wrong. Thus, although the intrinsic value calculation is an interesting exercise, it has little practical value.

However, Graham's formula can be very insightful when used in another way. If you substitute the current stock price for intrinsic value, and implied earnings growth for forecast growth, and then do some algebraic manipulation, you get

$$\text{implied growth rate} = \text{P/E} (\text{AAA} / 8.8) - 4.25$$

Implied growth, as I've defined it, is the long-term average annual earnings growth that the company would have to achieve to justify its current P/E.

To gain further insight, assume for the moment that the AAA corporate bond rate is 8.8 percent. Then the formula is simplified to

$$\text{implied growth rate} = \text{P/E} - 4.25$$

For example, using the simplified formula, a P/E of 50 implies a 46 percent average annual earnings growth rate.

The implied growth rate corresponding to a particular P/E moves in tandem with the corporate bond rate. For example, the market supports higher P/Es when interest rates drop. Table 5-1 shows how it works out. You can use this table to look up the long-term average annual growth rate corresponding to your stock's P/E. As you can see, the corporate bond rate makes a big difference. For instance, when the bond rate is 5 percent, a 50 P/E corresponds to a reasonable 24 percent annual EPS growth rate, but a usually unrealistic 46 percent growth rate for an 8.8 percent bond rate.

You can see the current AAA corporate bond rate at www.neatideas.com/aaabonds.htm.

TABLE 5-1   Implied Annual EPS Growth Rates for Various AAA Corporate Bond Rates

P/E	5%	6%	7%	8.8%
10	1%	2%	4%	6%
15	2%	6%	8%	11%
20	7%	9%	12%	16%
25	10%	13%	16%	21%
30	13%	16%	19%	26%
35	16%	19%	23%	31%
40	18%	23%	27%	36%
50	24%	30%	35%	46%
60	30%	37%	43%	56%
80	41%	50%	59%	76%
100	53%	68%	75%	96%

What's a reasonable annual earnings growth rate expectation?

It's better to start with sales growth, because earnings figures can be impacted by all sorts of nonrecurring charges related to acquisitions, loan refinancings, lawsuits, you name it. Consequently, the average annual earnings growth you calculate will come out too high if you pick a starting year with significant nonrecurring charges or too low if your ending year has one-time charges.

Table 5-2 shows average annual sales growth over the past five years and past ten years for a few well-known growth stocks.

As a rule of thumb, expect 25 to 40 percent annual sales growth from newer, small companies with new products and 15 to 25 percent from larger, established firms. Expect annual earnings growth to exceed sales growth by 2 to 5 percent for newer companies and to be even with sales growth for established firms.

TABLE 5-2   Average Annual Sales Growth (Data as of 3/16/09)

Company	Last Five Years	Last 10 Years
Amazon.com	29%	41%
Apple	39%	10%
Cisco Systems	16%	17%
Coach	27%	20%
Cognizant Tech	50%	47%
eBay	32%	58%
Google	72%	
Netflix	38%	100%
Starbucks	21%	23%
Urban Outfitters	29%	24%
Zimmer Holdings	17%	17%

You can look up the current AAA corporate bond rate on the Financial Forecast Center (www.neatideas.com/aaabonds.htm). What corporate bond rates should you assume for the future? Use history as your guide. Table 5-3 shows historical ranges dating back to the 1920s. You can draw your own conclusions, but my take is that barring a period of runaway inflation, rates are likely to hover in the 5 to 9 percent range.

TABLE 5-3   Historical AAA Corporate Bond Rates

Years	Low	High
1920–29	4.6%	6.4%
1930–39	2.9%	5.2%
1940–49	2.5%	3.0%
1950–59	2.6%	4.6%
1960–69	4.2%	7.7%
1970–79	7.1%	10.8%
1980–89	8.4%	15.5%
1990–94	6.7%	9.6%
1995–99	6.2%	8.5%
2000–04	7.0%	8.0%
2005–09	5.0%	6.3%

Source: Moody's via the Financial Forecast Center (www.neatideas.com)

Table 5-1 gives you the earnings growth rate implied by your stock's P/E. It's up to you to determine the reasonableness of the implied rate. However, a little common sense goes a long way.

For instance, say you're considering a value candidate with a 5 percent implied annual earnings growth rate. Based on your analysis, you expect the firm to achieve 10 to 20 percent annual earnings growth when it recovers from current problems. Thus, since it's currently valued at 5 percent growth, all else equal, it's a good candidate. You'll make money regardless of whether the market ends up pricing it as a 10 or 20 percent grower.

Growth at a Reasonable Price

Many growth investors don't spend much time worrying about the subtleties of stock valuations. Instead, they prefer a "keep it simple" philosophy. For them, valuation boils down to earnings and earnings growth.

These investors look for a balance between price and expected earnings growth. Specifically, they want to buy growth at a reasonable price. They determine the "reasonable price" by comparing a stock's price/earnings (P/E) ratio to its expected long-term annual earnings growth rate.

PEG and Fair Value

A stock is said to be "fairly valued" when its P/E equals its expected growth rate, "undervalued" when trading at a P/E below its growth rate, and "overvalued" when trading above. For example, a stock expected to grow earnings 25 percent annually is fairly valued when it's trading at a 25 P/E.

PEG is the acronym for the ratio of the stock's P/E divided by the expected earnings growth:

$$PEG = P/E \div \text{forecast annual EPS growth}$$

The PEG is 1 when the PE and growth rate are equal, above 1 when the P/E exceeds the growth rate (overvalued), and below 1 (undervalued) when the forecast growth exceeds the P/E. While it makes sense that faster-growing stocks should trade at higher P/Es than slower growers, I've never found any research or mathematical formulas that show why a stock is fairly valued when its P/E equals its growth rate.

Thus, it's understandable that growth investors, being pragmatic by nature, adjust their fair-value definition depending on market conditions. In strong markets, players consider stocks with PEGs of 2 (PE twice the earnings growth rate) to be fairly valued. In weak markets, they revert to defining PEGs of 1 as fair value. Adjusting fair value to the market makes sense. In the end, P/E measures the market's enthusiasm for a stock, and most stocks trade at higher valuations during a bull market.

While the definition sounds precise, not everyone uses the same value of earnings or growth to calculate the P/E.

The E in P/E

Everyone agrees that the E in P/E is 12 months' earnings, but which 12 months, and which earnings? Academics and individual investors often use the last four quarters' earnings (trailing earnings). However, most analysts and many money managers use analysts' consensus forecast earnings (forward earnings) for the current year. Since we're evaluating stocks expected to grow earnings, forecast earnings are higher than historical earnings. Also, forecast earnings usually exclude one-time or nonrecurring charges, which reduce earnings. Thus, the P/E calculated using forward earnings usually is lower than the P/E calculated using trailing earnings.

Keep in mind that this isn't rocket science. As you gain experience, you'll develop your own strategies for evaluating P/E and PEG. As long as you're consistent, it doesn't matter which version of earnings you use to calculate P/E.

Growth Rate

The earnings growth rate, the G in PEG, could be historical long-term earnings growth, but most participants use analysts' consensus growth forecasts. Here again, there's room for discussion. Some use analysts' five-year average annual earnings growth forecasts, while others prefer the current or next fiscal year's growth forecasts.

Pro Forma Earnings

When filing SEC reports, companies always calculate earnings following generally accepted accounting principles (GAAP).

However, many companies highlight pro forma earnings instead of GAAP earnings in their quarterly report press releases. The pro forma earnings calculation omits certain items, usually one-time (nonrecurring) costs that the reporting company deems not representative of its operating performance. No standards define which expenses should or should not be included in pro forma earnings. It's up to the discretion of the reporting company.

Despite the inaccuracies, many professional money managers rely on PEG because it's "close enough." In their view, this isn't rocket science. They're not calculating PEG down to decimals. If the P/E is 20 and forecast earnings growth is 40 percent, the stock is undervalued. If forecast earnings growth is 20 percent and the P/E is 50, it's overvalued. It's that simple.

Realistic Earnings Growth Estimates

Successful emerging growth companies often chalk up supercharged earnings growth in early years. Sales are growing rapidly, but more important, many are near the break-even point, and gross profits are just beginning to exceed fixed costs. As revenues grow, higher percentages of gross profits fall to the bottom line, driving up earnings faster than sales.

Eventually, sales growth slows to levels similar to the firm's market sector. When the market realizes that growth is slowing, the share price usually takes a massive hit, because investors value moderate-growth stocks much lower than rockets. The timing of the growth slowdown depends on the particulars, but it usually happens sooner than most expect.

Once a company is past that initial growth spurt, earnings growth, although volatile quarter to quarter, trends down toward the sales growth rate. That happens because a company can grow earnings faster than sales only by increasing its profit margins, and margin expansion opportunities diminish over time. That said, for the best companies you could probably expect annual earnings growth to exceed sales growth by approximately 10 percent on an ongoing basis. This means that a well-run company may be able to grow earnings around 22 percent annually on only 20 percent sales growth.

Table 5-4 shows expected annual sales growth rates for a few representative industries. The best companies exceed these industry averages by taking market share from weaker competitors. The forecasts assume normal economic conditions.

TABLE 5-4 Industry Expected Average Annual Sales Growth During Normal Economies

Industry		Industry	
Advertising	9%	Homebuilding	11%
Aerospace/defense	16%	Hotel/gaming	13%
Agricultural chemicals	18%	Household products	12%
Alternative energy	19%	Life insurance	0%
Apparel	7%	Medical services	14%
Banks	5%	Networking equipment	16%
Biotechnology	35%	Office equipment	9%
Drugs (generic)	11%	Restaurants	12%
Drugs (nongeneric)	6%	Retail stores	10%
E-commerce	20%	Securities brokerage	16%
Educational		Semiconductor equipment	13%
services (adult)	16%	Semiconductors	8%
Electric utilities	4%	Software	19%
Entertainment	15%	Telecommunications	
Food processing	9%	equipment	10%
Grocery	6%	Telecommunications	
Healthcare information		services	4%
systems	18%	Wireless networking	15%

Dividends

The valuation formulas described in this chapter do not include value added by dividends, if any. You can account for dividends by dividing the annual dividend payout by the AAA corporate bond rate. For instance, if a stock is paying $1.00 per share annually, and the corporate bond rate is 7 percent, the value added by the dividend is $14.28 ($1.00/0.07). That equation assumes that the dividend payout will continue indefinitely at the same level. Dividends growing over time would warrant a higher valuation.

Summary

Market analysts all too often ignore the earnings growth expectations built into the current price when they tell us to buy their favorite stocks. But you can check the reasonableness of their recommendations yourself. Simply look up the current AAA corporate bond rate on the web and then find the growth rate implied by a stock's P/E in Table 5-1.

6

Analysis Tool #3: Establish Target Prices

Before they buy a stock, many professional money managers compute a target price—the price they expect to sell it at if all goes well. The target price defines the potential profit on the investment, and if it isn't high enough to justify the risk, they don't buy the stock.

Computing target prices is not the same as determining the growth expectations implied by a stock's current trading price (as described in Chapter 5). Instead, the target price calculation forecasts a stock's trading range at some future time. How far depends on your goals and investing style. Value investors usually analyze distressed companies. Since they don't know when they will recover, they often look two to five years ahead. Growth investors usually have shorter time frames and may look only 12 to 18 months ahead, typically to the end of the next fiscal year (FY).

The beauty of the target price method is that it doesn't matter. The accuracy of your target prices depends on the accuracy of your assumptions, not the time span. Once you understand the process, you can vary the number of look-ahead years to suit your needs.

Here's why setting target prices can help you make better investing decisions. Assume that you're analyzing two stocks in similar businesses and both are trading for $30 per share.

Say that after analyzing relevant factors, if all goes according to plan, two years from now Stock A will be trading between $35 and $40, and Stock B will be trading in the $50 to $60 range. Your analysis could be wrong, of course, or events may not go as expected. But given that information, it's pretty obvious that Stock B presents the better opportunity.

The target price calculation isn't complicated. It involves forecasting a company's target-year sales and then uses historical price/sales ratios to predict minimum and maximum share prices after the target year results have been announced.

The Process

You can use the procedure to forecast target prices any number of years ahead. The only stipulation is that the target price date is always the day after a company reports its fiscal-year results. I call that fiscal year the target year.

Developing a target price involves five steps:

1. Estimate sales in the target year.
2. Estimate the number of shares outstanding in the target year.
3. Use steps 1 and 2 to compute the estimated target year sales per share.
4. Estimate the expected range of price/sale ratios.
5. Use steps 3 and 4 to compute the estimated target price range.

Why use sales and P/S instead of earnings and P/E ratios? First, sales growth is easier to predict than earnings growth. Moreover, if you look at historical data, you'll find that P/S ratios are more stable and hence easier to forecast than P/E ratios.

To demonstrate the process, I'll compute target prices for two stocks in completely different industries: grocery retailer Whole Foods and movie renter Netflix.

Whole Foods' fiscal year ends in September, and I'll use its 2011 fiscal year as its target year. Thus, I'll estimate its target price when Whole Foods reports its FY 2011 results, probably in November of that year.

Netflix's fiscal year ends in December, and I'll use 2011 for its target year. I'll estimate its target price when Netflix reports its 2011 results, probably in early February 2012.

You can find all the data you need to do the calculations on MSN Money's Key Ratios 10-Year Summary and Financial Statements 10-Year Summary reports. The process will go much faster if you first print those two reports for each stock you want to analyze.

Step 1: Start with Sales

Start by estimating each company's target year sales. The Financial Statements 10-Year Summary shows each company's fiscal year sales going back 10 years. Unlike analysts, who forecast sales growth in terms of year-over-year (YOY) percentage increase, I've found that it's more useful to analyze sales growth in terms of actual dollars instead of percentages.

Table 6-1 shows recent annual sales figures for Whole Foods.

TABLE 6-1   Whole Foods Historical Annual Sales and Year-Over-Year Sales Growth

Year	Revenues (in Millions of Dollars)	YOY Growth (in Millions of Dollars)
FY 9/03	3,149	
FY 9/04	3,865	716
FY 9/05	4,701	836
FY 9/06	5,607	906
FY 9/07	6,592	985
FY 9/08	7,594	1,002

Whole Foods' sales growth ranged from $716 million five years ago to $1,002 million in its most recent fiscal year. The dollar value of its growth has increased every year. However, Whole Foods' FY 9/08 growth figure included a major acquisition that probably won't be repeated. Eyeballing the year-over-year growth numbers, I figured that future growth would probably be between the FY 9/07 and FY 9/08 numbers, and I settled on $950 million.

Table 6-2 shows the Whole Foods numbers with my estimates. Adding $950 million sales growth for each year, I targeted Whole Foods sales at $9,494 million in FY 2010.

TABLE 6-2   Whole Foods Historical and Estimated Annual Sales and Sales Growth

Year	Revenues (in Millions of Dollars)	YOY Growth (in Millions of Dollars)
FY 9/03	3,149	
FY 9/04	3,865	716
FY 9/05	4,701	836
FY 9/06	5,607	906
FY 9/07	6,592	985
FY 9/08	7,594	1,002
FY 9/09	8,544 estimated	950 estimated
FY 9/10	9,494 estimated	950 estimated

Table 6-3 shows what the annual sales numbers look like for Netflix.

TABLE 6-3   Netflix Historical and Estimated Annual Sales and Sales Growth

Year	Revenues (in Millions of Dollars)	YOY Growth (in Millions of Dollars)
FY 12/03	270	
FY 12/04	501	231
FY 12/05	682	181
FY 12/06	997	315
FY 12/07	1,205	208
FY 12/08	1,365	160
FY 12/09	1,549	184 estimated
FY 12/10	1,733	184 estimated

Netflix's year-over-year sales growth has been all over the map, but it appears to be trending down. I averaged its last two numbers and settled on $184 million estimated year-over-year growth for the next two years. Thus, my estimated revenues in Netflix's FY 12/10 were $1,733 million.

My sales estimates assume that recent sales growth trends will continue. Obviously, that's not always the case. Modify your target-year sales if you have better numbers.

Step 2: Shares Outstanding

Next, I estimate each company's total shares outstanding at the end of its target year.

Again, I use history as my guide. Many companies consistently increase shares outstanding because they issue stock to raise cash, make acquisitions, or allocate shares for employee stock options.

Table 6-4 shows the historical numbers for Whole Foods. The data comes from MSN's Financial Statements 10-Year Summary.

TABLE 6-4   Whole Foods Historical Shares Outstanding

Year	Shares Outstanding (in Millions of Dollars)	YOY Growth (in Millions of Dollars)
FY 9/03	120.1	
FY 9/04	124.8	4.7
FY 9/05	135.9	11.1
FY 9/06	139.6	3.7
FY 9/07	139.2	−0.4
FY 9/08	140.3	1.1

Whole Foods was a prolific share issuer earlier, but it toned down things in recent years. I averaged its FY 9/06 through FY 9/08 numbers, coming up with an estimated 1.5 million new shares each year for the next two years. Table 6-5 shows the results.

**TABLE 6-5   Whole Foods Historical Shares and Estimated Future
Shares Outstanding**

Year	Shares Outstanding (in Millions of Dollars)	YOY Growth (in Millions of Dollars)
FY 9/03	120.1	
FY 9/04	124.8	4.7
FY 9/05	135.9	11.1
FY 9/06	139.6	3.7
FY 9/07	139.2	−0.4
FY 9/08	140.3	1.1
FY 9/09	141.8 estimated	1.5 estimated
FY 9/10	143.3 estimated	1.5 estimated

As shown in Table 6-5, I forecast 143.3 million shares outstanding at the end of fiscal 9/10.

Table 6-6 shows what the historical shares outstanding numbers looked like for Netflix.

TABLE 6-6   Netflix Historical Shares Outstanding

Year	Shares Outstanding (in Millions of Dollars)	YOY Growth (in Millions of Dollars)
FY 12/03	50.8	
FY 12/04	52.7	1.9
FY 12/05	54.8	2.1
FY 12/06	68.6	13.8
FY 12/07	64.9	−3.7
FY 12/08	58.9	−6.0

Netflix also was a prolific share issuer in earlier years but then went the other way and started buying back shares in 2007. I estimated that Netflix would continue that trend, buying back 4.0 million shares in each of the next two years. Table 6-7 shows what the numbers look like with those estimates added.

TABLE 6-7   Netflix Historical Shares and Estimated Future Shares Outstanding

Year	Shares Outstanding (in Millions of Dollars)	YOY Growth (in Millions of Dollars)
FY 12/03	50.8	
FY 12/04	52.7	1.9
FY 12/05	54.8	2.1
FY 12/06	68.6	13.8
FY 12/07	64.9	–3.7
FY 12/08	58.9	–6.0
FY 12/09	54.9 estimated	–4.0 estimated
FY 12/10	50.9 estimated	–4.0 estimated

With the buybacks, I estimated that Netflix's share count would drop to 50.9 million by the end of 2010.

Step 3: Sales Per Share

Just as earnings per share is annual earnings divided by the number of shares outstanding, sales per share is annual sales divided by the number of shares outstanding.

In step 1, I estimated target year sales for Whole Foods at $9,494 million. In step 2, I estimated its target year shares outstanding at 143.3 million.

Dividing target year sales by shares outstanding forecasts Whole Foods' target year sales per share at $66.25.

Using Netflix's estimated $1,733 million target year sales and estimated 50.9 million shares outstanding resulted in target year sales of $34.05 per share.

Step 4: Price/Sales Ratios

Some pundits advise judging the relative merits of companies in the same industry by comparing valuation ratios. For instance, Company A is the better buy if its P/E is only 20 compared to Company B's 35 P/E. But that doesn't work.

Competing firms often consistently trade at different valuations because one is more popular with investors. For instance, chipmaker Intel typically trades at higher valuations than competitor Advanced Micro Devices.

I've found that a stock's own history is the best indicator of its likely future trading range.

MSN's Key Ratios report shows historical average annual price/sales ratios for each stock going back ten years. It's best to focus on the most recent five years' valuations.

We can't predict the exact price/sales ratio for a stock when it reports its target year sales, or for any other time, for that matter. The best we can do is its normal trading range, in terms of its price/sales ratio, and assume that it would be trading within that range on the target date. Table 6-8 shows Whole Foods' average annual price/sales ratios going back five years.

TABLE 6-8   Whole Foods Historical Average Price/Sales Ratios

Year	Average P/S
FY 9/04	1.5
FY 9/05	1.9
FY 9/06	1.5
FY 9/07	1.1
FY 9/08	0.4

The Whole Foods ratio for FY 9/08 was much lower than previous years. That could be due to legal issues related to its acquisition of competitor Wild Oats Markets, or to the weak economy, or both. In any case, it's best to ignore numbers that far out of a stock's normal trading range.

So, ignoring the FY 9/08 ratio, my target range for the Whole Foods P/S ratio is 1.1 to 1.5.

Table 6-9 shows the price/sales ratio for Netflix.

TABLE 6-9   Netflix Historical Average Price/Sales Ratios

Year	Average P/S
FY 12/04	1.6
FY 12/05	2.6
FY 12/06	1.8
FY 12/07	1.5
FY 12/08	1.4

Using these numbers, Netflix's target P/S range is 1.4 to 2.6.

Step 5: Compute Target Price Ranges

If you do the algebra, you'll find that share price, price/sales ratio, and sales per share relate this way:

$$\text{share price} = \text{sales per share} \times \text{P/S}$$

In other words, you can compute the target price range by multiplying the target year sales per share by the target year high and low P/S ratios.

For Whole Foods, I estimated sales per share at $66.25 and its low and high P/S ratios at 1.1 and 1.5, respectively. Thus, for Whole Foods:

$$\text{FY 9/11 low target price} = \$66.25 \times 1.1 = \$72.88$$

$$\text{FY 9/11 high target price} = \$66.25 \times 1.5 = \$99.38$$

Given all the assumptions we've made along the way, it's silly to compute the targets down to pennies. So, when Whole Foods reports its fiscal year September 2011 results, I'm forecasting that it will be trading between $73 and $99 per share.

For Netflix, I estimated its sales per share at $34.05 and its low and high P/S ratios at 1.4 and 2.6. Thus:

$$\text{FY 12/11 low target price} = \$34.05 \times 1.4 = \$48$$

$$\text{FY 12/11 high target price} = \$34.05 \times 2.6 = \$89$$

When I did this analysis, Whole Foods was changing hands at $15 per share, and Netflix could be had for $39 per share.

Summary

Your target prices will be only as good as your estimates. But everybody who forecasts target prices is in the same boat. Even key company executives can't accurately forecast sales one or two years down the road. Errors are inevitable. Thus, it's important to review your assumptions whenever new data becomes available.

Even with the inherent errors, calculating target prices gives you insight into a stock's upside potential that will help you make better choices.

7

Analysis Tool #4:
Industry Analysis

The first three analysis tools dealt with abstract numbers such as earnings forecasts and P/E ratios and the like without regard to the company's business. Given the same numbers, your conclusions would have been identical whether you were analyzing a maker of chewing gum, buggy whips, solar cells, or wireless communication chips.

Now it's time to learn about your candidate's business, industry, and competition.

The Business

First, find out what the company does for a living. What products and/or services does it sell? That's a no-brainer if you're talking about Wal-Mart, but how many investors know what products or services F5 Networks or Zimmer Holdings offer?

For a concise overview, Morningstar's Snapshot report is a good place to start. For more details, check MSN Money's Company Report. For even more details, try Yahoo!'s Profile report. If you want still more information, Reuters' (www.reuters.com/finance/stocks) Company Profile report goes into considerable depth, describing each of the company's major products and services. It's probably more than you'll want to know at this stage, but you'll need it later.

Besides its free Snapshot report, Morningstar offers a longer review, written by a Morningstar analyst, for many, but not all, stocks. The review gives you the analysts' take on the company's business plan and competitive position. You must be a paid subscriber to see the analysts' reviews. It's a worthwhile read, usually giving you a better perspective on the company's operations than you'd otherwise have.

Industry Growth Outlook

Once you understand a company's line of business, your next step is to research its industry, starting with its growth prospects.

Why? If you're a growth investor, you want growing companies, and growing industries are the best place to find them. If the industry isn't growing, your picks will have to grow earnings by cutting costs, by taking market share from competitors, or by acquiring other industry players. Many firms have successfully practiced these strategies, but they are inherently riskier than participating in a growth industry.

The competition is less intense in a fast-growing market because there is plenty of business for all contenders. As an industry matures and growth slows, companies change their focus to increasing market share. That usually translates to price cutting, which leads to eroding margins and reduced earnings.

Value investors, although satisfied with a slower pace than growth investors, should still be concerned about their candidate's industry growth prospects. It's tough, even for value investors, to make money holding companies that are battling to survive in a declining industry.

Industry growth means sales growth, but industry sales growth forecasts are hard to find. However, analysts' consensus earnings growth forecasts are readily available for most industries. So we'll start with analysts' industry earnings growth forecasts and then convert the earnings growth numbers to sales growth.

Analysts' Forecasts Are Good Enough

Why would you want to rely on analysts' forecasts when few trust their buy/sell ratings?

For starters, most analysts strive to come up with accurate earnings growth forecasts for the companies they cover. Zacks and Thomson Reuters compile industry growth forecasts by averaging the individual forecasts for industry stocks. Since they are the average of many individual forecasts, the industry growth estimates are probably more accurate than those for individual stocks.

Furthermore, predicting long-term growth is easier said than done, and despite their failings, analysts' forecasts are probably as good as anyone's. Besides, you need ballpark figures, not precise estimates. In summary, analysts' growth forecasts are good enough for our needs.

MSN Money's Earnings Estimates report is a good place to find industry earnings growth forecasts. You get there by selecting Earnings Estimates and then Earnings Growth Rates. The report shows the last five years of historical growth, and consensus growth forecasts for the current and next fiscal year, as well as for the next five years, for both the company and its industry.

Convert Earnings Growth to Sales Growth

Once you have the industry forecast, you can convert the long-term earnings growth number to sales growth. On average, long-term industry earnings growth typically outruns sales growth by 10 to 15 percent or so. Also, analysts' long-term forecasts usually run high, probably also by 10 to 15 percent.

Taking those two factors together, discounting long-term earnings forecasts by 25 percent (20 percent earnings growth converts to 15 percent sales growth) is a reasonable rule of thumb for estimating industry sales growth. Sure, this method involves all kinds of assumptions, but so do everybody's forecasts. In reality, it's all guesswork, and this technique is probably as good as anyone's.

Table 7-1 lists suggested guidelines for evaluating industry growth rate forecasts.

The moderate 10 percent to 14 percent growth range is a favorite for many value investors, because to them, 14 or 15 percent is high, and they think it's unrealistic to expect more. Moderate-growth industries are suitable for growth investors, but only if they can pinpoint firms growing faster than their peers.

Growth investors generally need faster-growing industries than value investors. The best growth prospects are in industries growing at least 15 percent annually. Table 7-1 summarizes the suitability of various industry growth rates for value and growth investors.

TABLE 7-1   Industry Growth Guidelines for Value and Growth Investors

Expected Industry Annual Sales Growth	Value	Growth
Declining industry (less than 3%)	No good	No good
Slow growth (3 to 8%)	Good	No good
Moderate growth (9 to 14%)	Best	Fair
Fast growth (15 to 24%)	Good	Best
Super growth (25%+)	Poor	Good

Look at high industry growth forecasts skeptically, since analysts sometimes get carried away. That's especially true when an industry is experiencing super-heated growth, such as the alternative energy industry saw in 2008.

Industry and Sector Terminology

While we're on the subject of industries, here's a rundown on the terminology.

Technically, a sector is a major business category such as technology, and an industry is a subset of the sector, such as semiconductors. Sometimes, however, the terminology is used differently. For instance, someone might describe Panera Bread as being in the fast-food sector of the restaurant industry. The terminology doesn't matter as long as, in the end, you figure out that Panera Bread is an upscale casual restaurant.

Here are ten industries considered by many analysts as having the best long-term growth prospects:

Adult education

Alternative energy

Biotechnology

Consumer financial services

IT services and consulting

Medical devices and equipment

Mining: precious metals

Oil and gas operations

Retail: Internet

Security systems and services

Here are ten industries thought to have the worst long-term growth prospects:

Advertising

Automobile and truck manufacturing

Furniture and fixtures

Home improvement products

Insurance

Printing services: commercial

Publishing

Recreational products: outdoor

Recreational vehicles

Tobacco

Industry Concentration

Concentration refers to the number of major competitors in a given industry. The best industries, from an investing perspective, are near-monopolies—that is, highly concentrated industries.

Leading firms in concentrated industries—those with only two or three major competitors—typically report higher profit margins than companies in fragmented markets. These firms give higher priority to increasing profit margins than to gaining market share through price-cutting. Oil refiners and cellular phone service providers are examples of concentrated industries.

Fragmented markets with many participants vying for position are usually price-competitive, resulting in lower profit margins. For instance, the apparel industry, with dozens of companies battling for market share, generates net profit margins around 6 percent in normal times, compared to the 11 percent average margin for all companies making up the S&P 500 Index.

New high-growth industries start out fragmented and then concentrate over time as the winners emerge. Whether a fragmented market is a good thing or a bad thing depends on the industry's maturity and growth rate. Table 7-2 lists some guidelines for growth investors.

TABLE 7-2   Suitability for Growth Investors: Industry Fragmentation/Concentration Versus Growth Rates

Expected Industry Annual Sales Growth	Fragmented	Concentrated
Declining industry (less than 3%)	No good	No good
Slow growth (3 to 9%)	No good	Okay
Moderate growth (10 to 14%)	Fair	Good
Fast growth (15 to 20%)	Good	Best
Super growth (20%+)	Best	Best

Growth investors usually do well picking the strongest player in a concentrated high-growth industry. Microsoft and Intel during the early and mid-1990s are prime examples. However, picking the eventual winner in a still-fragmented emerging industry can be even more profitable, because the biggest stock market profits typically accrue to the winners. Here are some examples:

- Google's $120 billion market cap is more than five times number two Yahoo!'s $21 billion market capitalization.
- Intel's $85 billion market cap not only dwarfs number two Texas Instruments' $23 billion, but it also exceeds the combined value of all general-purpose chipmakers.
- Wal-Mart's $195 billion market cap similarly overwhelms second banana Target's $30 billion and Costco's $20 billion. Wal-Mart's market capitalization exceeds the combined value of all other discount variety stores.
- In the software industry, Microsoft's $180 billion is almost double number two Oracle's $95 billion.

Picking Winners in an Emerging Fragmented Industry

Picking the eventual winner starts with identifying the players.

Yahoo! is a good resource for identifying the major companies in each industry. After getting a price quote, select Industry and then scroll down to the list of top companies in the industry by market cap. You can pick up the names of additional competitors by checking the news headlines for the stock on Yahoo!. For instance, if you check the headlines for Target, Yahoo! also displays current headlines for Target's major competitors.

The SEC requires companies to include competitive information in their annual reports (but not in their quarterly reports). Most companies do a reasonably complete job of describing both major and lesser competitors, but they often don't say which is which. The competitive discussion is always included in a section titled "Competition." The annual reports are lengthy, so use your browser's find function (Ctrl-F on a PC and Cmd-F on a Mac) to search for "competition" rather than scrolling through the entire report.

Reuters frequently copies the annual report's competitive discussion almost verbatim into the last paragraph of its Company Profile, so check there first, because it's a quicker access. Also, Hoovers displays its view of the top three competitors on its free Company Overview.

Unfortunately, none of these sources consistently does a complete job of listing all significant competitors. So, if you're serious about a candidate, check all of them.

Identifying the Strongest Competitors

How do you pick the eventual winner in an up-and-coming industry? Here are four factors that, considered together, do the job for me:

- **Revenue** is total sales for the year. Obviously, the firm with the highest sales is the market leader, at least for the year measured.

- **Percentage of revenue growth** is the revenue growth for the listed year compared to the previous year. The firm with the highest revenue growth is gaining market share at the expense of the other industry players.

- **Operating margin** measures profitability, excluding interest expenses, income taxes, and income from investments. All else equal, the most profitable firm in an industry ends up with the most cash to fund new-product development.

- **SG&A percentage of sales** is often referred to as overhead. SG&A (sales, general, and administrative expenses) includes all expenses except research and development (R&D) and the direct costs of producing the company's goods or services. Computing the SG&A percentage of sales measures the company's operating efficiency. The lower the percentage, the more efficient the company.

Database Software Industry

Here's an example of how you could have used these four factors to analyze the database software industry during the mid-1990s when Oracle, although it was the market leader, was battling contenders Sybase and Informix for control of the still-young industry.

We'll pick up the story in 1993, when Oracle was still in a dogfight with Sybase and Informix. Table 7-3 summarizes the four performance items from 1993 to 1997.

TABLE 7-3   Database Software Industry Key Performance Measures

	Revenue (in Millions of Dollars)	% Revenue Growth	Operating Margin %	SG&A % of Sales
1993				
Oracle	2,001	33	21	44
Sybase	484	83	16	51
Informix	353	24	24	48
1994				
Oracle	2,967	48	22	43
Sybase	825	70	16	49
Informix	470	33	20	51
1995				
Oracle	4,223	42	21	42
Sybase	957	16	2	57
Informix	633	35	10	56
1996				
Oracle	5,684	35	22	40
Sybase	1,011	6	−7	59
Informix	735	16	−8	66
1997				
Oracle	7,144	26	17	38
Sybase	904	−11	5	59
Informix	664	−10	−54	76

By the end of 1993, Sybase had just ridden an 83 percent year-over-year sales gain to grab the number two spot from Informix. At that time, Informix was the slowest grower of the three but had recorded the highest operating margin, indicating that it wasn't giving away the store to gain sales. Oracle, however, was the most efficient operator of the bunch, with SG&A sapping only 44 percent of sales compared to Informix's 48 percent, and 51 percent for Sybase. From the data, it appears that Sybase sacrificed profits to gain market share in 1993.

Sybase increased market share again in 1994, racking up a 70 percent sales gain. But again, Sybase, with the lowest operating margin, was sacrificing earnings for market share. The numbers show that Informix, with increasing costs and diminishing operating margin, was struggling to stay in the game.

Oracle took over the market in 1995, gaining share while Sybase and Informix apparently slashed profits in a vain attempt to remain competitive.

Finally, in 1997, Sybase faltered, recording a drop in revenues, while Informix crashed and burned when its executives were caught cooking the books. From that point on, Sybase and Informix fell by the wayside.

Search Engine Wars: Google Versus Yahoo!

Here's another example illustrating how analyzing the same four factors would have helped you know that Google was a stronger pick than Yahoo! when the two battled for search engine supremacy in the mid-2000s.

Yahoo!, which operated a manually updated directory and charged for business listings, was the industry leader until Google came on the scene in late 1998. Google, which produced better search results, immediately began taking market share from Yahoo! and other search engines.

In 2000, Google began selling ads triggered by search keywords, but it didn't go public until 2004. In 2003, Yahoo! switched to an automatically updated, advertising-supported search engine, similar to Google.

Table 7-4 shows what you would have observed if you had analyzed Google and Yahoo! using the same four fundamental factors used to identify the strongest database software industry competitor. The table starts in 2003, when the two were roughly equal in terms of revenues.

TABLE 7-4   Key Performance Measures for Google and Yahoo!

	Revenue (in Millions of Dollars)	% Revenue Growth	Operating Margin %	SG&A % of Sales
2003				
Yahoo!	1,625	71	18.2	42.3
Google	1,466	234	23	12
2004				
Yahoo!	3,574	120	19	29
Google	3,189	118	20	15
2005				
Yahoo!	5,258	47	21	26
Google	6,139	93	33	14
2006				
Yahoo!	6,426	22	15	29
Google	10,605	73	34	15
2007				
Yahoo!	6,969	9	10	32
Google	16,594	57	31	17
2008				
Yahoo!	7,209	3	0	32
Google	21,796	31	25	17

As you can see, it wasn't even close. Google was consistently the faster grower, the more profitable as measured by operating margins, and the more efficient as gauged by SG&A percentage of sales.

Industry Scuttlebutt

The final step is to get up to speed on the current trends and issues facing the industry. You can do that by reading the news and in-depth reports usually found on industry trade magazine websites. You'd be hard-pressed to find an industry that isn't covered by at least one trade magazine. Appendix A lists trade magazine websites for a variety of industries. If you can't find the industry there, search for the industry name and the phrase "trade magazine" on Google (www.google.com). You can also use Google to search directly for stories about problems surrounding a candidate. Try searching for the company name plus terms such as "accused," "faltered," "problems," "rip-off," and "stumbled."

Summary

Growth investors will do best picking candidates in fast-growing industries. You can score the biggest profits by pinpointing the eventual winner in a still-fragmented emerging industry. Focusing on just four factors—sales (revenue), sales growth, operating margin, and SG&A compared to sales—will help you pick the winners.

Keeping tabs on industry happenings by reading industry trade magazine websites will keep you up to speed on industry developments and ensure that you haven't overlooked an important industry player or a significant event that might change the outlook for your candidate or for the industry as a whole.

8

Analysis Tool #5:
Business Plan Analysis

If you were considering buying a local business, such as a bicycle shop, would you base your purchase decision entirely on how much money the seller said he or she made last year or on the seller's profit forecast for this year?

I bet not. Instead, you'd probably want to know where the shop gets its bicycles, how much it pays for them, and whether the competition is paying the same prices.

You would check for alternative sources in case an important supplier goes out of business or decides to open its own outlet and stop selling to you. You'd also want to know something about your customers. Are they mostly individual consumers, or did one or two bicycle courier services account for a big hunk of last year's purchases?

Most people would explore such topics if they were, in fact, thinking of buying a bicycle shop. Yet all too often, investors skip this vital step when analyzing a stock.

For evidence, consider the dot-com start-ups that each raised hundreds of millions of dollars from millions of investors, both amateur and professional. Many of them had nonsensical business plans with zero chance of success. For instance, at least one web retailer planned to, and actually did, sell every product at cost or less.

In this chapter, you'll learn to analyze the pluses and minuses of your candidate's business model. Many of the concepts presented were inspired by the ideas of Harvard Business School Professor Michael Porter, considered by many to be the guru of competitive analysis.

Introduction

Nothing attracts competition more than big profits. But no matter how strong the market looks in the beginning, the unimpeded entry of new players leads to supply exceeding demand and tumbling profit margins as players fight for market share. That's why you need to consider a company's competitive advantages, or barriers to entry, in your analysis.

Barriers to entry discourage new players from entering the market. Without sufficient barriers to entry, a company's long-term success is problematic, because it will be easy for new competitors to enter the fray.

Barriers to entry can take many forms. The following sections describe some of the more common ones. You will uncover others when you analyze prospective candidates. A barrier to entry enjoyed by one company translates to a risk factor for its competition. Besides barriers to entry, every company's business model embodies a variety of additional risk factors.

To streamline the analysis, I've combined similar barriers to entry and risk factors into single rating factors. Most of the factors can be considered either an advantage or a disadvantage, depending on the circumstances.

Use the Business Plan Scorecard provided near the end of this chapter to assess each candidate's business model. Score each business plan factor as 1, –1, or 0, depending on whether you judge it to be an advantage, disadvantage, or not applicable, respectively.

Brand Identity

Many consumers will pay more for Nike shoes, a Sony TV, or an iPod than they would for lesser brands or generics. These products have achieved a combination of brand awareness and perceived superior quality in consumers' minds. A strong brand identity often translates into higher selling prices and higher profit margins.

Hewlett Packard's name is synonymous with computer printers, and HP enjoys a strong reputation for quality products. Those factors taken together equate to strong brand identity, explaining why HP printers outsell Lexmark by more than 5 to 1, even though Lexmark's products may be as good as or better than HP's.

As another example, consider the experiences of Oakley and Sunglass Hut. Oakley makes designer sunglasses, and Sunglass Hut, a retail chain, is the largest seller of designer sunglasses in the U.S. Back in 2001, Sunglass Hut was Oakley's largest customer, accounting for 19 percent of its sales. Then, in mid-2001, Luxottica Group, an Italian firm, acquired Sunglass Hut. That created a problem for Oakley, because Luxottica already owned Ray-Ban, a competing sunglasses brand. Sure enough, Luxottica dropped Oakley's products shortly after taking over Sunglass Hut.

But Sunglass Hut's shoppers wanted Oakley, not Ray-Ban. By mid-December, the chain was once again stocking Oakley's glasses, a testament to the power of the Oakley brand.

A strong brand identity gives its owner a competitive advantage and acts as a barrier to entry to new players. Give 1 point to companies with strong brand identities, and subtract 1 point for companies facing a competitor with strong brand identity.

Here is a list of highly regarded U.S. brands based on information compiled from a variety of sources:

Google	Toyota
Coca-Cola	Disney
Microsoft	McDonald's
IBM	Mercedes Benz
GE	HP
Intel	Gillette
Nokia	American Express

Other Barriers to Entry

You will uncover candidates with other barriers to entry in your analysis. Add 1 point for additional significant barriers to entry, and subtract 1 point from companies facing additional barriers. Add or subtract 1 point maximum for this category.

Distribution Model

In the early 1990s, PC makers Compaq and Dell were vying for market leadership. Although they offered similar products, the two companies had developed different distribution strategies.

Compaq adhered to the traditional model, selling to distributors that in turn sold to retail stores and systems builders. Compaq designed standard models, built them in bulk quantities, and warehoused the completed systems until it received orders. Each step of the process—building systems ahead of orders, warehousing, and selling through distributors and retailers—added costs.

Dell, in contrast, had no dealers, distributors, or warehouses stuffed with assembled computers. Instead, Dell allowed customers to pick and choose features, and then Dell built each computer to the buyer's specifications. Dell undoubtedly incurred higher costs, because it was dealing with thousands of individual customers instead of a few distributors. But on balance, it was the lowest-cost producer because it didn't have to pay for warehousing, and no middlemen were taking a cut. Dell's unique distribution system enabled it to overtake Compaq's once-commanding market share lead.

Eventually, Compaq floundered and was acquired by Hewlett Packard, but that's not the end of the story.

In the mid-2000s, as the technology evolved, consumers switched en masse from desktop computers to notebooks. That change transformed Dell's distribution strategy from an advantage into a liability. Here's why.

Notebook computers, no matter the brand, are all mass-produced in factories in China and Taiwan. A particular model's configuration is fixed—no customization can occur. Moreover, individual consumers became the most important market segment, whereas before it was large corporations. That was bad news for Dell, because many consumers prefer to buy notebooks in retail stores, where they can touch them and try them out before purchase.

Taken together, the switch to notebooks and the change in market demographics torpedoed Dell's direct distribution strategy, and the firm began selling PCs to retail stores, taking away its competitive advantage.

You may never find situations as clear-cut as Dell versus Compaq, but be on the lookout for companies with similar operational advantages in areas such as order processing, production techniques, marketing, and the like. Score 1 for companies enjoying such operational advantages and –1 for firms facing competitors with distribution model advantages.

Access to Distribution

If you were to start a new rock band, you could post your videos on YouTube and, if you were lucky, build up a big following and eventually sell your CDs on the web.

Contrast that scenario to starting a new line of laundry detergents, which are mostly sold in supermarkets where shelf space is at a premium. There's no room for a new detergent without eliminating an existing brand, and Procter & Gamble and its ilk deploy legions of salespeople to ensure that doesn't happen.

Same thing for cell phones. Most consumers buy their phones from wireless carriers such as AT&T or Verizon. So, if you wanted to bring a new cell phone to market, you'd be limited to a handful of possible distributors.

Locked-up distribution channels represent a strong barrier to entry. Award 1 business model point to companies enjoying distribution channel advantages, and subtract 1 point from companies facing competitors with those advantages.

Product Useful Life/Product Price

Long product-life items such as automobiles, home entertainment systems, computers, and washing machines are discretionary purchases that can usually be put off. However, food, healthcare products, cigarettes, and office supplies are quickly used up, and inventories must be frequently replenished. For example, it's unlikely that Bank of America stopped buying staples when it slashed spending to stay afloat in 2008 and 2009. Companies selling short-lived products have a business plan advantage.

This principle isn't limited to consumer products. Cabot Micro-electronics makes slurries, used in the semiconductor production process. Something like toothpaste, the slurries are used up in the process and must be continuously replenished. Consequently, despite the semiconductor industry ups and downs, as of the end of its September 2008 fiscal year, Cabot had grown sales 21 percent, on average, over the previous 10 years. In contrast, industry-leading chipmaker Intel had averaged only 4 percent annual growth over the same period.

Similarly, companies with inexpensive products have an advantage over companies with expensive products, especially in a weak economy. For instance, when times are tough, consumers put off buying a car or a new home, but they still buy breakfast cereal.

Award 1 point to companies with short-lived and/or low-priced products, and subtract 1 point from companies selling discretionary purchase products.

Access to Supply/Number of Suppliers

Most firms enjoy a choice of multiple vendors eager to supply needed services and materials. But sometimes you'll encounter companies where that is not the case.

For example, in March 2005, nutritional oils supplier Martek Bio-sciences' share price took a big hit after the company said problems at one of its sole supplier's plants would cause April-quarter sales to come in 26 percent short of earlier forecasts.

In other instances, companies may have multiple suppliers but face an industry-wide shortage of critical components. That happened in 2006 when notebook PC makers suffered earnings shortfalls because problems at Sony triggered a battery shortage, and again in 2007 when LCD panels were in short supply. Solar panel makers experienced similar problems in 2007 when they couldn't get enough polysilicon material.

Subtract 1 point from companies that face tight supply or allocated markets or that are dependent on only one or two suppliers.

Revenue Stream Predictability

It's much easier to forecast a company's future earnings if you have a good handle on its likely sales. Companies with long-term contracts or stable client bases have predictable revenue streams. Examples include health plans, credit card processors, telephone and cable TV companies, and utilities. Firms with predictable revenue streams suffer less year-to-year volatility in revenues, cash flow, and earnings than those that don't.

Conversely, media companies and makers of designer clothing, sporting goods, durable goods (such as stoves), video games, semiconductors, computers, computer software, and cameras all have unpredictable revenue streams. Hence, their earnings are equally unpredictable.

Award 1 point to companies with predictable revenues, and subtract 1 point from companies with unpredictable revenue streams.

Number of Customers

Companies with just a few customers accounting for a majority of sales are vulnerable to shifts in the growth rates of their customers and/or changes in their customers' strategies. Loss of a single customer to a competitor can severely impact a company's performance.

Furthermore, an important customer can squeeze a supplier's profit margins by insisting on lower prices. Suppliers to the cable TV, aircraft, and automobile industries fall into this category.

Give 1 point to companies with thousands of customers, and award 0 points to companies with a few hundred customers. Subtract 1 point if fewer than 10 customers account for 50 percent or more of the firm's sales.

Product Cycle

The product cycle is how long a product is on the market before it's replaced by a newer version. Companies with short product cycles—including women's clothing makers, automobile companies, and most technology manufacturers—are riskier investments than those with long product cycles, such as candy makers. The short product cycle companies must continuously develop new products and run the risk of seeing their creations made obsolete by a hotshot new competitor.

Give 1 point to companies with long product cycle products, and subtract 1 point from makers of high-tech and other short-cycle products.

Product/Market Diversification

Firms offering just a single product line are riskier than companies with a variety of products, because something unforeseen can happen to unexpectedly kill the sales of almost any product.

Similarly, companies serving a single business segment—such as the automotive, construction, and energy industries—would suffer when those industries go into a downturn.

Firms producing multiple products serving a variety of markets are less susceptible to those sorts of mishaps and to economic downturns than less diversified companies.

Award 1 point to companies with multiple products serving diversified markets, and subtract 1 point from single-product or single-market firms.

Growth by Acquisition

In the beginning, most firms grow organically. Their growth comes from selling more products or opening new stores. Eventually growth slows as supply catches up with demand or new competition appears. When that happens, management must find new ways to sustain the growth rate; otherwise, the slowing growth will sink the firm's stock price.

At that point, most firms develop new products or enter additional markets, but others turn to an acquisition strategy to maintain growth.

Growth by acquisition is an appealing strategy. Purchasing an established company already serving a market saves the acquirer the time and expense of learning the business and developing products from scratch. The process is relatively inexpensive because the acquirer often uses its own newly issued shares to pay for the acquisition.

The strategy is often successful early on, and the acquiring firm is able to maintain a strong growth rate, keeping the market happy and its share price up. The latter is important because the firm's stock is the currency enabling the acquisitions.

Eventually, however, the numbers get too big. Consider the math. A company with $100 million in annual sales can achieve a 25 percent sales increase by acquiring a company selling $25 million annually. However, once it reaches the $200 million level, it must acquire $50 million in annual sales to maintain the same growth rate. Compounding the problem, the bigger it gets, the fewer the acquisition candidates.

Sooner or later, something goes wrong. Perhaps the acquirer overpays. Maybe the acquired company doesn't perform to expectations, or expected cost-cutting synergies fail to materialize. Perhaps a clash between corporate cultures disenchants key employees in the acquired company, and they leave.

Whatever the cause, the serial acquirer fails to meet earnings growth forecasts, torpedoing its stock price. The lower stock price takes away its acquisition currency, further slowing growth and thereby putting more pressure on its share price. In essence, it's game over!

Easy-to-Spot Serial Acquirers

When making an acquisition, the acquirer usually pays more than the accounting book value for the target firm. The difference between the purchase price and book value is added to either goodwill or intangibles on the acquirer's balance sheet. The goodwill and intangibles totals will be close to 0 for firms that have never made any acquisitions.

Thus, you can gauge a firm's acquisition history by comparing its goodwill and intangibles to its total assets. For brevity, call the result of dividing goodwill plus intangibles by total assets the GI/A ratio. The higher the ratio, the more acquisitive the firm.

Drugstore chains Walgreens and CVS afford a good example. Both are relatively fast-growing firms. Walgreens relies almost entirely on internal growth, while CVS depends mostly on acquisitions to increase sales.

According to their December 2008 balance sheets, Walgreens' GI/A ratio was 5 percent, compared to 59 percent for CVS.

Table 8-1 shows GI/A ratios for firms that have employed acquisitions for much of their recent growth. For comparison, Table 8-2 shows the GI/A ratios for firms that have grown mostly organically.

TABLE 8-1   Goodwill Plus Intangibles Divided by Total Assets (GI/A) for Serial Acquirers (as of 12/08)

Company	GI/A
CACI International	62%
CVS Caremark	59%
eBay	50%
Expedia	74%
Express Scripts	64%
Fortune Brands	56%
J M Smucker	52%
L-3 Communications	58%
Laboratory Corp. of America	64%
Medtronic	45%
Oracle	56%
Procter & Gamble	65%
Walt Disney	48%
WD-40	53%
Weight Watchers	76%
Zimmer Holdings	50%

As you can see, a wide divide exists between the ratios of serial acquirers and organic growers. As a rule of thumb, organic growers usually show ratios below 5 percent, and ratios of 15 percent or more identify firms growing at least partly by acquisition.

TABLE 8-2   Goodwill Plus Intangibles Divided by Total Assets (GI/A) for Organic Growers (as of 12/08)

Company	GI/A
Apple	1%
Bed Bath & Beyond	0%
Bob Evans Farms	4%
Bunge	2%
CARBO Ceramics	1%
Caterpillar	4%
Columbia Sportswear	3%
ConocoPhillips	3%
Digital Globe	1%
Harley Davidson	2%
Home Depot	3%
Kohl's	2%
Microchip Technology	2%
Pegasystems	4%
PetSmart	2%
Seacor Holdings	2%
XTO Energy	4%

Award 1 point to companies with GI/A ratios less than 5 percent, and subtract 1 point for companies with ratios greater than 15 percent.

Overblown Competitive Advantages: Factors That Should Make a Difference But Often Don't

Some supposed competitive advantages sound good but somehow never amount to much in practice. The following are two competitive advantages that you'd be better off ignoring unless you're an expert in the field.

Patents

The pharmaceuticals industry effectively employs patents as a barrier to entry. However, pharmaceuticals are more the exception than the rule. For instance, tech companies file hundreds, if not thousands, of patents annually. Yet new competitors constantly pop up, and it's hard to think of a tech name that has turned its patents into an effective barrier to entry.

Few investors have the expertise to judge a patent's value as a barrier to entry. Even in the pharmaceuticals industry, it's difficult to assess the value of a particular patent. A new drug may sound miraculous, but an even better treatment could be on the way from a competitor.

Ignore patents as a significant barrier to entry unless you are an expert in the field *and* a patent attorney.

Proprietary Technology/Production Processes

In theory, a company's superior production processes or equipment could be an effective barrier to entry. In practice, these advantages rarely produce the expected results.

For example, again comparing Lexmark to Hewlett Packard, Lexmark enjoys laser printer production cost advantages compared to HP because Lexmark makes its own printer engines (the guts of the printer), while Hewlett Packard buys its engines from Canon. Somehow, that advantage has never meant much. Hewlett Packard still dominates the industry, and Lexmark has failed to gain significant market share.

Every CEO, given the opportunity, will tell you why his or her company's products are technologically superior. That's their job. Many market analysts repeat that same dogma as truth. As with patents, unless you're an expert, you'd be well advised to remain skeptical about touted technological advantages.

Business Plan Scorecard

As discussed earlier, award 1 point for each category where a company has a significant advantage, and subtract 1 point for categories where it is at a disadvantage. Score 0 where the category is irrelevant. See Chapters 15 and 16 for further details on the relevance of the categories to each strategy.

Business Plan Scorecard	
Brand identity	____
Other barriers to entry	____
Distribution model	____
Access to distribution	____
Product useful life/product price	____
Access to supply/number of suppliers	____
Revenue stream predictability	____
Number of customers	____
Product cycle	____
Product/market diversification	____
Growth by acquisition	____
Serial acquirers	____
Total score	____

Summary

Professional money managers routinely evaluate a firm's business plan before investing, and you should too. Technology candidates usually score lower than other industries, because many do not enjoy strong brand identity that separates them from the field, most offer expensive products with short life cycles, and many depend on acquisitions for growth.

9

Analysis Tool #6:
Evaluate Management Quality

Many professional money managers consider management quality an important consideration in their analysis. They often visit the company and spend a day or two talking with management to determine if its key officers are in tune with stockholders' best interests. It's impractical for individual investors to visit companies and meet with management. However, we still have clues at our disposal to accomplish the job.

Key Executive and Board Quality

Start by reviewing key officers' resumes. Reuters' Officers and Directors report includes biographies of key executives and board members.

Look for officers with relevant experience. At least some should be crusty veterans with years of experience in the same industry. Imagine that you're doing the hiring. Would you hire these people based on their experience? Notice how long the key executives have been on the job. Numerous recent management changes signal problems.

Look at the makeup of the board of directors. The best boards are filled mostly with CEOs of successful firms in the same field, not consultants and venture capitalists.

During the Internet bubble heyday, many hot startups were run by investment bankers rather than experienced managers. Here's an extreme example.

Webvan was a web-based grocery retailer offering home delivery that went public in November 1999 and filed for bankruptcy less than two years later. Its CEO had previously been a management consultant. Its senior VP of corporate operations and finance, a lawyer, came from stockbroker Merrill Lynch. The VP of merchandising, the man responsible for ordering the groceries, came from General Electric. Nobody on the board of directors had experience in selling groceries.

Unfortunately, things haven't changed much. You'll still find the boards of many companies filled with private equity investors, stockbrokers, lawyers, and consultants.

Clean Accounting

Many market pros consider clean and straightforward accounting a hallmark of good management. For them, repeated one-time, non-recurring, and extraordinary charges are red flags signaling questionable accounting practices.

The reason that some corporate executives like nonrecurring expenses is that they don't have to count them when they tabulate pro forma earnings. Thus, the more expenses that can be defined as non-recurring, the higher the reported pro forma earnings.

There's nothing wrong with pro forma earnings when they are used appropriately. Such uses might include presenting the results of recently merged companies "as if" they had always been a single company, or excluding the effects of one-time events such as income tax refunds or legal expenses.

The problem comes in when managers use them inappropriately, and repeatedly, simply to boost pro forma earnings. Unfortunately, analysts often accept management's definition of what's appropriate without questioning it.

It's easy to spot nonrecurring charges. Both Reuters and MSN Money list nonrecurring items on a separate line of each company's income statement. The entries are labeled Unusual Expense/ Income on both.

The raw numbers don't mean much by themselves, so it's best to compare nonrecurring expenses to total sales, also shown on the income statement. You do that by dividing the nonrecurring expenses by sales and computing the result as a percentage. For instance, the ratio would be 10 percent if a company recorded sales of $1,000 and listed $100 in nonrecurring charges (100/1,000).

Table 9-1 lists the nonrecurring expenses to sales percentages for a sampling of companies. I compiled the data using MSN Money's income statement, which combines several separate line items into Total Extraordinary Items. If you use the MSN Reports, add unusual expenses to total extraordinary items, and divide that total by revenues.

Use the Reuters income statements if you want to see more details. If you do, consider all charges labeled unusual, restructuring, purchased R&D, extraordinary, accounting changes, and discontinued operations in the calculation.

TABLE 9-1   Unusual Expenses and Extraordinary Charges as a Percentage of Annual Sales

Company	2008	2007	2006	2005	2004
Adobe Systems	1%	0%	1%	9%	0%
Alleghany	68%	41%	39%	69%	58%
American Water Works	32%	23%	11%	18%	37%
Applied Materials	1%	0%	2%	0%	2%
Avalonbay Communities	42%	17%	17%	37%	29%
Boston Scientific	34%	14%	53%	17%	2%
Caterpillar	0%	0%	0%0	0%	0%
Google	5%	0%	0%	0%	05
MDC Holdings	20%	25%	2%	0%	0%
Walt Disney	0%	0%	0%	0%	0%

Figures shown are from fiscal year data closest to the calendar year columns, compiled from MSN Money income statements. Charges considered include unusual expenses and total extraordinary items.

Judging management quality is a subjective exercise. Most firms from time to time incur costs that are truly nonrecurring, such as charges associated with losing a lawsuit, closing factories, or writing off worthless patents. The trick is to differentiate those from the companies that persistently come up with nonrecurring expenses to boost pro forma earnings.

Looking for recent years' patterns is more significant than any single year's number. You can do that by simply eyeballing the results or averaging the past five years' ratios. Consider companies with five-year average ratios much above 4 percent as suspected nonrecurring expense abusers.

For a historical perspective, Table 9-2, taken from the first edition of this book, shows the same information for a selection of companies as found in early 2002.

TABLE 9-2   One-Time, Nonrecurring, and Extraordinary Charges as a Percentage of Annual Sales as of Early 2002

Company	2001	2000	1999	1998	1997
Bed Bath & Beyond	0%	0%	0%	0%	0%
Cisco Systems	9%	7%	4%	7%	8%
Computer Associates		–4%	13%	23%	0%
Dell Computer	2%	1%	1%	0%	0%
Intel	1%	0%	1%	1%	0%
Lucent Technologies	57%	3%	–8%	4%	5%
Microsoft	0%	1%	0%	0%	2%
Tyco International	45%	15%	7%	15%	12%

Figures shown are from fiscal year data closest to the calendar year columns, compiled from Reuters' income statements. Charges considered include unusual expenses, restructuring, purchased R&D, extraordinary items, accounting charges, and discontinued items.

Tyco's CEO, Dennis Kozlowski, and CFO, Mark Swartz, were convicted of grand larceny. Lucent flirted with bankruptcy but didn't file and eventually merged with Alcatel.

Earnings Growth Stability

Looking at a firm's historical earnings pattern can also help you evaluate management quality. Every company has its bad years, but overall, solid managers turn out relatively consistent earnings growth. Conversely, some firms' roller coaster earnings histories make you wonder whether management is really in control.

Both MSN Money's Financial Results Highlights Report and Reuters' Financial Highlights reports list up to three years' reported earnings per share in formats that make it easy to visually evaluate earnings growth stability. They show each fiscal year's quarterly earnings in a column so that you can compare the same quarter of each year (such as the March quarter) and thus eliminate seasonal variations. That's good for a quick overview, but you really need at least four, and ideally five, years worth of data to analyze earnings growth stability. Earnings.com is a good resource for quarter earnings per share data going back five years or so. On the downside, Earnings.com shows the EPS data in list form, so you have to build your own table.

Table 9-3 shows an example of a company with consistent earnings history. Always compare earnings to the year-ago period, not the previous quarter, to rule out seasonal distortions. Don't be too hard of a grader. Even well-managed companies have occasional bad quarters.

TABLE 9-3   Earnings Per Share, Quarterly Results; Consistent Earnings History Reflects Quality Management

	FY 12/08	FY 12/07	FY 12/06	FY 12/05	FY 12/04
1st quarter	$0.32	$0.24	$0.14	$0.12	$0.09
2nd quarter	$0.38	$0.29	$0.26	$0.20	$0.14
3rd quarter	$0.35	$0.30	$0.26	$0.35	$0.35
4th quarter	$0.67	$0.53	$0.40	$0.35	$0.29
Totals	$1.72	$1.36	$1.06	$1.02	$0.87

Table 9-4 shows an example of a company with an erratic earnings history, casting doubt on management quality.

TABLE 9-4   Earnings Per Share, Quarterly Results; Inconsistent Earnings Growth

	FY 12/08	FY 12/07	FY 12/06	FY 12/05	FY 12/04
1st quarter	−$0.27	$0.09	−$0.04	$0.07	$0.05
2nd quarter	$0.15	$0.14	$0.02	$0.14	$0.08
3rd quarter	−$0.20	$0.12	−$0.17	$0.11	$0.14
4th quarter	−$0.05	−$0.05	$0.01	$0.35	$0.31
Totals	−$0.37	$0.30	−$0.18	$0.67	$0.58

Stock Ownership

It's reassuring to know that key management, particularly the CEO and CFO, hold large positions in a firm. What constitutes a large position varies with company size, but think millions of shares for the CEO and hundreds of thousands for the CFO. It's disconcerting if key officers hold only a few thousand shares and sell immediately after they exercise stock options.

Yahoo!'s Insider Roster report is a good place to see how many shares insiders own. Reuters' Officers and Directors reports show the stock options held by each insider. Low shareholdings by key officers isn't a deal breaker per se, but it should be considered along with the other management quality factors.

Summary

Management quality is probably the single most important determinate of a company's success. Reviewing key officers' resumes is a good check on management's qualifications for the job. Analyzing the firm's accounting cleanliness tells you whether its officers are a conservative lot looking out for the firm and its shareholders' long-term interests, or are bending the rules to achieve short-term gains. Analyzing earnings growth stability and key officers' shareholdings gives you further perspective on management quality.

10

Analysis Tool #7: Analyze Financial Fitness

Picking financially strong stocks is critical to investing success. This chapter describes how to achieve that goal.

Financial Fitness Counts

Stocks move up or down on a daily basis for any number of reasons. But in the long term, only two factors account for most stock losses:

- Earnings growth expectations drop.
- The market believes that the company is running low on cash and might file for bankruptcy.

Most analysts and individual investors concentrate on the first one and don't worry much about the second.

For proof, look no further than Fannie Mae, Freddie Mac, or AIG. All three were taken over by the U.S. government in 2008 to prevent them from filing for bankruptcy. Yet, despite numerous warning signals and plunging stock prices, many analysts continued to advise buying these stocks until shortly before they imploded.

A company doesn't have to file for bankruptcy to ruin your day. Just coming close would drive its share price into the ground.

Given the consequences, you'd think that financial strength would be an important consideration when market analysts decide on their buy/sell ratings. But all too often, it isn't, so you're on your own in this department.

Fortunately, the information you need to do the analysis is readily available. Moreover, you don't have be a bond analyst to do the job. You only need to determine if a company is a potential bankruptcy candidate, not whether its bonds should be rated AAA or AA. The process is straightforward; anyone can do it. This chapter describes two different methods of evaluating financial fitness, depending on whether it's a low- or high-debt firm.

Low-debt companies are relatively easy to analyze, while high-debt firms require spending some time with your calculator. Thus, if working with numbers is not your idea of fun, consider confining your candidate list to low-debt stocks. That shouldn't be a problem—you'll find plenty that fit the bill.

If you don't want to do either of those analyses, we describe two alternative checks later in this chapter: looking up the firm's current bond ratings, and checking to see if bond traders are pricing a risk premium into the firm's bond prices, indicating perceived default risk.

Pinpointing Financially Challenged Companies

Bankruptcy candidates typically fall into one of three categories:

- **Busted cash burners** are newer firms that have never made it to the stage where they consistently turn a profit. They may have little or no long-term debt because they were originally funded via IPOs and follow-on stock offerings. Now they are running short of cash and can't raise more.

- **Overburdened debtors** typically are large, mature companies with a history of using debt to enhance productivity. Then something happens and they can no longer generate sufficient cash to service their debt.

- **Solvent and/or profitable companies** may be established firms that file for bankruptcy to avoid crippling lawsuits, such as asbestos-related claims.

We'll focus on tools to detect the first two categories. But neither would protect you from firms that misrepresent their financial condition. For instance, our analysis procedures would not detect that assets held are worth less than shown on the balance sheet.

Simplify the Problem

You can analyze low-debt firms using the Busted Cash Burner analysis, which is simpler than the Detailed Fiscal Fitness Exam required for high-debt firms. So the first order of business is determining whether your stock falls in the low- or high-debt category.

Measuring Debt

What's the best way to measure debt? I suggest using the financial leverage ratio, often simply called "leverage" or "leverage ratio." Whatever you call it, the formula is total assets divided by shareholders' equity. The concept of using assets to measure debt probably sounds backwards, but it works. Here's why.

If you do the algebra, you'll find that financial leverage is also equal to $1 + TL / SE$, where TL is total liabilities and SE is shareholders' equity. In other words, financial leverage is total liabilities divided by shareholders' equity, plus 1. So it's equivalent to comparing liabilities to assets.

The advantage of using financial leverage instead of TL/SE is that you don't have to do the math. MSN Money, Morningstar, Forbes, and possibly others do the calculation and list it on their financial ratios reports.

A leverage ratio of 1 equates to no debt, and the higher the ratio, the higher the debt. The median (as many stocks above as below) leverage ratio for all stocks is around 2.5. However, banks and other financial institutions carry higher ratios, typically between 5 and 15. For them, borrowed cash is their inventory.

The financial leverage ratio is a better debt measure than the more common debt/equity ratios. The debt/equity ratio counts only long-term debt, while the total debt/equity ratio counts both short-

and long-term debt. You'd think that the total D/E would cover all the
bases, but it doesn't. Some firms list certain debt items in categories
that don't get counted by the D/E ratios. By contrast, the leverage
ratio counts everything.

Table 10-1 lists the financial leverage ratios for Fannie Mae,
Freddie Mac, and AIG as of June 30, 2008, shortly before they
imploded.

TABLE 10-1 Financial Leverage Ratios

Company	Leverage
Fannie Mae	21.5
Freddie Mac	66.9
AIG	13.4

Table 10-2 lists the financial leverage ratios for the 11 publicly
traded firms that filed for bankruptcy during the first three months of
2009. The ratios were taken from each firm's last financial report
before filing.

TABLE 10-2 Financial Leverage Ratios for Firms That Filed for Bankruptcy in Early 2009

Company	Leverage
BearingPoint	Negative equity
Fleetwood Enterprises	13.9
Magna Entertainment	4.3
Milacron	Negative equity
Nortel Networks	Negative equity
Pacific Energy Resources	Negative equity
Smurfit-Stone Container	Negative equity
Tarragon	Negative equity
Tronox	4.3
Trump Entertainment Resorts	2,649
Young Broadcasting	Negative equity

Negative equity means that liabilities exceed assets; in other words, the company is technically insolvent. However, that doesn't necessarily mean that it is a bankruptcy candidate. That depends on whether it is generating sufficient cash to service or, even better, pay down its debt.

Use the leverage ratio to determine if you can apply the Busted Cash Burner analysis or if you need to do the Detailed Fiscal Fitness Exam. Table 10-3 gives the rules.

TABLE 10-3   Financial Leverage Ratio Determines the Required Fiscal Fitness Analysis

Leverage Ratio	Suggested Analysis
Negative	Detailed Fiscal Fitness Exam
Less than 2.5	Busted Cash Burners
2.5 or greater	Detailed Fiscal Fitness Exam

Detecting Potential Busted Cash Burners

Determining if a stock is a potential busted cash burner involves comparing its operating cash flow to working capital. The following sections explain what those terms mean.

Operating Cash Flow

Operating cash flow is the cash that moved into or out of a firm's bank accounts as a result of its main operations during a specified period. Operating cash flow excludes cash flows resulting from adding or paying down debt, buying capital equipment, selling more shares, and so on.

It's better to analyze operating cash flow than earnings, because a firm could be reporting positive earnings but still be burning cash (cash is flowing out, not in). The following sections describe three ways that could happen.

Example #1

Say that Company A reports a $1,000 sale to Customer B. Next, say that Company A recorded the $1,000 order as shipped, but Customer B hadn't paid for the goods by the end of the quarter.

Following the rules, Company A records the $1,000 as a completed sale, deducts the product cost and other expenses, and logs the difference—say, $200—as net income. Because it hadn't yet received any cash from Company B, Company A added the $1,000 unpaid bill to accounts receivables.

Thus, Company A showed the $1,000 sale and the $200 profit on its income statement, but it didn't receive any cash from the customer. In fact, Company A actually spent $800 in real cash. Consequently, its operating cash flow was a negative $800.

Example #2

Let's modify that scenario and assume that Customer B did pay before the books were closed. But to get the best prices, Company A ordered enough materials to build two of the products—say, $600 worth. So Company A had an extra $300 worth of materials in its inventory. Assuming that Company A paid cash for the materials, it ended up with $100 less in the bank ($200 net income (profit) on the product sold, less $300 for extra inventory). So it recorded $200 income on the sale, but its operating cash flow was a minus $100.

Example #3

Finally, assume a third scenario in which Customer B paid before the end of the quarter, but Company A had to buy a new machine costing $2,000 to produce the product. So Company A's operating cash flow was $200, but after shelling out $2,000 in capital expenses, it was, in fact, $1,800 poorer for the transaction. Free cash flow is accounting terminology for operating cash flow minus capital expenses (plants and equipment). In this example, Company A's free cash flow was a negative $1,800.

Since capital expenses generally are an optional expense, we'll use operating cash flow to analyze potential busted cash burners.

Working Capital

Examining cash flow tells only half the story. You must also determine if the company has enough cash to run its business. For that, we'll check working capital, which is current assets minus current liabilities. In accounting terminology, "current" refers to assets and liabilities that are short-term (less than one year) in nature.

Current Assets

Current assets include cash plus inventories and accounts receivables. It doesn't include nonliquid assets such as buildings, capital equipment, and patents.

Cash includes cash in the bank plus short-term investments that can be readily converted to cash. Inventory includes finished products ready to be shipped to customers, raw materials, and partially built products (work in process). Accounts receivables are the monies owed by customers for goods that have been shipped but not paid for.

Current Liabilities

Current liabilities include unpaid taxes, accounts payables, short-term debts, and anything else the company will have to pay out during the next 12 months.

Comparing Current Assets to Current Liabilities

Working capital is simply current assets minus current liabilities, which is the cash available to run the business. Working capital is positive when current assets exceed current liabilities and negative when liabilities exceed assets.

Current ratio is another term that gives you the same information. Instead of subtracting, current ratio is current assets divided by current liabilities. The current ratio is greater than 1 when current assets exceed current liabilities and less than 1 when liabilities exceed assets.

Cash Burner Analysis

You can do the analysis using balance sheet and cash flow data offered by a variety of financial websites. However, Morningstar compiles the data into a readily usable format. Especially important, Morningstar displays the trailing 12 months (TTM) operating cash flow, a figure you need for the analysis.

It shouldn't take you longer than a minute or two to complete the entire busted cash burner analysis using Morningstar's oddly named "5-Yr Restated" financial report, shown in Figure 10-1. Morningstar's balance sheet breakdown lists cash and other current assets on separate lines. Calculate current assets by adding together those two items. Then calculate working capital by subtracting current liabilities from current assets. Using Morningstar's terminology:

working capital = cash + other current assets – current liabilities

Cash Flow $Mil				
Fiscal year-end: 1			TTM = Trailing 12 Months	
	2007	2008	2009	TTM
Operating Cash Flow	3,969	3,949	1,894	1,894
– Capital Spending	896	831	440	440
= Free Cash Flow	3,073	3,118	1,454	1,454

Balance Sheet			
Assets	$Mil	Liabilities and Equity	$Mil
Cash	8,352.0	Current Liabilities	14,859.0
Other Current Assets	11,799.0	Long-Term Liabilities	7,370.0
Long-Term Assets	6,349.0	Shareholders' Equity	4,271.0
Total	26,500.0	Total	26,500.0

Figure 10-1　Morningstar's cash flow and balance sheet breakdown for Dell as of March 2009. You can find it on Morningstar by selecting Financial Statements and then 5-Yr Restated.

Next, estimate the current year's operating cash flow. Morningstar lists the last three fiscal years and the TTM operating cash flow. Usually, the TTM number is a good estimate.

However, you may need to modify it if the historical cash flows are inconsistent from year to year. For instance, say that the TTM cash flow is 30 but the last three fiscal years' numbers are –50, 50, and –20, respectively. That much inconsistency makes the TTM number suspect. You have to exercise judgment in those instances. I'd probably estimate 0 current year operating cash flow in that case.

Based on the working capital and estimated operating cash flow, each company falls into one of four categories:

- Cash flow positive and working capital positive
- Cash flow positive and working capital negative
- Cash flow negative and working capital positive
- Cash flow negative and working capital negative

Cash Flow Positive and Working Capital Positive

This is the best result. You wouldn't go wrong requiring that all your stocks meet this requirement. These companies already have enough working capital to pay their bills, and they are consistently adding more cash to the pile.

Software giant Microsoft's March 2009 financials, shown in Figure 10-2, illustrate the point. The company had $7,285 million in cash and another $33,439 million in other current assets on its balance sheet. Subtracting the $23,823 million current liabilities left Microsoft with working capital of $16,901 million. Furthermore, Microsoft generated $19,281 million in TTM operating cash flow. Comparing the TTM cash flow to the last three fiscal years shows the TTM number to be reasonable.

Cash Flow $Mil				
Fiscal year-end: 6			TTM = Trailing 12 Months	
	2006	2007	2008	TTM
Operating Cash Flow	14,404	17,796	21,612	19,281
- Capital Spending	1,578	2,264	3,182	3,470
= Free Cash Flow	12,826	15,532	18,430	15,811

Balance Sheet			
Assets	$Mil	Liabilities and Equity	$Mil
Cash	7,285.0	Current Liabilities	23,823.0
Other Current Assets	33,439.0	Long-Term Liabilities	8,087.0
Long-Term Assets	28,129.0	Shareholders' Equity	36,943.0
Total	68,853.0	Total	68,853.0

Figure 10-2   Morningstar's 5-Yr Restated report for Microsoft

There may be other reasons why Microsoft's shares might not have been a smart buy, but from a fiscal fitness perspective, Microsoft looks like a winner.

Table 10-4 lists 15 consistent positive cash flow generators that had strong working capital and carried virtually no debt. OCF stands for operating cash flow (in millions of dollars). LFY is the last fiscal year. LFY-1 is the previous fiscal year.

TABLE 10-4   Cash-Rich Stocks (Data as of May 15, 2009)

Company	Current Ratio	LFY OCF	LFY-1 OCF
Bankrate	5.3	43	78
Cabot Microelectronics	11.3	71	65
CoStar Group	7.7	41	52
Cree	8.9	103	111
Dorchester Minerals	21.7	83	58
Gentex	9.3	121	149
Hittite Microwave	14.6	60	53
Intersil	5.4	204	232
Intrepid Potash	6.2	158	39
Martek Biosciences	6.3	107	46
MKS Instruments	7.7	90	119
Neutral Tandem	10.4	35	24
Pioneer Southwest Energy Partners	15.9	101	72
Simpson Manufacturing	8.4	16	36
Techne	14.9	16	8

Cash Flow Positive and Working Capital Negative

These may be former cash burners that have turned the corner and are now generating excess cash. However, they are still in the hole in terms of working capital. To pass this test, current cash flow must be sufficient to overcome the working capital deficit.

Security software maker Symantec offers a good example (see Figure 10-3). As of December 31, 2008, Symantec's balance sheet showed current assets of $2,943 million compared to $3,471 million in current liabilities, so in terms of working capital, it was $528 million in the hole.

Cash Flow $Mil				
Fiscal year-end: 3				TTM = Trailing 12 Months
	2006	**2007**	**2008**	**TTM**
Operating Cash Flow	1,537	1,666	1,819	1,738
- Capital Spending	267	420	274	280
= Free Cash Flow	1,270	1,246	1,545	1,458

Balance Sheet				
Assets	**$Mil**	**Liabilities and Equity**		**$Mil**
Cash	1,449.0	Current Liabilities		3,470.8
Other Current Assets	1,494.0	Long-Term Liabilities		3,180.5
Long-Term Assets	7,899.0	Shareholders' Equity		4,190.7
Total	10,842.1	Total		10,842.1

Figure 10-3   Morningstar's 5-Yr Restated report for Symantec

However, the company posted positive TTM operating cash flow of $1,738 million. Assuming that it keeps generating cash at that clip, it could make up the deficit in six months.

To pass this test, the estimated annual operating cash flow, at a minimum, should equal the working capital deficit.

Cash Flow Negative and Working Capital Positive

Most cash burners that you encounter will have positive working capital. In these instances, you need to estimate how long the company can continue operating at its present burn rate before it runs out of cash.

The best way to get a handle on that is to convert the TTM operating cash flow to a monthly burn rate (divide by 12) and then compare the burn rate to the working capital. For example, a company has a 10 months' supply of cash if it's burning $10 million monthly and has $100 million in working capital.

How much is enough? As a rule of thumb, a company probably has a good shot at surviving if it has enough cash to last at least two years. If its business plan makes sense, the firm is likely to attract more capital or, better yet, become cash-flow-positive in that time frame.

Conversely, firms with less than 12 months of working capital are in dangerous waters unless they can raise additional funds in short order.

To illustrate, consider medical device maker Abiomed (see Figure 10-4). Abiomed had burned $25 million in the four quarters ending in December 2008, around $2 million per month. However, Abiomed had current assets totaling $97 million versus $14 million of current liabilities, so its working capital totaled $83 million, enough to last about 3.5 years at its current burn rate. With that much time, chances are that Abiomed would get its new products on the market before it ran out of cash.

Cash Flow $Mil				
Fiscal year-end: 3			TTM = Trailing 12 Months	
	2006	2007	2008	TTM
Operating Cash Flow	-9	-20	-29	-25
- Capital Spending	3	2	4	3
= Free Cash Flow	-12	-22	-33	-29

Balance Sheet			
Assets	$Mil	Liabilities and Equity	$Mil
Cash	3.0	Current Liabilities	13.6
Other Current Assets	94.0	Long-Term Liabilities	2.2
Long-Term Assets	46.0	Shareholders' Equity	126.3
Total	142.1	Total	142.1

Figure 10-4   Morningstar's 5-Yr Restated report for Abiomed

Cash Flow Negative and Working Capital Negative

Companies in this condition are in bad shape; normally you wouldn't find many in such dire straits. However, they were plentiful in 2008 and 2009.

Racetrack owner Magna Entertainment is one such example. According to its September 2008 report, Magna had burned $63 million in the previous four quarters (see Figure 10-5), leaving it with a $196 million working capital deficit. Magna never got around reporting its December 2008 results. It filed for bankruptcy in March 2009.

Cash Flow $Mil				
Fiscal year-end: 12			TTM = Trailing 12 Months	
	2005	2006	2007	TTM
Operating Cash Flow	-57	-64	-62	-63
- Capital Spending	---	---	80	48
= Free Cash Flow	---	---	-141	-111

Balance Sheet			
Assets	$Mil	Liabilities and Equity	$Mil
Cash	21.0	Current Liabilities	420.1
Other Current Assets	203.0	Long-Term Liabilities	471.0
Long-Term Assets	939.0	Shareholders' Equity	272.7
Total	1,163.7	Total	1,163.7

Figure 10-5   Morningstar's 5-Yr Restated report for Magna Entertainment

Simple Analysis Is Good Enough

This simple analysis assumes that the TTM cash flow burn rate will continue into the future, and that each company's working capital will be completely converted to cash in time to pay its operating expenses.

In practice, a firm running close to the edge will figure out how to reduce its cash burn rate. On the other hand, not all of its working capital will convert to cash, not all of its inventory will be sold, and not all of its accounts receivables will be collected. In the end, the assumption errors tend to be self-canceling, and the estimate is close enough for our purposes.

Some Will Survive

Not all busted cash burner candidates will file for bankruptcy. Some will find additional financing, and others will be acquired.

You can do more research to identify likely survivors. Start by checking the news for each company. Firms that have found additional funding will say so in a press release.

If you don't find out anything by checking the news, you could continue your research by reviewing each company's SEC reports. But first you should decide whether your time wouldn't be better spent locating more promising candidates.

Detailed Fiscal Fitness Exam

A landmark study done in the early 1990s showed that value-priced stocks outperformed growth stocks. Later, Joseph Piotroski, an accounting professor at the University of Chicago business school, took another look at that study.

He found that a few strong stocks accounted for the value portfolio's outperformance. In fact, more stocks underperformed the market than outperformed.

Piotroski wondered about the relevance of a strategy that "relies on the strong performance of a few firms while tolerating the poor performance of many deteriorating companies." For instance, say five stocks out of a hundred account for the outperformance. What are the chances of picking one of those outperformers if you buy only 10 or 15 stocks?

Piotroski reasoned that since value stocks got that way because something went wrong, many were financially distressed and might not survive. Piotroski wondered if you could boost the performance of the value portfolio by getting rid of the weakest players. To find out, he devised a simple nine-step test, using financial statement factors to evaluate financial strength.

Each step posed a question and awarded 1 point if the company passed. For instance, did the company earn money last year? Give it 1 point for a yes and 0 for a no. Same thing for operating cash flow—1 point if it was positive last year and 0 if not. The remaining seven questions looked at performance measures such as return on assets, gross margins, asset turnover ratio, working capital, and so forth. Each question was worth 1 point, so the total score ranged between 0 and 9.

Piotroski classified companies scoring below 5 as financially weak. Those that scored 5 and above were strong. He compared the performance of a portfolio limited to strong firms to a portfolio of all value-priced stocks. He found that the strong firms outperformed the all-stock portfolio by 7.5 percent annually. Most significant, he found that weak (low-scoring) firms were five times more likely to delist for performance-related reasons than strong firms.

You could use Piotroski's formula to find value candidates. The American Association of Individual Investors (AAII) maintains a stock screen based on the formula in the Screens section of its website (www.aaii.com). However, with some modifications, Piotroski's scoring system can be used to evaluate the financial strength of all high-debt companies, not just value-priced distressed firms.

I tested Piotroski's scoring formula on a variety of stocks, both value and growth, and further researched the factors common to financially stressed firms. Based on that research, I devised a modified version that is applicable to a wide range of medium- to high-debt companies. However, it breaks down when applied to very low-debt firms, sometimes giving failing scores to financially solid companies that recently reported negative cash flow and earnings.

Consequently, the detailed fiscal fitness exam should be applied only to high-debt firms (financial leverage ratios of 2.5 or higher).

I'll explain the modifications I made to Piotroski's original scoring formula as I describe the revised version.

Measuring Fiscal Fitness

Piotroski's scoring formula consisted of nine tests, each worth either 0 or 1 point. I modified some of his original tests and added two new ones. One of my new tests can have a score of –1, 0, or 1, and the other can have a score of 0 or 1. So the range of possible scores is from –1 to 11.

Piotroski grouped his nine tests into three categories: profitability, leverage and liquidity, and operating efficiency. All tests measure the company's performance over a 12-month period—either the last four reported quarters or the last fiscal year. It's easier to compute the scores using fiscal-year data, but the last four reported quarters' data may be timelier.

Many of Piotroski's tests involve comparing ratios at the beginning of the test period to the same ratio at the end. For instance, did the return on assets (net income divided by total assets) increase during the period? I take some shortcuts rather than computing the beginning and ending ratios. For instance, to find out if the ROA increased, I compare the percentage increase in net income to the percentage increase in total assets. It's mathematically identical to comparing ratios, but easier to compute.

When computing the scores, always measure revenues, income, and cash flow over 12 months. For balance sheet items, such as assets and debts, always compare values at the beginning and end of the 12-month period.

The following sections provide detailed descriptions of Piotroski's original nine tests plus the two that I added.

Profitability

Profits are, of course, the key to financial strength. Without profits, most companies would eventually fail. This section describes four profitability tests, each essentially identical to Piotroski's tests. The first two determine if the company is profitable in terms of net income and operating cash flow. Tests 3 and 4 gauge the quality of the reported profits.

1. **Net income**: Net income is the bottom-line after-tax profit. Award 1 point if net income is a positive number.
2. **Operating cash flow**: Reported net income is subject to a variety of arbitrary accounting decisions. By contrast, operating cash flow measures real-cash profits. Award 1 point if operating cash flow is positive.
3. **Return on assets**: ROA (net income divided by total assets) measures management's effectiveness in converting available resources into profits. Piotroski wanted to see a year-over-year increase in ROA. I measure that by requiring that the net income growth exceed the growth in total assets. Award 1 point if that condition is met.
4. **Quality of earnings**: Operating cash flow should exceed net income because depreciation and other noncash items subtract from income, but not from cash flow. If net income exceeds cash flow, noncash accounting entries may be inflating income. Award 1 point if operating cash flow exceeds net income.

Debt and Capital

Is the company sinking deeper into debt, or is it digging its way out? Tests 5 and 6 award points for declining debt levels. If debt dropped, was it due to profitable operations, or did the company raise cash by selling more stock? Test 7 penalizes companies that sold shares to raise cash. As a byproduct, the test also penalizes firms that issued shares to grow by acquisition, rather than organically.

5. **Total liabilities to total assets**: Comparing total liabilities to total assets measures the overall debt load. Increasing debt isn't necessarily a problem for strong companies, but Piotroski, dealing mostly with financially distressed firms, preferred shrinking debt. I substituted total liabilities where Piotroski called for long-term debt, because TL counts debt that the long-term debt figure might miss. Award 1 point if the percentage increase in total assets exceeds the percentage increase in total liabilities.

6. **Working capital**: Current assets minus current liabilities. Piotroski looked for growing working capital to signal a strengthening balance sheet. However, there's no reason why healthy companies should increase working capital beyond needed levels. I modified Piotroski's requirement and penalize only companies with shrinking working capital.

   The current ratio (current assets divided by current liabilities) measures working capital. The ratio is 1 when current assets equal current liabilities and increases when working capital increases. Award 1 point if the latest current ratio is equal to or greater than the year-ago ratio.

7. **Shares outstanding**: Figuring that they sold stock to raise cash or to make an acquisition, Piotroski penalized companies that increased the number of shares outstanding. However, employee stock options, a normal course of business, inflate the shares outstanding total, even if the firm didn't use stock for acquisitions or to raise cash. Stock option activities typically inflate the number of shares outstanding by less than 2 percent annually. I modified Piotroski's test to award 1 point if the number of shares outstanding increased less than 2 percent.

Operating Efficiency (Productivity)

These two tests, in effect, take the company's operational pulse. Rising gross margins along with improving asset turnover signals that both the company's competitive position and its productivity are improving.

8. **Gross margin**: Declining gross margins (gross income divided by sales) warn of a deteriorating competitive position, a problem regardless of the company's financial condition. Piotroski rewarded firms with increasing gross margins, and I kept that requirement. Award 1 point if the gross margin (trailing 12 months) is higher than the year-ago figure.

9. **Asset turnover**: Asset turnover, which is revenues divided by total assets, is a productivity measure. Piotroski rewarded companies with improving asset turnover ratios. I implement the test by comparing sales growth to asset growth, and I award 1 point if the percentage sales increase exceeds the percentage increase in assets.

Added Tests: Current Financial Strength

Piotroski's scoring system weighs factors that predict which way a firm's fiscal fitness is trending (stronger or weaker). But he doesn't discriminate between strong balance sheet firms and those on the ropes. That worked for identifying the stocks most likely to rise from the dead, which was his goal. However, extending Piotroski's strategy to evaluate all stocks requires taking into account existing financial strength. It's counterproductive to penalize firms for carrying high debt as long as they are generating sufficient cash to service the debt. To accomplish that, I added two more checks:

10. **Total liabilities/EBITDA**: A gauge favored by lenders, EBITDA measures income before deducting for interest, taxes, depreciation, and amortization. Credit analysts believe that EBITDA best measures the ability to service debt. Lenders often require debtor companies to maintain a specified debt/EBITDA ratio (typically 7 or 8). Failure to maintain the required ratio gives lenders the option to call their loans, meaning that they want their money back immediately.

Credit analysts use the debt/EBITDA ratio to gauge credit quality. They consider firms with ratios below 5 as investment-quality, qualifying them to borrow at the lowest rates. Analysts' and lenders' reliance on the debt/EBITDA ratio makes it more important than any other single factor, so I give it more weight. I substituted total liabilities for Piotroski's total debt because it's a more complete debt measure. Award 1 point to companies with ratios up to 5. Award 0 points for ratios of 6 or 7. Deduct 1 point for ratios of 8 or above.

11. **Total liabilities to operating cash flow**: This test awards firms that generate significant cash flows compared to their liabilities (cash flow at least 25 percent of total liabilities). They are in little danger of insolvency as long as that condition persists. Add 1 point if the TL/OCF ratio is less than 4.

Add up the individual test results to determine the test score.

A Passing Grade

In Piotroski's original 9-point system, 5 points constituted a passing grade. My changes didn't affect Piotroski's passing criteria. I found that companies that ended up in bankruptcy court almost always scored between 1 and 4 points. This was based on my analysis of the most recent financial statements the company filed prior to filing for bankruptcy.

The goal is to highlight companies most at risk of facing solvency problems. Obviously, not all companies with low scores will end up in financial trouble, but all the troubled companies I analyzed had low scores.

Piotroski's research found that, in terms of scores, higher is better. For instance, firms scoring 7 recorded better future performance than those scoring 6, and so on. However, Piotroski's value-priced distressed-stock universe is not representative of all stocks. I haven't found any evidence that 10-point stocks perform better than 6-point stocks.

Table 10-5 lists scores for the 14 largest publicly traded companies that filed for bankruptcy during the first three months of 2009. The Date column shows the date of the financial statements analyzed. For instance, 12/08 means that I analyzed data for the 12 months ending 12/31/08.

TABLE 10-5   Companies That Filed for Bankruptcy in Early 2009

Company	Date	Score
BearingPoint	9/08	3
Charter Communications	12/08	4
Fleetwood Enterprises	4/08	3
General Growth Properties	12/08	3
Magna Entertainment	9/08	1
Milacron	9/08	2
Nortel Networks	12/08	1
Smurfit-Stone Container	12/08	3
Spansion	9/08	1
Spectrum Brands	9/08	2
Tarragon	9/08	3
Tronox	9/08	2
Trump Entertainment Resorts	12/08	2
Young Broadcasting	9/08	1

Table 10-6 lists the scores for 14 well-known stocks.

TABLE 10-6   Well-Known Stocks

Company	Date	Score
Amazon.com	12/08	7
Apple	9/08	8
Cisco Systems	7/08	9
eBay	12/08	8
ExxonMobil	12/08	7
Google	12/08	10
H&R Block	4/08	5
Intuit	7/08	7
Netflix	12/08	8
PALM	5/08	2
Rite Aid	11/08	2
Simon Property Group	12/08	5
Starbucks	12/08	8
UAL	12/08	0

Of the stocks listed, only PALM, Rite Aid, and UAL scored low enough to qualify as bankruptcy candidates. The fact that Netflix scored higher than ExxonMobil highlights that once you get up to 6 or so, higher isn't necessarily better. Keep in mind that these tests measure financial strength, not business outlook or stock appreciation prospects.

Computing Fiscal Fitness Scores

Computing EBITDA can be time-consuming, so if possible, use financial statements that do the math for you and display EBITDA as a line item. You also need to know the number of shares outstanding for each stock.

Smart Money (www.smartmoney.com), Forbes (www.forbes.com), MarketWatch (www.marketwatch.com), and CNN Money (money.cnn.com) all list EBITDA on their income statements and shares outstanding on their balance sheets.

A fiscal fitness worksheet is included at the end of this chapter. Make copies and use the worksheet to tally the scores when you analyze a company. The process looks formidable, but you should be able to score a company in less than ten minutes after you've done it a couple of times.

The worksheet is divided into two sections. The top section is used to gather the data and make necessary calculations, and the lower section is used to tabulate the scores.

Figuring Percentages

The worksheet requires two types of percentage calculations: simple percentages and year-over-year comparisons.

To calculate simple percentages, divide one number by the other. For instance, gross margin is gross profit divided by sales. If the gross profit is 10, and the sales are 25, the gross margin is

$$10 / 25 = 0.40 \text{ or } 40\%$$

Calculate year-over-year percentage growth by dividing the latest figure by the year-ago value, and subtract 1 from the result. For instance, if the recent value is 10, and the year-ago number is 7:

$$\text{percentage growth} = (10 / 7) - 1 = 1.43 - 1 = 0.43 \text{ or } 43\%$$

Do this calculation when A versus B is indicated—for instance, this year versus a year ago. Do all calculations in millions, and compute numbers to only one decimal place.

The following sections show a sample Fiscal Fitness Score calculation using Amazon.com's December 2008 fiscal year results. Figure 10-6 shows the Smart Money annual income statement, which provided the data.

Income Statement (Non-Cumulative)					Print Current View
	Fiscal Year Ending 2008	Fiscal Year Ending 2007	Fiscal Year Ending 2006	Fiscal Year Ending 2005	Fiscal Year Ending 2004
Revenues	19,166,000	14,835,000	10,711,000	8,490,000	6,921,124
Cost of Revenues	14,609,000	11,447,000	8,230,000	6,330,000	5,243,403
Gross Income	**4,557,000**	**3,388,000**	**2,481,000**	**2,160,000**	**1,677,721**
Selling, General & Admin. Expenses	2,395,000	1,880,000	1,405,000	1,156,000	918,341
Research & Development	1,033,000	818,000	662,000	451,000	251,195
Ebitda	**1,129,000**	**690,000**	**414,000**	**553,000**	**508,185**
Depreciation & Amortization	287,000	35,000	25,000	121,000	75,724
Operating Income	**842,000**	**655,000**	**389,000**	**432,000**	**432,461**
Interest Expense	71,000	77,000	78,000	92,000	107,227
Income Taxes/(Credit)	247,000	184,000	187,000	95,000	-232,581
Minority Interest	0	0	0	0	0
Other Income	47,000	-8,000	7,000	44,000	2,439
Het Income From Continuing Operations	**645,000**	**476,000**	**190,000**	**333,000**	**588,451**
Het Income From Discontinued Operations	**0**	**0**	**0**	**0**	**0**
Het Income From Total Operations	**645,000**	**476,000**	**190,000**	**333,000**	**588,451**
Other Gains/(Losses)	0	0	0	26,000	0
Total Het Income	**645,000**	**476,000**	**190,000**	**359,000**	**588,451**

Figure 10-6   A portion of Smart Money's display of Amazon.com's annual income statement. Smart Money shows EBITDA as a separate line item, avoiding the need to calculate the figure.

Gathering and Calculating

The form is organized so that you can gather the needed data from the income statement, balance sheet, and cash flow statement in sequence. A sample Fiscal Fitness Exam Worksheet appears at the end of this chapter. The following sections break the worksheet into individual portions, using Amazon as an example.

Income Statement

The Income Statement portion of the Fiscal Fitness Exam Worksheet lists the following:

---

a) Sales Growth: TTM Sales _____ vs. Year-Ago TTM Sales _____ = ____%

b) TTM Gross Margin: Gross Profit _____ / Sales _____ = ____%

c) Year-Ago Gross Margin: Year-Ago Gross Profit _____ / Year-Ago Sales _____ = ____%

d) TTM EBITDA: _____

e) Net Income Growth: TTM Net Income _____ vs. Year-Ago NI _____ = ____%

---

a) Record the most recent year's and previous year's sales (revenues), and compute the percentage increase. For Amazon, the sales figures were 19,166 million (latest) and 14,835 million (year-ago) for a year-over-year increase of 29.2 percent [(19,166 / 14,835) – 1]:

Sales Growth: TTM Sales vs. Year-Ago TTM Sales: 19,166 vs. 14,835 = 29.2%

b) Record the latest period's gross profit (gross income on smart money) and sales. For Amazon, the gross profit was 4,557, and sales were 19,166:

TTM Gross Margin: Gross Profit / Sales (%): 4,557 / 19,166 = 23.8%

c) Repeat step b) using year-ago figures:

Year-Ago Gross Margin: Year-Ago Gross Profit / Sales (%): 3,388 / 14,835 = 22.8%

d) Record the EBITDA figure from the Income Statement:

TTM EBITDA: 1,129

e) Record the most recent year's and previous year's total net income, and compute the percentage increase. For Amazon, the income figures were 645 (latest) and 476 (year-ago) for a year-over-year change of 35.5 percent:

Net Income Growth: TTM Net Income vs. Year-Ago NI: 645 vs. 476 = 35.5%

Balance Sheet

Next, fill in the Balance Sheet data:

---

f) Asset Growth: Total Assets _____ vs. Year-Ago Total Assets _____ = ____%

g) Total Liabilities Growth: Latest TL _____ vs. Year-Ago TL _____ = ____%

h) Current Ratio (Latest): Current Assets _____ / Current Liabilities _____ = ____

i) Current Ratio (Year-Ago):

   Year-Ago Current Assets _____ / Year-Ago Current Liabilities _____ = ____

j) Shares Outstanding: Latest _____ Year-Ago _____ Year-Ago × 1.02 _____

k) Total Liabilities to EBITDA Ratio: Total Liabilities (Latest) _____ / EBITDA _____ = _____

---

f) Record the latest and year-ago total asset figures, and compute the percentage change. For Amazon, the numbers were 8,314 (latest) and 6,485 (year-ago):

> Asset Growth: Total Assets / Year-Ago Total Assets: <u>8,314</u> vs. <u>6,485</u> = <u>28.2%</u>

g) Record the latest and year-ago total liabilities, and compute the percentage change. For Amazon, the numbers were 5,642 (latest) and 5,288 (year-ago):

> Total Liabilities Growth: Latest TL / Year-Ago TL: <u>5,642</u> vs. <u>5,288</u> = <u>6.7%</u>

h) The current ratio is the current assets divided by the current liabilities. By custom, the current ratio is not expressed as a percentage. This step computes the latest period current ratio. For Amazon, the current assets are 6,157 and the current liabilities are 4,746:

> Current Ratio (latest): Current Assets / Current Liabilities: <u>6,157</u> / <u>4,746</u> = <u>1.3</u>

i) Compute the year-ago current ratio. For Amazon, the year-ago current assets were 5,164, and the current liabilities were 3,714:

> Current Ratio (year-ago): Year-Ago Current Assets / Year-Ago Current
> Liabilities: <u>5,164</u> / <u>3,714</u> = <u>1.4</u>

j) The number of (common) shares outstanding at the end of each period is shown near the bottom of the balance sheet. Record the number of common shares outstanding for the current and year-ago periods. Multiply the year-ago figure by 1.02 (a 2 percent increase):

> Shares Outstanding: Latest <u>428 million</u> Year-Ago <u>416 million</u> ¥ <u>1.02</u> = <u>424 million</u>

k) Compute the ratio of total liabilities to EBITDA by dividing the total liabilities (item g) by the EBITDA (item d):

> Total Liabilities to EBITDA ratio: TL / EBITDA: <u>5,642</u> / <u>1,129</u> = <u>5.0</u>

Cash Flows

Only two entries are required on the Cash Flows portion of the worksheet:

l) TTM Operating Cash Flow (OCF): _____

m) Total Liabilities vs. OCF Ratio < 4: TL _____ / OCF _____ = _____

l) The operating cash flow (net cash from operating activities) is listed about midway down the cash flow statement. Record the most recent four quarters' (TTM) operating cash flow:

TTM Operating Cash Flow (OCF): <u>1,697</u>

m) Compute the total liabilities to operating cash flow ratio by dividing the total liabilities (item g) by the OCF (item l):

Total Liabilities to OCF Ratio: <u>5,642</u> / <u>1,697</u> = <u>3.3</u>

Tabulating the Score

. That was the hard work. Now all that remains is filling in the blanks on the rating form.

The Tabulate Score section of the worksheet is divided into four sections: Profitability, Debt and Capital, Operating Efficiency, and Added Tests.

Profitability

The Profitability section of the worksheet shows the following:

---

1) Net Income (NI) Positive? _____   _____

2) Operating Cash Flow Positive? _____   _____

3) Net Income Growth > Total Asset Growth:

   NI Growth _____% Asset Growth _____%   _____

4) Operating Cash Flow > Net Income: OCF _____ NI _____   _____

---

1) Net income: Use the TTM net income (item e). Score 1 point if the income is a positive number, no matter how small:

Net Income (NI) Positive? <u>645</u> = <u>1</u>

2) Operating cash flow: Use the most recent year's operating cash flow (item l). Score 1 point if it is a positive number:

Operating Cash Flow Positive? <u>1,697</u> = <u>1</u>

Fire Your Stock Analyst!

3) Return on assets (ROA): Record the net income growth (item e) and the total asset growth (item f). Score 1 point if the income growth exceeds the asset growth (if the ROA increased). If both growth figures are negative, score 1 point if the NI growth dropped less than the asset growth:

Net Income Growth > Total Asset Growth: NI Growth <u>35.5</u>% TA Growth

<u>28.2</u>% = <u>1</u>

4) Quality of earnings: This test compares operating cash flow to net income. It's a positive if cash flow exceeds net income and a negative if it doesn't. This holds true even when both are negative numbers. For instance, it is still worth a point if net income is –$100 million but cash flow is only –$10 million. Score 1 point if operating cash flow (step 2) exceeds net income (step 1):

Operating Cash Flow > Net Income: OCF <u>1,697</u> NI <u>645</u> = <u>1</u>

Debt and Capital

Next, fill in the Debt and Capital portion of the score:

5) Asset Growth > Total Liabilities Growth:

  Asset Growth _____% TL Growth _____%   _____

6) Current Ratio >= Year-Ago CR:

  Latest CR _____ Year-Ago CR _____   _____

7) Shares Outstanding <= Year-Ago Shares Out + 2%:

  Latest _____ Year-Ago + 2% _____   _____

5) Growth of assets versus debt: It's a positive if assets grow faster than debt, and vice versa. Award 1 point if the assets growth (item f) exceeds the total liabilities growth (item g). If liabilities growth is negative, award 1 point if asset growth is less negative than liabilities growth:

Asset Growth > Total Liabilities: Asset Growth <u>28.2</u>%

Total Liabilities Growth <u>6.7</u>% = <u>1</u>

6) Working capital: Award 1 point if the latest current ratio (item h) equals or exceeds the year-ago ratio (item i):

Current Ratio >= Year-Ago CR: Latest CR <u>1.3</u> Year-Ago CR <u>1.4</u> = <u>0</u>

7) Shares outstanding: Award 1 point if the latest number of shares outstanding (item j) is less than or equal to the year-ago figure plus 2 percent (item j):

Shares Outstanding <= Year-Ago Shares Outstanding + 2%: Latest <u>428</u>

Year-Ago + 2% <u>424</u> = <u>0</u>

Operating Efficiency (Productivity)

Next, record the Operating Efficiency (Productivity) scores:

8) Gross Margin > Year-Ago GM: GM _____% Year-Ago GM _____%   _____

9) Sales Growth > Asset Growth: Sales Growth _____% Asset Growth _____%   _____

8) Gross margin: Award 1 point if the latest GM (item b) exceeds the year-ago GM (item c):

GM > Year-Ago GM: GM <u>23.8</u>% Year-Ago GM <u>22.8</u>% = <u>1</u>

9) Asset turnover: Ideally, sales should rise faster than assets. Award 1 point if the sales (revenue) growth (item a) exceeds total assets growth (item f). Both figures can be negative. In those cases, award 1 point if the sales shrinkage is less than the asset shrinkage:

Sales Growth > Asset Growth: Sales Growth <u>29.2</u>% Asset Growth <u>28.2</u>% = <u>1</u>

Added Tests: Current Financial Strength

Finally, enter the scores for the Current Financial Strength tests:

10) Total Liabilities / EBITDA: Ratio _____ (0 to 5 = 1; 8 and above = –1)   _____

11) Total Liabilities vs. OCF Ratio _____ (< 4 = 1; negative cash flow = 0)   _____

10) Total-liabilities-to-EBITDA ratio: EBITDA is a measure of cash available to service debt and pay taxes. Thus, the lower the debt-to-EBITDA ratio, the better. Record the total liabilities/EBITDA ratio (item k). Award 1 point if the ratio is equal to or less than 5.0. Subtract 1 point if the ratio is 8.0 or higher, or if EBITDA is a negative number:

Total Liabilities / EBITDA: Ratio <u>5.0</u> = <u>1</u>

11) Total liabilities compared to operating cash flow: Award 1 point if the ratio of total liabilities (item g) divided by operating cash flow (step 2) is less than 4.0. Score 0 if the ratio is 4.0 or higher or if cash flow is negative:

Total Liabilities / OCF Ratio <u><4.0 = 1</u>: <u>5,642</u> / <u>1,697</u> = Ratio <u>3.3</u> = <u>1</u>

Total Score: <u>9</u>

Amazon's 9 score signals that you don't have to worry about the online retail giant's financial strength—at least until its next quarterly report. Companies scoring 4 or less are risky from a financial fitness perspective and should be avoided. Firms scoring 5 or higher are not high bankruptcy risks, but that's all the score means. No data shows that the stocks of high-scoring firms outperform lower-scoring stocks.

Bond Ratings

The fiscal fitness exam is a thorough analysis, but it takes some time and effort. Another way to get a reading on a firm's financial health is to piggyback on bond analysts' research.

Rating agencies, such as Moody's Investors Service (www.moodys.com), Standard & Poor's (www.standardandpoors.com), and Fitch (www.fitchratings.com), perform in-depth financial strength analyses of corporations that raise funds by issuing bonds or similar credit instruments. The company being rated pays for the analysis because it needs the rating to sell its bonds. So you won't find bond ratings for companies that raise funds strictly by selling stock.

Don't confuse bond ratings with the stock analysts' buy/sell ratings. Unlike stock analysts, who are concerned mainly with earnings growth prospects, bond analysts focus on the company's ability to service its debt. They evaluate financial statements, management quality, the competitive environment, and overall economic conditions. Where stock analysts are optimists, bond analysts—in theory, at least—focus on what can go wrong.

Bond ratings reflect the agencies' view of the risk that a company will default on its bond payments. That information is important to stock investors as well as bond investors because a bond default always destroys the issuing company's stock price. Also, the rating determines a firm's access to, and its cost of, borrowing. A lowered bond rating can impact the company's earnings by increasing its interest expenses, and lack of access to new borrowings can stifle growth or even drive a firm into bankruptcy.

The agencies use a combination of letters, numbers, and plus or minus signs, such as AAA, BA1, and B–, to rate corporate bonds:

- The combination of symbols used by each rating service varies somewhat, but AAA always indicates the highest quality rating, and any rating starting with A signifies high-quality debt. Three-letter ratings starting with B, such as BAA and BBB, indicate lower-quality debt than A ratings but are still considered investment-quality. Companies with A or three-letter B ratings probably could raise additional funds without problems.
- Two-letter B ratings, such as BB and BA1, signify noninvestment-grade or junk-bond securities. Corporations with bonds in the junk category may be able to raise additional funds, but this is problematic, and they will have to pay higher interest rates.
- Single-letter B ratings, such as B1, and all double or triple C-rated bonds, such as CC and CCC, signify substantial risk. Companies with bonds carrying these ratings probably couldn't raise funds from normal sources.
- Single-letter C ratings indicate that the company has filed for bankruptcy, and D ratings signify that the company has defaulted on its bond payments.

S&P often adds a + or – to the rating to indicate that it falls at the top or bottom of its rating group. For instance, a + indicates that the rating falls at the top end. Moody's adds the numbers 1, 2, and 3 to fine-tune their ratings, where 1 indicates rating at the top end of the range, 2 signifies midrange, and 3 indicates the lower end of the rating category. Rating agencies frequently place a rating on credit watch or under review if they are considering changing a rating.

Any A or triple letter B rating is good enough for our purposes, because it signals that the rating agency sees little risk of default. There is no evidence that stocks issued by AAA-rated companies outperform BBB-rated companies' stocks.

Rating agencies also publish ratings that apply to the issuer's general creditworthiness instead of to a specific bond issue. Moody's uses the same rating codes for corporate credit as for specific bond issues, but S&P uses different codes for corporate credit:

- **A-1, A-2, and A-3**: Best or good quality
- **B**: Risky credit
- **C**: Riskier than B
- **D**: Already in default

You can see each of the three major rating services' ratings on their own websites. However, it's easier to use sites such as Finra (www.finra.org), BuySellBonds (www.buysellbonds.com), or the Securities Industry and Financial Markets Association website (www.investinginbonds.com). On those sites, you can frequently see all three major ratings, as well as the bond trading prices, at one time.

The downside of relying on bond ratings is that they can be too slow to change in fast-moving situations, or they can be wrong for other reasons. The rating services were famously slow to downgrade Enron's investment-grade ratings until just a few weeks before the energy trader filed for bankruptcy in December 2001. The Enron debacle was a huge embarrassment for the rating agencies, and you would have thought that the experience would have compelled them to rethink their rating strategies.

But it didn't happen. The agencies were equally slow to catch on to the problems brewing at mortgage insurers Ginnie Mae and Freddie Mac. The agencies kept them rated at investment grade until a month or so before the U.S. government took control of both.

Use Bond Prices to Identify Risky Debtors

As was the case with Enron, Fannie Mae, Freddie Mac, and others, bond buyers often know of problems before bond analysts change their ratings. When that happens, bond buyers demand a higher bond yield, or a risk premium, to compensate for the added risk before they'll buy the bonds. Thus, a drop in bond prices often signals a change in the issuing firm's fundamental outlook. So, a quick check on bond prices will give you a read on income investors' take on a company's outlook.

Bonds are usually sold in $5,000 denominations but are quoted as if the bonds were traded in $100 increments. For instance, a bond price of $105 means that the bond traded at $105 per $100 of face value, or at a 5 percent premium.

Most corporate bonds are bought and sold by individual dealers. Unlike stocks, there is no national quotation system for bonds, and you'll find different quotes for the same bond on different websites.

The maturity date is the date when the issuing corporation must redeem the bond for its face value. Bonds with maturities of four years or less are termed short-term bonds, those with maturities of more than 12 years are deemed long-term, and those in between are medium-term bonds. When comparing a particular firm's bond prices to other bonds, stick with similar maturity dates.

Most corporate bonds pay a specified fixed interest rate, called the coupon rate, based on the issue price. The current yield is the return rate a new buyer would receive. For instance, say a bond with a 6 percent coupon (original interest rate) is currently selling for $95. A new buyer would receive $6 in interest annually, which would equate to a 6.3 percent yield, since the buyer paid only $95 for the bond. The difference between the original (coupon) interest rate and the current rate also reflects the risk bond investors see in holding the bond.

A bond is callable if the issuer can redeem it before the maturity date. Most bonds are noncallable. Since callable and noncallable might trade at different prices, stick with noncallable bonds for your analysis.

Summary

Few would argue that checking a firm's financial health should be done for every investment candidate. You'd think that stock analysts would take that step before advising investors to buy a stock, but since they don't, you have to do it on your own.

You can simplify the task by sticking with low-debt firms showing positive cash flow and positive working capital. You can get a quick read on a high-debt firm's financial health by checking its bond ratings, but the detailed Fiscal Fitness Exam is the best way to detect a potential financial basket case.

FISCAL FITNESS EXAM WORKSHEET

COMPANY _____ as of (financial statement date): _____

Income Statement

a) Sales Growth: TTM Sales _____ vs. Year-Ago TTM Sales _____ = ____%

b) TTM Gross Margin: Gross Profit _____ / Sales _____ = ____%

c) Year-Ago Gross Margin: Year-Ago Gross Profit _____ / Year-Ago Sales _____ = ____%

d) TTM EBITDA: _____

e) Net Income Growth: TTM Net Income _____ vs. Year-Ago NI _____ = ____%

Balance Sheet

f) Asset Growth: Total Assets _____ vs. Year-Ago Total Assets _____ = ____%

g) Total Liabilities Growth: Latest TL _____ vs. Year-Ago TL _____ = ____%

h) Current Ratio (Latest): Current Assets _____ / Current Liabilities _____ = ____

i) Current Ratio (Year-Ago): Year-Ago Current Assets _____ / Year-Ago Current Liabilities _____ = ____

j) Shares Outstanding: Latest _____ Year-Ago _____ Year-Ago × 1.02 _____

k) Total Liabilities to EBITDA Ratio: Total Liabilities (Latest) _____ / EBITDA _____ = _____

Cash Flows

l) TTM Operating Cash Flow (OCF): _____

m) Total Liabilities vs. Operating CF Ratio < 4: TL _____ / OCF _____ = _____

Tabulate Score

Profitability

1) Net Income (NI) Positive? _____   _____

2) Operating Cash Flow Positive? _____   _____

3) Net Income Growth > Total Asset Growth: NI Growth _____% Asset Growth _____%   _____

4) Operating Cash Flow > Net Income: OCF _____ NI _____   _____

Debt and Capital

5) Asset Growth > Total Liabilities Growth: Asset Growth _____% TL Growth _____%   _____

6) Current Ratio >= Year-Ago CR: Latest CR _____ Year-Ago CR _____   _____

7) Shares Outstanding <= Year-Ago Shares Outstanding + 2%: Latest _____ Year-Ago + 2% _____ _____

Operating Efficiency

8) Gross Margin > Year-Ago GM: GM _____% Year-Ago GM _____%   _____

9) Sales Growth > Asset Growth: Sales Growth _____% Asset Growth _____%   _____

Added Tests

10) Total Liabilities / EBITDA: Ratio _____ (0 to 5 = 1; 8 and above = –1)   _____

11) Total Liabilities vs. OCF Ratio _____ (< 4 = 1; negative cash flow = 0) _____

TOTAL   _____

11

Analysis Tool #8:
Profitability and Growth Analysis

When a company reports quarterly results, the market focuses on earnings. All else equal, the share price moves up if the company reports better than expected earnings and down if it doesn't.

But, earnings don't come out of thin air. In this chapter, you'll learn how to analyze quarterly financial statements to determine if the firm had to stretch to make its numbers and, most important, what happens next. Is the company more likely to beat or fall short of analysts' forecasts when it reports its current quarter's results? This chapter focuses on four factors that, taken together, will help you answer those questions:

- Sales and sales growth
- Profit margins
- Profitability ratios
- Cash flows

The first two determine reported earnings. The last two tell you what's behind those numbers.

Where Do Earnings Come From?

Sales and profit margins combine to produce earnings. It takes both. Here's the formula:

$$\text{earnings} = \text{sales} \times \text{profit margin}$$

This formula tells you that sales and profit margins, taken together, determine earnings. That's very important to remember. Here's why.

A company can't report consistent earnings growth if sales rise but profit margins drop. Same problem if profit margins rise but sales drop. Let's flesh out the concept with numbers.

Suppose that a company sold $1,000 worth of products during the last quarter at a 15 percent profit margin. The company earned $150:

$$\text{earnings} = \$1,000 \times 0.15 = \$150$$

If nothing changes in the next quarter, the company will again rack up sales of $1,000, and it will again earn $150.

That would be a problem for shareholders if it did happen, because earnings growth, or the expectation of earnings growth, is usually what drives up share prices.

The profit formula tells us that the only way to boost earnings is to grow sales and/or profit margins. In the best case, good management grows both sales and profit margins. When that happens, earnings grow faster than sales, often beating forecasts.

The bottom-line number that gets all the attention on earnings report day is earnings per share (EPS). It's net income divided by the number of outstanding shares:

$$\text{earnings per share} = \text{net income} / \text{shares outstanding}$$

A company with lackluster growth can boost its EPS by buying back its stock, thereby reducing the number of shares outstanding.

Table 11-1 shows the long-term (10-year) relationship between average annual sales growth and earnings per share growth for a sampling of larger companies.

The table shows that, long-term, earnings typically grow about 10 percent faster than sales (such as 20 percent versus 18 percent). "Long-term" is the operative word. Earnings tend to be volatile from quarter to quarter and even year to year. That's why sales growth is a better growth measure than earnings growth.

TABLE 11-1   10-Year Average Annual Sales and EPS Growth for a Sampling of Large-Cap Companies

Ticker	Company	10-Year Average Annual Sales Growth	10-Year Average Annual Earnings Growth
ABC	AmerisourceBergen Corp.	22.1	20.3
APOL	Apollo Group Inc.	23.4	27.1
AXP	American Express Co.	5.3	4.9
BBBY	Bed Bath & Beyond Inc.	18.0	17.1
BBY	Best Buy Co. Inc.	16.2	17.9
BG	Bunge Limited	19.2	17.4
CAT	Caterpillar Inc.	9.4	10.7
CB	Chubb Corp.	7.6	8.9
COST	Costco Wholesale Corp.	11.6	11.1
CTSH	Cognizant Technology Solutions	47.3	47.1
DE	Deere & Co.	7.5	8.5
DNA	Genentech Inc.	28.9	33.8
DO	Diamond Offshore Drilling Inc.	11.4	13.5
EBAY	eBay Inc.	58.4	67.5
EMR	Emerson Electric Co.	6.3	8.4
EXC	Exelon Corp.	13.5	13.5
FAST	Fastenal Co.	16.6	18.3
FDX	FedEx Corp.	9.1	8.0
GD	General Dynamics Corp.	14.8	15.6
GE	General Electric Co.	6.2	6.7
HD	Home Depot Inc.	9.0	6.9
HON	Honeywell International Inc.	4.5	4.8
HPQ	Hewlett-Packard Company	11.6	9.9
HRB	H&R Block Inc.	13.2	12.5
JCI	Johnson Controls Inc.	11.7	10.4
KO	Coca-Cola Co.	5.4	5.8
KSS	Kohl's Corp.	16.1	17.2
LOW	Lowe's Companies Inc.	13.7	16.1
MCK	McKesson Corp.	16.5	12.8
MDT	Medtronic Inc.	14.7	14.5

TABLE 11-1   Continued

Ticker	Company	10-Year Average Annual Sales Growth	10-Year Average Annual Earnings Growth
MSFT	Microsoft Corp.	14.8	16.2
NOV	National-Oilwell Varco Inc.	24.9	23.5
NSC	Norfolk Southern Corp.	9.6	10.6
NUE	Nucor Corp.	18.6	23.1
NWS	News Corp.	9.6	11.7
ORLY	O'Reilly Automotive Inc.	19.2	15.3
PAYX	Paychex Inc.	15.4	18.9
PEP	PepsiCo Inc.	6.8	9.4
PFE	Pfizer Inc.	7.6	8.9
PG	Procter & Gamble Co.	8.4	11.0
PSA	Public Storage	11.6	12.4
SPLS	Staples Inc.	12.5	15.2
TGT	Target Co.	7.8	10.9
UPS	United Parcel Service Inc.	7.6	6.5
UST	UST Inc.	3.4	3.3
WAG	Walgreen Co.	14.5	15.0
WMT	Wal-Mart Stores Inc.	11.3	13.0
WYE	Wyeth	7.3	7.4
XOM	Exxon Mobil Corporation	10.9	22.4

Since nothing works every time in the stock market, a rule of thumb such as "Earnings grow 10 percent faster than sales" doesn't apply to all stocks.

For instance, Table 11-2 lists a sampling of stocks that have grown earnings faster than sales, even over 10 years. They accomplished that by consistently growing profit margins.

TABLE 11-2   10-Year Average Annual Sales and EPS Growth for Companies That Consistently Grow Earnings Faster Than Sales

Ticker	Company	10-Year Average Annual Sales Growth	10-Year Average Annual Earnings Growth
ADI	Analog Devices Inc.	7.7	17.5
AMAT	Applied Materials Inc.	6.5	13.9
AZO	AutoZone Inc.	7.2	21.1
BA	Boeing Co.	0.8	12.3
CALM	Cal-Maine Foods Inc.	11.5	41.4
CLX	Clorox Co.	3.1	8.3
COH	Coach Inc.	19.8	43.0
CSX	CSX Corp.	1.7	10.7
CVX	Chevron Corp.	14.1	29.6
DNB	Dun & Bradstreet Corp.	2.0	18.7
FMC	FMC Corp.	2.8	10.0
GMT	GATX Corp.	1.3	5.6
GYMB	Gymboree Corp.	8.1	28.7
HAS	Hasbro Inc.	2.0	7.1
IBM	International Business Machines	2.4	10.5
KR	Kroger Co.	5.8	12.3
LMT	Lockheed Martin Corp.	5.2	11.8
MHP	McGraw-Hill Companies Inc.	5.5	11.4
MMM	3M Co.	5.3	12.7
NKE	NIKE Inc.	6.9	18.6
NWSA	News Corp.	9.2	24.2
OLN	Olin Corp.	1.6	10.1
PTEN	Patterson-UTI Energy Inc.	19.5	43.9
SCHW	Charles Schwab Corp.	4.9	13.3
TXN	Texas Instruments Inc.	3.5	18.6
XOM	Exxon Mobil Corp.	10.9	22.4
XRAY	DENTSPLY International Inc.	10.6	24.1
YUM	Yum! Brands Inc.	2.9	10.7

On the other side of the coin, Table 11-3 lists companies that recorded strong sales growth, but earnings didn't follow. That happens when profit margins fall, typically because costs rise faster than sales.

TABLE 11-3   10-Year Average Annual Sales and EPS Growth for Companies Whose Earnings Growth Doesn't Translate to Similar Sales Growth

Ticker	Company	10-Year Average Annual Sales Growth	10-Year Average Annual Earnings Growth
ATO	Atmos Energy Corp.	23.9	0.8
CCL	Carnival Corp.	17.1	7.6
CMVT	Comverse Technology Inc.	23.7	4.3
COO	Cooper Companies Inc.	21.9	-2.8
CREE	Cree Inc.	27.4	12.9
DBD	Diebold Inc.	10.3	3.3
DF	Dean Foods Co.	14.1	2.3
EAT	Brinker International Inc.	10.4	0.8
FRED	Fred's Inc.	11.6	4.9
GNTX	Gentex Corp.	10.9	2.6
HAIN	Hain Celestial Group Inc.	17.7	7.1
INTC	Intel Corp.	3.6	0.7
JBL	Jabil Circuit Inc.	24.0	6.4
LG	Laclede Group Inc.	14.7	5.3
LM	Legg Mason Inc.	18.0	7.8
LUV	Southwest Airlines Co.	10.2	-7.8
MAC	Macerich Co.	12.3	1.5
NAVG	Navigators Group Inc.	19.5	8.4
PLT	Plantronics Inc.	13.8	6.9
SGR	Shaw Group Inc.	30.2	10.2
SYMC	Symantec Corp.	27.1	11.4
T	AT&T Inc.	10.4	-0.4
TEX	Terex Corp.	23.1	-7.8
UAM	Universal American Corp.	55.6	18.5
UMPQ	Umpqua Holdings Corp.	25.8	2.9
USM	United States Cellular Corp.	12.4	-16.9
VZ	Verizon Communications Inc.	5.5	1.6
WFMI	Whole Foods Market Inc.	19.8	8.6
WPI	Watson Pharmaceuticals Inc.	15.4	5.6
WSM	Williams-Sonoma Inc.	11.2	-5.1

Analyzing Sales (Revenue) History

Despite the inevitable exceptions, for most companies, sales growth powers earnings growth.

Thus, you'll be most productive by starting your analysis with sales growth. First, analyze long-term sales growth trends, and then zero in on the most recent data.

MSN Money's 10-Year Summary report is a good resource for long-term sales data. Table 11-4 shows the data for a sampling of companies.

TABLE 11-4   Examples of Long-Term Sales Histories (in Millions of Dollars)

Year End	Amazon	GameStop	Green Mountain Coffee	Strayer Education	SanDisk	VeriSign	Cerner
12/08	19,166	8,806	500	396	3,351	962	1,676
12/07	14,835	7,094	342	318	3,896	847	1,520
12/06	10,711	5,319	225	264	3,258	983	1,378
12/05	8,490	3,092	162	221	2,306	1,605	1,161
12/04	6,921	1,843	137	183	1,777	1,121	926
12/03	5,264	1,579	117	147	1,080	1,017	840
12/02	3,933	1,353	100	117	541	1,222	780
12/01	3,122	1,121	96	93	366	984	561
12/00	2,762	757	84	78	602	475	404
12/99	1,640	553	65	70	247	85	319

Growth investors should focus on candidates with at least 15 percent average annual sales growth over the past three years, and higher is better. Value investors don't need fast growth. For them, 5 percent average annual sales growth is sufficient, but, as with growth investors, more is always better.

If you did the math, you'd see from Table 11-4 that Amazon.com racked up 25 percent sales growth every year, except for 2001. Especially impressive, sales grew 29 percent in 2008, a year when sales growth faltered for most firms.

Video game retailer GameStop, although more erratic than Amazon, also recorded impressive growth over 10 years.

Coffee seller Green Mountain Coffee, a slow grower in the mid-2000s, took off in 2006 when it chalked up 39 percent year-over-year growth, up from 18 percent in 2005. Especially impressive, Green Mountain registered 46 percent sales growth in 2008.

Adult educator Strayer Education, recording steady 20 to 25 percent annual growth every year since 2001, doesn't generate the kind of growth numbers that attract the "hot money," making it an ideal long-term growth candidate.

Healthcare computer systems maker Cerner, although in a good sector, generated only 10 percent year-over-year revenue growth in 2007 and 2008, far below the two prior years. That kind of inconsistency might qualify Cerner as an interesting value candidate, but growth investors should avoid stocks with inconsistent growth.

Flash memory maker SanDisk is the major player in a hot industry. But, as its sales record shows, hot tech stocks attract too much competition to qualify as viable growth candidates. Value investors, however, might find SanDisk an interesting player whenever it reports a disappointing quarter.

VeriSign's numbers tell us that the keeper of Internet names is a failed growth stock, another potential value candidate.

Based on those summaries, Strayer Education looks like an interesting growth candidate. Table 11-5 shows its recent sales history expressed as year-over-year growth percentages.

TABLE 11-5   Strayer Education's Recent Annual Sales Growth History

Fiscal Year	12/08	12/07	12/06	12/05	12/04
YOY Sales Growth	25%	20%	19%	21%	24%

These annual growth rates help you spot potential candidates, but those trends could turn on a dime. So, your first order of business is to determine whether the historic revenue growth trend is continuing, slowing, or accelerating. You can do that by examining the most recent quarterly revenue reports.

MSN Money and Reuters are the best resources for that information. Both display up to three years of quarterly sales data on their Financial Highlights reports. I'll use the MSN Money report to illustrate the process. Table 11-6 shows the revenue history portion of the report for Strayer that was available in April 2009.

TABLE 11-6   Strayer Education's Quarterly Revenues (in Millions of Dollars)

	FY (12/08)	FY (12/07)	FY (12/06)
1st quarter	97.1	80.2	67.1
2nd quarter	97.9	78.9	65.6
3rd quarter	87.0	69.8	56.7
4th quarter	114.3	89.1	74.3
Totals	396.3	318.0	263.6

Always compare sales to the same quarter in the previous year (year-over-year), rather than comparing to the preceding quarter. For instance, compare Strayer's 2008 fourth quarter (December) sales to December 2007 instead of to September 2008 (third quarter). For many industries, revenues fluctuate depending on the time of year. By always comparing the same time of year, you automatically eliminate seasonal variations from your analysis.

Rather than using the revenue totals, you'll get a better perspective by computing the year-over-year percentage sales growth for each quarter. I haven't found a website that calculates the percentages, so you have to do the math yourself. Table 11-7 shows the sales growth percentages that I computed for Strayer.

TABLE 11-7   Strayer Education's Quarterly Year-Over-Year Revenue Growth

Quarter	2008	2007
1st quarter (March)	21%	20%
2nd quarter (June)	24%	20%
3rd quarter (September)	25%	23%
4th quarter (December)	28%	20%

Doing the Math

Calculate year-over-year growth by dividing the most recent figure by the year-ago number and subtracting 1 from the result. For instance, to calculate Strayer's March 2008 quarter's growth, divide 97.1 by 680.2, yielding 1.321, and then subtract 1, which gives you 0.21, or 21 percent.

Strayer's recent revenue growth was unusually consistent. Even better, since the December 2008 quarter showed the strongest growth, revenue growth appears to be accelerating. Based on revenue growth alone, this looks like the ideal time to consider Strayer.

For contrast, consider SanDisk. Table 11-8 shows its recent sales in terms of year-over-year percentage sales growth, tabulated from the data in Table 11-4.

TABLE 11-8   SanDisk's Annual Revenue Growth

Fiscal Year	12/08	12/07	12/06	12/05	12/04
YOY Sales Growth	−14%	20%	41%	30%	65%

SanDisk has enjoyed some good years, but its revenue growth slowed in 2007 and turned negative in 2008. Table 11-9 shows recent quarterly sales.

TABLE 11-9   SanDisk's Quarterly Revenues (in Millions of Dollars)

	FY (12/08)	FY (12/07)	FY (12/06)
1st quarter	850.0	786.1	623.3
2nd quarter	816.0	827.0	719.2
3rd quarter	821.5	1,037.4	751.4
4th quarter	863.9	1,245.8	1,163.7
Totals	3,351.4	3,896.4	3,257.5

Table 11-10 shows the year-over-year revenue growth percentages.

TABLE 11-10   SanDisk's Quarterly Year-Over-Year Revenue Growth

Quarter	2008	2007
1st quarter (March)	8%	26%
2nd quarter (June)	–1%	15%
3rd quarter (September)	–21%	38%
4th quarter (December)	–31%	20%

SanDisk's revenue growth, already in negative territory, plunged in its December 2008 quarter. The worldwide recession undoubtedly contributed, but SanDisk's revenue growth was already trending down. For growth investors, SanDisk is not a viable candidate. However, the flash memory market has unlimited potential, and SanDisk is the main player. Value investors—do you see opportunity here?

Growth Investors

Pick candidates with recent sales growth consistent with or higher than historical sales growth. Look for at least 15 percent recent year-over-year growth. Higher—up to 45 percent or so—is better. Make sure that analysts are expecting historical growth rates to continue or, even better, accelerate. But beware—annual sales growth expectations of 50 percent or higher are unrealistic. That doesn't mean you can't make money on such stocks. Just be willing to sell at the first hint of bad news.

Value Investors

Your best prospects are stocks that have recently tripped up in terms of sales growth. Avoid perpetual losers that never generated significant revenue growth (less than 10 percent). Instead, focus on former "rock-star" stocks that have the potential to resume earlier growth rates.

The analysts' consensus revenue growth forecasts available on Yahoo! and Reuters can help you pinpoint stocks with good future revenue growth potential. See Chapter 12 for details.

Analyzing Margins

You can use three different margins to gauge profitability: gross margin, operating margin, and net income margin. All three divide a particular profit measure by total sales:

$$\text{margin} = \text{profit} / \text{total sales}$$

In theory, you could compute profit margins for any period (days, weeks, months). However, for stock analysis, the last quarter (three months), the last four reported quarters (TTM), or the last fiscal year are the only periods of interest.

The only difference between gross margin, operating margin, and net income margin are the specific profit figures that are compared to sales.

Gross Margin

Gross income—in theory, at least—is the profit made on a product considering only the costs of materials and labor to produce the product. These costs are called "cost of sales." Thus, gross income (profit) is sales less cost of sales:

$$\text{gross profit} = \text{total sales} - \text{cost of sales}$$

Gross margin is the gross profit divided by total sales:

$$\text{gross margin} = \text{gross profit} / \text{sales}$$

Here's how that translates to the real world. When Home Depot sells a hammer, its gross profit is the difference between the sales price and the price that Home Depot paid for the item. Home Depot's cost of putting the hammer on the shelves, advertising it, and all the other costs involved in selling the hammer are operational expenses and don't figure into the gross margin calculation. HD labels it gross product costs as cost of goods sold, or cost of sales on its operating statement.

The hammer example works for retail and service stocks. Manufacturing companies, however, add to their cost of sales depreciation and amortization (D&A) charges related to plants and equipment used to make the products. The D&A charges that are added to the cost of sales are not listed separately on the income statement.

Operating Margin

Operating expenses include costs of goods sold, plus selling, general, and administrative (SG&A) expenses; research and development; depreciation and amortization (if not in cost of sales); and most other costs of doing business, except interest expenses and taxes.

Operating income is sales less operating expenses:

operating income = total sales – operating expenses

Because it doesn't account for interest expenses and income taxes, operating income is also called EBIT, an acronym for earnings before interest and taxes.

Operating margin is

operating margin = operating income / total sales

Net Profit Margin

The net profit margin calculation takes into account all other expenses not included in the operating margin calculation—namely, interest expenses and income taxes.

Net income is operating income less interest expenses and income taxes:

net income = operating income – interest expenses – income taxes

The net profit margin is net income divided by total sales:

net profit margin = net income / total sales

The net profit margin is often simply called the profit margin. Net income is the bottom line, and EPS is the net income divided by the number of outstanding shares.

Comparing Margins

This section describes how to use the gross, operating, and net profit margins to evaluate investment candidates.

Gross Margins

Since gross margins gauge the difference between product costs and selling price, companies that have lower production costs or that are producing in-demand products that command higher prices should report higher gross margins than competitors. Table 11-11 compares microprocessor chipmakers Intel and Advanced Micro Devices' recent gross margins. Advanced Micro produces microprocessors that are technically competitive with Intel's, but Advanced Micro's brand identity is inferior to Intel's. The gross margins reflect their different competitive positions. Advanced Micro, the perennial number two, had to undercut Intel's prices to maintain market share.

Consider the implications. In 2008, our example, Intel, had 56 cents for every dollar of sales that it could apply to research and development, advertising, and administrative costs, or add to profits. Advanced Micro, by contrast, had only 40 cents left over for those items.

TABLE 11-11   Gross Margins for Intel and Advanced Micro Devices

Fiscal Year	Intel	AMD
2008	56%	40%
2007	52%	37%
2006	51%	50%
2005	59%	41%
2004	58%	39%
2003	57%	34%
2002	50%	22%

As another example, Table 11-12 compares automakers Ford, General Motors, and Toyota.

TABLE 11-12   Gross Margins for Ford, General Motors, and Toyota

Fiscal Year	Ford	GM	Toyota
2008	6%	2%	18%
2007	11%	8%	20%
2006	2%	9%	20%
2005	13%	5%	20%
2004	16%	16%	20%
2003	16%	18%	20%
2002	18%	18%	24%

Toyota had consistently recorded higher profit margins than Ford or General Motors, but the spread widened markedly in 2005.

Gross margins work best for analyzing manufacturing companies. They are not as useful for evaluating retail stores and other industries that sell directly to consumers. Competitive retail stores usually buy from the same manufacturers and sell their products at similar markups.

For example, Table 11-13 shows annual gross margins for electronics superstores Best Buy and Circuit City, which filed for bankruptcy in late 2008.

TABLE 11-13   Annual Gross Margins for Electronics Superstores Best Buy and Circuit City

Year	Best Buy	Circuit City
2008	24%	
2007	24%	21%
2006	24%	24%
2005	25%	24%
2004	24%	25%

Operating Margins

Operating margins are more useful than gross margins for retail and service businesses. Even for manufacturing companies, operating margins can reveal important clues pointing to the eventual dominator of a previously competitive industry.

Table 11-14 shows the annual operating margins for search engine operators Google and Yahoo!. In 2002, Yahoo!'s $950 million in revenues almost doubled Google's $440 million figure. By 2004, with revenues for Yahoo! at $3.6 billion and Google at $3.2 billion, the two were neck-and-neck in terms of both operating margins and revenues. But in 2005, Google pulled away in both measures. By 2008, Google dominated the industry with revenues of $21.8 billion compared to Yahoo!'s $7.2 billion.

TABLE 11-14   Operating Margins for Google and Yahoo!

Fiscal Year	Google	Yahoo!
2008	25%	0%
2007	31%	10%
2006	34%	15%
2005	33%	21%
2004	20%	19%
2003	23%	18%
2002	42%	9%

There could be many reasons why Google overcame Yahoo!'s lead and, for all intents and purposes, took over the web search industry. But profitability was a big factor. The more profitable the company, the more cash available to improve and expand its product lines.

That cash, termed "operating cash flow," is the cash left over after paying all operating expenses. Table 11-15 shows the annual operating cash flow figures for Google and Yahoo!.

TABLE 11-15   Annual Operating Cash Flow for Google and Yahoo! (in Millions of Dollars)

Fiscal Year	Google	Yahoo!
2008	$7,850	$1,880
2007	$5,780	$1,920
2006	$3,580	$1,370
2005	$2,460	$1,710
2004	$980	$1,090
2003	$400	$430
2002	$160	$300

The table tells you that in 2006, for example, Google had $2.2 billion more cash available to expand and improve its business than Yahoo!. By 2007, Google's cash advantage ballooned to $3.9 billion. By then, Yahoo! didn't have a chance.

Analyzing Margins

While gross margins are useful for detecting deterioration in a company's competitive position, and profit margins are a key ingredient in the target price calculation, I've found that operating margins are the most useful of the three measures for detecting profitability trends.

Table 11-16 lists the quarterly operating margins for SanDisk for calendar years 2004–2006.

TABLE 11-16 SanDisk Quarterly Operating Margins

Period	2006	2005	2004
March	9.3%	26.2%	25.5%
June	17.9%	20.6%	25.5%
September	17.1%	26.9%	23.0%
December	1.0%	26.4%	23.0%

Except for a dip in the second quarter of 2005, SanDisk's operating margin held steady in the mid-20 percent range during 2004 and 2005. However, everything went sour in 2006. SanDisk's March quarter operating margin dropped 65 percent versus year-ago (9.3 versus 26.2). June was down 13 percent, and SanDisk's September quarter margin fell 36 percent versus year-ago to 17.1 percent.

Operating margin percentage declines as little as 5 percent (such as 19 versus 20) are significant. The June 2005 drop would have been a red flag unless unusual one-time costs sank the margin. In any case, anyone paying attention would have dumped SanDisk after seeing the March and June 2006 results. SanDisk's share price peaked at $80 or so in January 2006. But it traded mostly in the $50 to $60 range until October 2006. Then it weakened, hitting the mid-$30 range in February 2007. So, you would have had plenty of time to analyze the March and June 2006 reports and still get out before the share price tumbled.

The SanDisk example illustrates the importance of analyzing the most recent quarter's margins to spot signals pointing to future shortfalls. Compare the quarterly margins to the year-ago number, not the annual data, to allow for seasonal variations. However, expect more volatility in the quarterly data.

Growth Investors

Observe trends in both annual and quarterly operating margins. In terms of annual margins, avoid companies with a decline of 5 percent or more (such as 19 versus 20) year-over-year. For quarterly margins, compare to the year-ago quarter, and avoid the company if its recent quarter's margin dropped 10 percent or more (such as 18 versus 20).

Value Investors

Value investors typically find their candidate's margins depressed compared to historical levels. But the historical margins are useful for estimating earnings when the company recovers.

High Versus Low Margins

Intuitively, you'd surmise that it's a good idea to pick the most profitable company in an industry. That strategy works for growth investors, especially when analyzing competing firms in fast-growing emerging markets. But value investors should take the opposite view. In other words, they should seek out companies with margins below industry averages or, better yet, their own historical averages.

Bear with me while I state the obvious: The market typically values stocks higher when the market perceives them as winners than when they are out of favor. Table 11-17 shows the average price/sales ratios for pharmaceutical giants Merck and Pfizer over a 10-year timeframe.

TABLE 11-17 Historical Price/Sales Ratios for Pharmaceutical Makers Pfizer and Merck

	2008	2007	2006	2005	2004	2003	2002	2001	2000	1999
Merck	2.7	5.3	4.2	3.2	3.1	4.6	6.0	6.4	5.5	4.9
Pfizer	2.5	3.3	3.9	3.7	4.2	5.8	5.9	8.7	11.3	7.5

The table shows that the market valued Pfizer more than four times higher for each dollar of revenues in 2000 than it did in 2008. Similarly, investors were willing to pay more than twice as much for each dollar of Merck sales in 2001 than in 2008.

You can capitalize on the market's fickleness when it comes to valuing stocks. Here's an example.

Suppose a company is generating a subpar 3 percent net profit margin (net income divided by revenues) in an industry where most players are generating 7 percent. Assuming $1,000 in annual revenues, the company earned $30 for the year.

Revenues	$1,000
Net Profit Margin	3%
Net Income	$30

To keep it simple, assume that the company has only one share of stock outstanding. Furthermore, because of its low profit margin, it's trading at only a 10 price/earnings ratio versus its industry average 20 P/E.

If you do the math, you'll see that a company's stock price is equal to its P/E multiplied by its earnings per share:

$$P = P/E \times EPS$$

In this example, I've stipulated that the P/E is 10 and the EPS is 30, so the share price is $300:

$$P = 10 \times 30 = 300$$

Now suppose a year goes by and the company reports 25 percent sales growth. Even better, its net profit margin recovers to 5 percent—still low, but closer to the 7 percent industry average. So you have the following:

Sales	$1,250
Net Profit Margin	5%
Net Income	$62.50

The net income more than doubled, even though sales increased only 25 percent, thanks to the higher profit margin.

But that's not the whole story. The market likes the higher profit margin and, sensing that it will be even better next year, rewards the company's stock with a 15 P/E. So the stock price goes up to $937.50:

$$P = P/E \times EPS = 15 \times 62.50 = \$937.50$$

The bottom line is that a 25 percent sales increase combined with an improving profit margin tripled the share price.

Analyzing Overhead Expenses

Sales, general, and administrative (SG&A) is a catchall category that includes most of a firm's operating expenses except for cost of sales, research and development, and depreciation and amortization. SG&A expenses are, in effect, overhead.

Some companies list marketing expenses on a line separate from other SG&A expenses on the income statement. Consider all operating expenses except cost of sales, research and development, and depreciation/amortization charges as SG&A for this analysis.

The lower the SG&A, the tighter the ship that management is running. Comparing competitors' SG&A expenses can give you important insight into each company's operations. The best way to compare SG&A between companies is to divide the total SG&A by sales:

$$SG\&A \% \ sales = SG\&A \ / \ total \ sales$$

For instance, in 2008, Google's SG&A totaled 17.2 percent of revenues compared to Yahoo!'s 31.5 percent. How significant is that 14.3 percent difference? Yahoo!'s revenues totaled $21.796 billion in 2008. So a 14.3 percent reduction in costs would have amounted to $3.117 billion ($2.20 per share). Yahoo!'s 2008 pretax income totaled $95.8 million. So saving that 14.3 percent would have increased pretax income to $3.118 billion. I'd say that's significant.

Observing trends in SG&A percentage of revenues can also be useful for detecting operational problems within a company. However, out-of-control SG&A expenses will likely also be reflected in deteriorating operating margins.

Profitability Ratios

Legendary investor Warren Buffet is often quoted as advising investors to analyze purchasing a company's shares as if you were buying the whole company.

One of the items you'd probably evaluate if you were buying a company is your return on investment:

return on investment = annual profits / total investment

For instance, your return on investment is 10 percent if you bought a company with a $100,000 cash investment and you made $10,000 in profits annually (10,000 / 100,000).

Return on Equity

Return on equity measures a company's returns on its shareholders' investments in the same manner. ROE is a company's annual net income divided by its shareholders' equity.

ROE = net income / shareholders' equity

ROE is widely followed. Many money managers rely on it as a key profitability gauge. In fact, many managers I interviewed for this book would not consider a stock with less than 15 percent ROE. Why is ROE so widely used? The way the math works, a company can't internally fund annual earnings growth higher than its ROE. Here's an example.

In the return-on-investment example, I described a situation where a $100,000 investment (equity) yields a $10,000, or 10 percent, annual return on your equity. Let's postulate that you could earn a 10 percent return on any additional cash you put into the business. Further assume that you are willing to invest your profits into growing the business, but you're not willing to put in additional cash or borrow more money.

Based on those assumptions, you'd invest your first year's 10 percent return ($10,000) on equity back into the business. So the second year, the company would earn 10 percent on $110,000 equity, 10 percent more than the first year's $100,000 equity, and so on.

Your 10 percent return on equity defined the maximum annual growth that your company can achieve given the assumptions. In the same way, ROE determines the maximum achievable growth for a corporation, assuming that it doesn't raise additional cash by borrowing or selling more stock.

Implied Growth

Suppose that instead of reinvesting all your profits, you decide to take $1,000 out of the business annually. Thus, your $1,000 dividend is unavailable to fund future growth. The term "implied growth" defines a corporation's maximum achievable growth, accounting for dividends paid out:

$$\text{implied growth} = (\text{net income} - \text{dividends}) / \text{shareholders' equity}$$

Implied growth is the same as ROE if the firm doesn't pay dividends.

As discussed earlier, assuming no dividends, ROE defines a firm's maximum internally funded growth rate. For instance, a 15 percent ROE firm that doesn't pay dividends can't internally fund annual growth faster than 15 percent.

Of course, companies often do raise additional funds through borrowings or stock sales. But stockholders are better off if a company doesn't have to resort to those measures to grow. Here's why.

Selling additional stock dilutes per-share profits. For instance, a company with one million shares outstanding and $1 million net income earns $1 per share. However, its EPS drops to $0.67 if the company makes the same profit after selling another 500,000 shares.

Similar results occur if the firm borrows instead of selling shares. For example, say that a year earlier, the same company had borrowed $1 million at 8 percent interest. It would earn $920,000 ($1 million less $80,000 interest), bringing its EPS down to $0.92.

All that said, using ROE to evaluate a company's profitability has limitations.

Recall that ROE is calculated by dividing net income by shareholders' equity. By the way, book value is shareholders' equity expressed on a per-share basis.

The problem lies in the shareholders' equity or book value calculation. From the name, you might conclude that book value represents the value of the company's hard assets, give or take asset depreciation or appreciation. There is such a balance sheet figure— total assets—but it's not the same as equity or book value.

According to accounting rules, total assets must equal the sum of total liabilities plus shareholders' equity:

total assets = total liabilities + shareholders' equity

or

shareholders' equity = assets – liabilities

Say a firm has current assets such as cash and inventories totaling $1,000 and long-term assets such as plants and equipment adding up to $2,000. The assets portion of the balance sheet would look like this:

Assets

Current Assets	1,000
Long-Term Assets	2,000
Total Assets	3,000

Here's how the liabilities would look if the company owed $800 for accounts payable and other short-term debts and $300 for a long-term loan:

Liabilities

Current Liabilities	800
Long-Term Liabilities	300
Total Liabilities	1,100

Since assets exceed liabilities by $1,900, that's the shareholders' equity. Here's the complete balance sheet:

Assets

Current Assets	1,000
Long-Term Assets	2,000
Total Assets	3,000

Liabilities

Current Liabilities	800
Long-Term Liabilities	300
Total Liabilities	1,100
Shareholders' Equity	1,900

If the company earned $250 last year, its ROE is 13 percent:

ROE = net income / shareholders' equity = 250 / 1,900 = 13%

Now consider another company with a similar balance sheet, except that its long-term debt totals $1,500 instead of $300:

Assets

Total Assets	3,000

Liabilities

Current Liabilities	800
Long-Term Liabilities	1,500
Total Liabilities	2,300
Shareholders' Equity	700

If the second company earned the same $250 as the first company, its ROE would be 36 percent instead of 13 percent:

ROE = net income / shareholders' equity = 250 / 700 = 36%

Thus, all else equal, the company with more debt has the higher ROE.

For real examples, Table 11-18 compares measurement systems maker National Instruments to funeral home and cemetery product provider Matthews International.

TABLE 11-18   ROE Calculation for National Instruments and Matthews International

National Instruments (FY 12/08)	
Revenues	$821 million
Net Income	$84.8 million
ROE	12.8%
Matthews International (FY 9/08)	
Revenues	$819 million
Net Income	$79.5 million
ROE	18.3%

Both firms reported nearly the same revenue, but National Instruments generated higher net income. Nevertheless, investors insisting on a minimum 15 percent ROE would reject National Instruments in favor of Matthews. Why is Matthews' ROE higher? Debt! National's liabilities totaled only $168 million compared to $480 million for Matthews. That debt brought Matthews' shareholders' equity down to $434 million versus $665 million for National Instruments.

It's clear that using ROE to measure profitability works only when you compare firms carrying similar debt levels. Otherwise, the ROE calculation treats debt backwards. It penalizes efficiently run firms that grow without borrowing and rewards companies that are hooked on debt. In fact, if a company pays down its debt, its ROE goes down, not up!

A Check on ROE

Even with that downside, many money managers believe that ROE is the best profitability measure. If you fall into that camp, you can overcome the debt anomaly by comparing growth in shareholders' equity to ROE. That is, if management is properly reinvesting ROE, shareholders' equity should be increasing at the same rate as the ROE. You can use book value growth in place of shareholders' equity growth if that number is more readily available.

Return on Capital

The return on capital (a.k.a. return on invested capital) formula corrects the debt anomaly by adding long-term debt to the equity figure in the ROE equation:

return on capital = net income / (shareholders' equity + long-term debt)

Table 11-19 shows that ROC paints a different picture than ROE.

TABLE 11-19   Return on Invested Capital (ROC) for National Instruments and Matthews International

National Instruments (FY 12/08)
ROC   12.2%

Matthews International (FY 9/08)
ROC   10.6%

The ROC formula makes it easier to compare companies carrying different amounts of long-term debt. However, ROC doesn't count liabilities listed as short-term debt, or as "other long-term liabilities." That could be significant when you're evaluating firms that substitute continuously renewed short-term instruments for long-term debt.

Return on Assets

Return on assets overcomes that shortcoming by considering all debt, no matter where it's listed on the balance sheet.

Let's take another look at the basic accounting equation:

total assets = total liabilities + shareholders' equity

Total liabilities is just what it says—everything the company says it owes, regardless of where it's listed on the balance sheet.

The return on assets (ROA) formula divides net income by total assets, which includes shareholders' equity plus all borrowings:

return on assets = net income / total assets

Table 11-20 shows how National Instruments and Matthews International measure up as far as ROA.

TABLE 11-20   Return on Assets (ROA) for National Instruments and Matthews International

National Instruments (FY 12/08)

ROA   10.3%

Matthews International (FY 9/08)

ROA   8.8%

Since return on assets counts short-term debt, and almost all firms will have something listed in that category, return on capital will always be higher than return on assets for the same stock. Similarly, because ROA takes liabilities into account, and ROE doesn't, ROE will always be higher than ROA. Shareholders' equity is negative when liabilities exceed assets. In those instances, only ROA is meaningful.

When I checked, the median (as many stocks above as below) five-year average ROE was 9.5. The median five-year average ROA was 3.5, and the median ROC was 4.4.

Do profitability ratios matter?

In April 2009, I listed the best 50 and worst 50 members of the S&P 500 Index (excluding banks and insurance companies), in terms of share price performance, over the previous 12 months. Then I separately averaged the five-year profitability ratios for the best-50 and worst-50 lists.

I excluded banks and insurance companies because stocks in those industries, as a group, were crushed during the previous 12 months and would have distorted the results.

Table 11-21 shows the average five-year profitability ratios for each list.

TABLE 11-21   Average Five-Year Profitability Ratios for the 50 Best-Performing and 50 Worst-Performing Members of the S&P 500 Index

	ROE	ROC	ROA
Top 50	23.2	12.7	8.0
Bottom 50	7.7	4.0	2.9

This table shows that the profitability ratios for the best-performing stocks were generally triple the ratios for the worst performers.

Cash Flow Analysis

Cash flow is easy to understand. If you had $5,000 in your bank account on January 1, and only $1,000 on December 31, your cash flow for the year was a negative $4,000, regardless of how much income you reported to the IRS. Corporate accounting follows the same rules, except that the numbers are bigger.

Interestingly, companies were not required to include cash flow statements with their financial reports until 1987.

Accountants construct the cash flow statement by starting with reported earnings. Then they add back noncash items that were subtracted from earnings to figure income but did not actually result in cash moving out of the firm's bank accounts.

Expenses, such as depreciation and amortization, for example, represent a reduction in the book value of capital equipment and other assets but require no actual cash outlays.

Working Capital Changes

Another operating cash flow category, changes in working capital, represents real cash outflows and inflows that are not reported on the income statement.

For instance, cash used to buy raw materials isn't charged against income until the goods are incorporated into finished products and sold. The net change in cost of *inventories* during the reporting period *subtracts* from cash flow because the monies were spent but not deducted from reported income.

Accounts receivables, the money owed the company by its customers, is recorded as income when it's billed, usually long before the actual cash is received from the customer. Since the company doesn't really have the cash, net increases in accounts *receivables subtract* from operating cash flow.

Accounts payables are monies owed to suppliers and service providers. Those charges are deducted from income when the company is billed (or the items are billable), not when it's actually paid. Since the firm didn't pay out the cash, increases in accounts *payables* (unpaid bills) add to the firm's bank balance and thus *add* to operating cash flow.

Cash Tells the Story

While creative accountants can do all sorts of things to manipulate reported earnings, outside of outright fraud, there's little they can do to fudge bank balances. Because the cash flow statement must balance to real cash, savvy investors pay more attention to cash flows than to reported net income.

Ambassadors International owns a fleet of cruise ships that operate mostly in North American rivers and other waterways. On December 31, 2006, Ambassadors' shares changed hands at $45, up almost 200 percent for the year. That price run-up reflected Ambassadors' apparently great fundamentals.

For 2006, it recorded net income of $5.63 million ($0.53 per share), up 79 percent for the year, propelled by a 435 percent surge in revenues. Alas, those numbers didn't translate to cash in the bank. Anyone checking Ambassadors' operating cash flow would have noticed that by that measure, Ambassadors actually lost $955,000 in 2006.

Ambassadors released its 2006 numbers on February 28, 2007. Its share price peaked at $47 on March 12 and was still changing hands at $46 or so on March 31. Thus, investors who checked the 2006 cash flow statement had plenty of time to act on that information. In April, the share price started dropping, and Ambassadors ended 2007 at $14.60, down 69 percent from March.

Reporting corporations have some room to fudge their operating cash flow numbers, but all inflows and outflows must be listed somewhere on the cash flow statement. Otherwise, the cash flow total won't balance to the bank account totals.

The cash flow statement consists of three sections: operating, investing, and financing activities:

- Operating cash flow, in theory, includes all items related to operating the firm's main business.
- Investing cash flows are supposed to be restricted to capital expenditures and other investments.
- Financing activities theoretically include cash flows from stock sales or buybacks and changes in debt levels.

However, accounting rules require that certain items end up in funny places on the cash flow statement, as you'll soon see.

Dubious Allocations

Deferred taxes—that is, income taxes that were deducted from income but not actually paid—logically a financing item, are added to operating cash flow.

Accounting rules give companies the option of capitalizing most software development expenses. The capitalized software development costs are treated similarly to capital expenses. They are depreciated over time rather than being charged against income in the year the money was spent. Since some firms capitalize software development and others don't, deduct software development cash flows listed in the investing section from operating cash flow before you compare competing companies' operating cash flows.

Using Operating Cash Flow

Operating cash flow offers a better picture of profitability than reported earnings. In most instances, the dubious allocations just mentioned will not significantly affect your analysis.

However, it's best to review the detailed cash flow statements filed with the SEC if you do want to perform a thorough analysis and check for dubious items. Subtract dubious items, such as deferred income taxes and others that you may discover from the reported operating cash flow, before performing your analysis.

Several academic studies found that stocks of companies with positive operating cash flow outperform those with negative cash flow. However, negative operating cash flow doesn't always signal problems. Small, fast-growing firms often soak up cash to finance burgeoning, but necessary, inventories and receivables. However, slower growers—say, firms growing sales less than 25 percent annually—should be generating positive operating cash flow. Mature companies—those growing sales in the 10 percent to 15 percent range—should be generating large operating cash flows. Many investors consider positive operating cash flow (OCF) a prerequisite for considering a stock.

How much operating cash flow is enough? Table 11-22 shows some examples of strong cash flow generators.

Recent research has found that observing the relationship between operating cash flow and net income can help pinpoint stocks with potential earnings quality issues. Normally, operating cash flow exceeds net income because noncash depreciation and amortization charges that were deducted from net income are added back to operating cash flow.

Operating cash flow less than net income signals possible inflated accounts receivables or inventory levels, both indicators of potential future earnings disappointments. Rising net income accompanied by declining operating cash flow was found to be the most dangerous signal. This subject is covered in detail in Chapter 12.

Still, OCF doesn't tell the whole story. Depreciation accounts for the aging of previous capital expenditures. The OCF formula adds back the depreciation deducted from net income but doesn't account for new capital spending.

Free Cash Flow

Free cash flow is the excess cash after accounting for capital spending on plants and equipment, software development, and similar items. To put it another way, free cash flow is extra cash that the firm doesn't need for running and expanding its current businesses. It's surplus cash that the company can use to acquire other companies, expand into new business areas, or pay out to shareholders as dividends.

Despite its wide use, free cash flow is not shown on cash flow statements; you have to calculate it:

free cash flow = operating cash flow – capital spending

For this analysis, capital spending includes the capital spending line item plus all its variants, including capitalized software expenses, cost of acquisitions, and so forth.

Free cash flow is the bottom line for many investors, and some want to see large positive numbers in that category. However, many fast growers spend almost all available cash to fund expansion. How much free cash is enough? For free cash flow, more is always better, but any number in the billions gets my attention.

Table 11-22 lists a sort of honor roll of cash flow generators. To qualify, a firm must have converted at least 25 percent of its annual revenues to operating cash flow and must have generated at least $100 million of annual free cash flow.

TABLE 11-22   Cash Flow Honor Roll (as of 4/24/09)

Company	OCF % of Revenues	Last FY Free Cash Flow (in Millions of Dollars)
Adobe Systems Inc.	36	1,169
Akamai Technologies Inc.	43	228
Altera Corp.	33	409
American Express Co.	38	9,643
Amgen Inc.	40	5,316
Anadarko Petroleum Corp.	44	1,641
Apple Inc.	30	8,505
AT&T Inc.	30	13,321
Cisco Systems Inc.	31	10,824
Comcast Corp.	30	4,481
Corning Inc.	36	207
Diamond Offshore Drilling Inc.	46	953
Dolby Laboratories Inc.	41	251
eBay Inc.	34	2,316
Eli Lilly & Co.	36	6,348
Genentech Inc.	29	3,204
Gen-Probe Inc.	38	139
Gilead Sciences Inc.	41	2,090
Google Inc.	36	5,494
Intel Corp.	29	5,729
Intuitive Surgical Inc.	32	216
Linear Technology Corp.	45	495
McDonald's Corp.	25	3,782
Merck & Co. Inc.	28	5,273
Microsoft Corp.	36	18,430
NetApp Inc.	31	821
Oracle Corp.	33	7,159
Paychex Inc.	37	552
Pfizer Inc.	38	16,537
QUALCOMM Inc.	32	2,161

Company	OCF % of Revenues	Last FY Free Cash Flow (in Millions of Dollars)
Questar Corp.	43	990
Symantec Corp.	31	1,545
TD Ameritrade Holding Corp.	36	1,084
Tidewater Inc.	39	136
VeriSign Inc.	50	363
Verizon Communications Inc.	27	9,382

Is it difficult to combine positive cash flows and fast growth? Yes, but not impossible. Table 11-23 lists a sampling of firms that grew year-over-year sales at least 20 percent in their last fiscal year and generated at least $1 billion in both operating cash flow and free cash flow.

TABLE 11-23   Fast-Growing Companies Recording Positive Operating Cash Flow and Positive Free Cash Flow (in Millions of Dollars)

	Revenue Growth	Operating Cash Flow	Free Cash Flow
Amazon.com Inc.	29%	1,697	1,364
Apache Corp.	24%	7,065	1,092
Apple	35%	9,596	8,397
Biogen Idec Inc.	29%	1,564	1,289
Bunge	39%	2,543	1,647
Chevron Corp.	24%	29,632	9,966
Fiserv Inc.	22%	1,442	1,243
Gilead Sciences Inc.	26%	2,205	2,090
Google Inc.	31%	7,853	5,494
Monsanto Co.	36%	2,799	1,881
Mosaic Co.	70%	2,547	2,175
National-Oilwell Varco	37%	2,294	1,916
Nucor	43%	2,499	1,480
Oracle	25%	7,402	7,159
QUALCOMM Inc.	26%	3,558	2,161
Schering-Plough Co.	46%	3,364	2,617

This table illustrates that it is possible to find fast growers that manage to produce billion of dollars of both operating cash flow and free cash flow.

Positive cash flow is how small companies become large. Cash burners have to regularly raise more cash, by either selling stock or borrowing. Both cut existing shareholders' earnings. Why not put the wind at your back and require positive operating cash flow at a minimum, and at least close to break-even free cash flow?

That said, sometimes fast growers temporarily burn cash for justifiable reasons, such as to build a new plant or acquire needed technology. The management discussion in the SEC reports should explain why cash is flowing out rather than in.

Quarterly Cash Flow Reports

Unlike income statements that show each quarter's results separately, the cash flow statements filed with the SEC list only year-to-date numbers. The second quarter's cash flow statement shows the combined first- and second-quarter totals, the third quarter's statement shows the totals for the first three quarters, and so on. Most financial websites that display the cash flow report show it in this same cumulative format.

Using the cumulative format, to see the third-quarter results, you must subtract the second-quarter year-to-date figures from the third-quarter totals. That's a pain, but it is doable using websites such as MSN Money and Reuters, which show the five most recent quarters' data side by side. It's much harder using the reports filed with the SEC, because those cash flow statements do not show the previous quarter's numbers.

Yahoo! lists the actual quarterly cash flow figures (not cumulative) on its Quarterly Data report. That's a big advantage. On the downside, Yahoo! lists only the four most recent quarters. That's a problem. When analyzing quarterly statements, you need to see five quarters to compare recent figures to year-ago. That limitation applies to Yahoo!'s income statements and balance sheets, as well as to its cash flow statements.

EBITDA Versus Operating Cash Flow

EBITDA stands for earnings before interest, taxes, depreciation, and amortization. Similar in purpose to OCF, EBITDA describes the cash generated by a company's main business, but it calculates it differently.

Unlike OCF, which starts with net income on the top line, the EBITDA calculation starts with operating income, which is also known as EBIT, earnings before interest and taxes. EBITDA is EBIT plus depreciation and amortization expenses.

EBITDA is not defined by generally accepted accounting principles (GAAP), and it is not listed on most financial statements. Forbes, Smart Money, Market Watch, and CNN Money are the only websites I've found that display EBITDA as a separate line item on their income statements.

Calculating EBITDA is not difficult, because operating income (EBIT) is listed on most income statements. Compute EBITDA by adding depreciation and amortization charges to operating income:

EBITDA = operating income (EBIT) + depreciation + amortization

Depreciation and amortization charges are listed on the cash flow statement.

Many companies report a figure that they call EBITDA in their earnings press releases. However, since EBITDA isn't an officially defined term, they often change the definition to suit their needs. If you decide to use EBITDA, ignore the press release figure, and either look it up on one of the websites that lists it or calculate it yourself.

A major difference between EBITDA and operating cash flow is that EBITDA does not count changes in working capital. That's both a disadvantage and an advantage.

Recall that comparing operating cash flow to net income helps you identify potential earnings quality issues—namely, abnormal increases in accounts receivable and inventory levels. Thus, using EBITDA in place of operating cash flows requires that you do the math and compare accounts receivables and inventory levels to sales to warn of the earnings quality issues described in Chapter 12.

Some analysts ignore working capital changes, believing that receivables and inventories change in response to short-term market conditions. But in the long run, they end up pretty much where they started. For them, EBITDA is a better measure than operating cash flow. Another advantage of using EBITDA is that it isn't inflated with dubious entries such as deferred income taxes.

Summary

Sales growth, operating margins, profitability ratios, and cash flows all figure into the profitability equation. Many of the analysis tools described in this chapter can serve a dual purpose. They help you determine a company's absolute profitability, and they help you pinpoint the most profitable players in a market sector. Analyzing an investing candidate's profitability is something that professionals almost always do but individual investors often overlook.

12

Analysis Tool #9:
Detect Red Flags

The best growth stock candidates grow sales and earnings at least 15 percent annually, and faster is better. Table 12-1 shows recent year-over-year revenue growth rate trends for a variety of stocks that meet that requirement. I didn't list 2008 growth rates because in 2008, global economic problems overwhelmed individual company fundamentals.

I divided the stocks into four categories:

- **Big bang stocks** register high double-digit, even triple-digit, year-over-year revenue growth at the start. Of course, those rates are unsustainable, and growth slows quickly. However, they are worth considering again when growth stabilizes. Many chalk up steady 25 to 30 percent annual revenue growth for years after the initial slowdown.

- **Slow starters** are similar to big bang stocks, except rather than starting fast, it takes them a few years to achieve significant revenue growth numbers.

- **Steady eddies** generate sustainable 20 to 30 percent annual revenue growth for years. However, as the table shows, growth eventually slows for them too.

- **Bumpy ride** stocks have good years and bad years in terms of growth. They make ideal value stock candidates.

TABLE 12-1   Year-Over-Year Revenue Growth Rates

Company	2007	2006	2005	2004	2003	2002	2001	2000	1999	1998	1997
Big Bang Stocks											
Amazon.com	39	26	23	32	34	26	13	68	169	313	839
Chipotle Mexican	32	31	33	49	54	56	94				
Crocs	131	227	703	1061	4574						
eBay	29	31	39	51	78	62	74	92	161	108	
Google	56	73	92	118	234	409	352				
Netflix	21	46	36	85	77	101	111	617			
P.F. Chang's	16	15	15	31	33	28	36	53	96	96	116
Slow Starters											
Gilead Sciences	40	49	53	53	86	100	20	16			
Green Mountain Coffee	52	39	18	18	17	5	14	14	29	16	
Hansen Natural	49	74	93	63	20	14	12	−1			
Steady Eddies											
Apollo Group	10	10	25	34	33	31	26	22	30	38	32
Cheesecake Factory	15	11	22	25	19	21	23	26	31	27	30
Panera Bread	29	29	34	32	29	40	33				
Bumpy Ride											
GameStop	33	72	68	17	17	21	40	37			
Symantec	26	60	38	33	31	26	15	26	11	18	2
Intuitive Surgical	61	64	64	51	27	40	94				
Yahoo!	9	22	47	120	71	33	−36	88	141	191	291

One element common to all categories is that revenue growth peaks at some point in time and then tapers off. Unfortunately, stock prices typically reflect expectations that recent growth rates will continue unabated for the foreseeable future. Thus, stocks always get hit hard when the market realizes that growth is slowing.

Since their wealth is usually tied to the stock price, company executives have great incentive to hide any clues that growth might be tailing off while they scramble to get things back on track.

Given those realities, priority number one for growth investors should be detecting clues that management is working the numbers to mask faltering growth.

Chapter 4 describes how to detect clues embedded in analysts' earnings forecasts. Here, we'll focus on the financial statements. We'll check revenue trends for signals that growth might be slowing, and we'll look for red flags in the financials warning that management might be resorting to creative accounting to keep up the growth numbers.

Although management reports results only quarterly, the sooner you detect and act on these red flags, the better. You can't wait for the next earnings report. These days, probably encouraged by lawyers, management often warns of oncoming shortfalls by "reduced guidance" press releases weeks ahead of report time.

Less urgent, you'll also learn how to analyze financials for yellow flags, which are conditions pointing to potential problems down the road.

Sales Growth Trends

Although mentioned before, it's worth repeating that although the market prices stocks based on earnings expectations, you can't have earnings without first selling something.

That's important, because a slowdown in revenue growth often precedes an earnings disappointment.

Adult Educator Apollo Group provides a good example. Table 12-2 shows Apollo's revenues and earnings from 2003 through 2006. Depending on where you are in a company's fiscal year, you can get two to three years' quarterly data in summary form similar to Table 12-2 on MSN Money or Reuters. You can find older data on Smart Money's income statement (click "previous five quarters").

TABLE 12-2 Quarterly Earnings and Revenues for Apollo Group

Quarter	2003	2004	2005	2006
Revenues (in Millions of Dollars)				
February	295.2	396.9	506.3	570.6
May	364.2	497.0	617.8	653.4
August	371.3	492.8	592.2	624.9
November	411.8	534.9	628.7	667.8
Earnings Per Share				
February	0.24	0.35	0.38	0.45
May	0.39	0.56	0.76	0.75
August	0.37	−0.59	0.61	0.43
November	0.44	0.59	0.72	0.65

It's always best to compare revenues or earnings to the same year-ago quarter, rather than to the previous quarter. For example, you would compare the November 2006 quarter to November 2005, not to August 2006. Otherwise, seasonal variations may distort the results.

The numbers show that except for August 2004, when it took an acquisition-related special charge, Apollo recorded reasonably consistent earnings growth from 2003 through 2005. In 2006, however, quarterly earnings fell short of year-ago in the May, August, and November quarters.

Table 12-3 illustrates how you could have seen that coming. Instead of showing the actual revenue and earnings numbers, Table 12-3 lists the year-over-year percentage growth. Since I didn't collect the 2002 numbers, I didn't calculate the 2003 year-over-year growth. However, Table 12-1 shows that Apollo grew revenues 33 percent that year.

TABLE 12-3   Apollo Group Year Versus Year Percentage Change in Quarterly Earnings and Revenues

Quarter	2004	2005	2006
Revenues			
February	35%	28%	13%
May	36%	24%	6%
August	33%	20%	6%
November	30%	18%	7%
Earnings Per Share			
February	46%	9%	18%
May	48%	36%	–1%
August	Loss		–30%
November	34%	22%	–10%

While earnings often fluctuate wildly from quarter to quarter, revenues are a steadier gauge. In fact, revenue growth often moves in relatively long-term trends.

Apollo continued its historic mid-30 percent revenue growth pace during its February, May, and August 2004 quarters. By November, however, growth slowed, but not enough to trigger red flags. But February 2005 was down 20 percent (28 percent versus 35 percent), May was down 33 percent, and August and November both dropped around 40 percent.

A revenue growth slowdown warns of a coming earnings shortfall. However, revenue growth naturally varies from quarter to quarter, so don't be alarmed by relatively small changes. Consider a 20 percent drop as cause for concern and 25 percent and above as a red flag signaling slowing growth.

It's the percentage change in revenue growth, not the absolute values, that matters. For instance, a drop from 20 percent to 15 percent in year-over-year growth (a 25 percent drop) is just as significant as a drop from 60 percent to 45 percent (also a 25 percent drop).

It's natural to excuse a fall from, say, 150 percent to 75 percent as understandable, because 150 percent growth is obviously unsustainable. Besides, 75 percent year-over-year growth is plenty. That's all true, but it doesn't matter—the sales growth slowdown still signals a forthcoming earnings disappointment.

Analyzing historical revenue growth is helpful, but it can be misleading. Maybe the strong growth was triggered by nonrecurring events, such as a new product introduction, an acquisition, or a competitor dropping out of the business. Also, the company may not be able to maintain the historical pace into the future because it's saturating the market, new players are entering the fray, or any number of other reasons.

Checking the analyst consensus revenue forecasts available on both Yahoo! and Reuters will alert you to such circumstances.

Allscripts Healthcare, a provider of information systems to healthcare clinics, offers a good example.

In May 2007, Allscripts reported blockbuster March quarter results. Earnings soared 160 percent on a 54 percent increase in sales. Those results, though great, were not surprising. Allscripts had reported 100 percent or so year-over-year revenue growth in each of its previous three quarters.

However, the consensus revenue forecasts warned that the party was nearing an end. Analysts were forecasting only 25 percent or so revenue growth in each of the next two quarters, compared to the year-ago 100 percent growth figures. Why the low forecasts? Some analysts had noticed that the number of new orders received in the March quarter was low. Whatever the reason, analysts were expecting a growth slowdown, which almost always leads to missed expectations.

As it turned out, Allscripts reported good June quarter results. But it not only missed its September quarter numbers, it cut its guidance (forecasts) as well. All in all, Allscripts ended the year around 40 percent off its May 2007 peak.

When looking at revenue forecasts, pay the most attention to the current and next quarter. Ignore the next fiscal year's forecast. The further out the forecast, the less reliable it is. In fact, analysts usually increase their next quarter's sales forecast if the company makes its current-quarter numbers.

Apply the same limits to forecast revenue growth as for historical figures. A 25 percent drop in forecast year-over-year growth (such as from 25 percent to 18 percent) is a red flag.

Accounts Receivables and Inventories

Analyzing accounts receivable and inventory levels is the most widely used method of spotting red flags.

Accounts Receivables

Unlike when it sells to us, a company doesn't usually require payment in advance when it sells to another firm. Instead, it bills the customer and specifies a payment due date. Accounts receivables are the monies owed by customers for goods already shipped and billed. Normally, receivables more or less track sales. For instance, if sales double, receivables should also double.

You can compare a company's accounts receivables to an earlier period, or even to a different company's receivables, by dividing the receivables by revenues. You can use either the most recent quarter's revenues or the last four quarters' revenues in the denominator. The result is usually expressed as a percentage, such as 45 percent of revenues.

Days Sales (Revenues) Outstanding

Days Sales Outstanding (DSO) is a popular method of gauging receivables. You calculate the DSO by dividing the end-of-quarter receivables by 12 months' sales and multiplying the result by 365 instead of converting to a percentage. For example, assume receivables totaled $100, and the last four quarters' sales totaled $500. Dividing 100 by 500 gives you 0.2, and multiplying 0.2 by 365 gives you 73 DSO.

Every industry has its own payment customs, so you can't compare receivables percentages of companies serving different markets. Many corporations prefer to delay paying their bills for as long as they can because they view those unpaid bills as an interest-free loan. Often, companies within the same industry exhibit differing receivables percentages due to differences in billing or collection procedures.

Accounts receivables should track revenues. It's a red flag when receivables increase significantly faster than revenues. Receivables analysis doesn't apply to retail stores or restaurants, because they sell on a cash basis and don't have significant receivables.

There are several reasons why receivables grow faster than revenues:

- The accounts receivables department has fallen behind in billing or dunning customers.
- Unhappy customers are withholding payments.
- Channel stuffing.
- Customers cannot pay their bills.

The last two reasons are the more serious, and they are the only two we will describe in detail. But all we'll be able to determine from this analysis is that a receivables problem exists, not the cause.

Channel Stuffing

Channel stuffing occurs when a company realizes that it will not meet its sales goals by following its normal practices. At that point, management devises incentives to spur sales. One approach is to offer customers better terms. For example, it could offer six months to pay instead of the usual 60 days. If that doesn't work, it might offer even longer terms, and furthermore, allow them to return the goods with no penalty if, in the end, the customer doesn't need the product.

That's a deal that's hard to refuse. If it's accepted, the company ships the goods, and the transaction appears on the income statement the same as any other sale, helping it meet sales and earnings numbers for the quarter.

More extreme examples of channel stuffing involve shipping goods that customers didn't order or recording nonexistent shipments.

Customers Can't Pay

The telecommunication equipment industry's experiences in 2000 and 2001 illustrate a situation where customers wanted the products but couldn't come up with the cash to pay for the goods.

In the late 1990s, a new breed of telephone company appeared on the scene. They intended to compete with the entrenched Baby Bell incumbents and thought they could teach the old fogies a thing or two about the business. By mid-2000, the upstarts ran out of cash, and most eventually folded. That stuck equipment suppliers with receivables that would never be paid.

Calculate Receivables/Sales Percentage

Regardless of the cause, inflated receivables can be easily detected by comparing the most recent receivables/sales percentage to the year-ago figure. Start by dividing the accounts receivables (A/R) total from the most recent balance sheet by the last quarter's sales, or by the last four quarters' sales.

receivables percentage of sales = accounts receivables / total sales

Use the most recent quarter's sales unless there is an overriding reason to use the 12 months number. In some instances, a full year's sales might be the best choice, possibly for industries with strong seasonal variations, such as patio furniture. Using the last quarter's sales is easier, and that's what I usually do.

Except in the healthcare field, accounts receivables typically run between 40 percent and 80 percent of one quarter's sales. A number in excess of 100 percent is cause for concern by itself. Firms selling to hospitals and other healthcare providers typically show receivables running as high as 150 percent of quarterly sales.

Always compare the current A/R percentage of sales to the year-ago figure. There is no red flag if the current receivables percentage is equal to or less than the year-ago figure. Variations of 5 percent or so (such as 52 versus 50) are common and are not a cause for concern. It's a red flag if the current quarter's A/R-to-sales percentage exceeds the year-ago ratio by 20 percent (such as 60 versus 50), and it's a potential red flag if the current figure exceeds the year-ago number by 10 percent or more.

Medical imaging software provider Vital Images illustrates this principle. Vital released its December 2005 quarterly results in March 2006, when its shares were changing hands for around $30. Vital reported December quarter earnings above analysts' forecasts and more than double the year-ago figure on a 38 percent rise in sales. Table 12-4 shows Vital's December quarter revenues, receivables, and the receivables percentage of revenues for December 2005 and for the year-ago period.

TABLE 12-4   Vital Images December 2005 Receivables Analysis

	12/2005	12/2004
Revenues (in millions of dollars)	15.3	11.1
Receivables (in millions of dollars)	14.3	8.1
Receivables percentage of revenues	93.8%	72.9%

December quarter receivables rose 77 percent, far outpacing the 38 percent revenue gain, driving a 29 percent increase in the receivables/revenues ratio (93.8 versus 72.9). Vital's share price dropped around 30 percent in May 2006 after missing March quarter numbers.

Companies often give reasons for an outsized receivables increase in the management's discussion section of their SEC reports. Also, the topic is often raised in the question-and-answer portion of the analysts' conference call following the earnings report. Management always presents a plausible reason for increasing receivables. One common excuse is that a new product line targets a slower-paying industry than existing products. Pay attention to the numbers. It's usually a mistake to ignore a receivables red flag.

Inventory Analysis

Inflated Inventories Equal Higher Profits

Motivated management can manipulate inventory values to artificially boost reported earnings. You have to understand the gross profit calculation to see how that works. The formula for gross margin is

$$GM = \text{gross profit} / \text{sales}$$

where

$$\text{gross profit} = \text{sales} - \text{cost of sales}$$

Assume that no labor is involved in producing a product—only raw materials. Accountants don't calculate the cost of sales by adding up the cost of the raw materials used to build the products. Instead, they compare the values of the inventory on hand at the beginning and end of the period. To keep it simple, assume that the firm didn't buy any raw materials during the period. Then:

$$\text{cost of sales} = \text{beginning inventory} - \text{ending inventory}$$

where beginning inventory is the total value of all inventories at the beginning of the quarter (or fiscal year), and ending inventory is the value at the end of the period.

If the beginning inventory was $100 and the ending inventory was $50, the cost of sales would be

$$\text{cost of sales} = \$100 - \$50 = \$50$$

If the firm sold its products for $75, its gross profit is $25 (75 – 50).

But if the ending inventory is $75 instead of $50:

$$\text{cost of sales} = \$100 - \$75 = \$25$$

If the firm again sold its products for $75, its gross profit would now be $50 (75 – 25) instead of $25. You can see that increasing the value of the ending inventory figure on the books can be a tempting way to boost profits.

Inflated Inventories Can Mean Slower Sales

Rising inventory levels (compared to revenues) don't necessarily imply creative accounting. Inventory levels can increase because the company is producing more than its customers want to buy, causing finished products to pile up. If that were the case, you'd probably see slowing revenue growth along with the higher inventory levels.

You can analyze inventories by comparing inventory levels to sales, exactly the same as described for accounts receivables.

Broadband communications equipment maker Acme Packet offers an example. Acme announced its September 2007 quarter's results in early November when its stock was fetching $11 per share. Revenues rose 33 percent versus year-ago. Pretax income (income tax rate change distorted net income figures) rose a less-impressive 15 percent, but that number beat analysts' forecasts.

Table 12-5 shows Acme's September quarter revenues and inventories for 2007 compared to 2006.

TABLE 12-5   Acme Packet September Quarter 2007 Inventory Analysis

	9/2007	9/2006
Revenues (in millions of dollars)	29.6	22.3
Inventory (in millions of dollars)	5.9	3.7
Inventory percentage of revenues	19.8%	16.8%

Acme's inventory level rose 59 percent, outpacing its 33 percent revenue gain. Acme's share price dropped to the $8 range in February after offering disappointing revenue growth guidance for 2008. It dropped again to $4.50 per share in early July when it said that its yet-to-be-announced June quarter results would fall short. (This was before the economy fell off a cliff in September.)

Manufacturing companies divide inventory into three categories—raw materials, goods in process, and finished goods—in the financial statements they file with the SEC. However, they usually don't provide that breakdown in their earnings press release, and most websites don't show the inventory details on their financial statements.

If you do access statements showing inventory breakdowns, make note of where the buildup occurred if inventories grew more than sales. Sometimes a firm stocks up on hard-to-get parts in times of shortages, inflating raw-materials levels. If that's the case, management will probably make note of that in its discussion of results. An abnormal rise in finished goods is the worst case, signaling that product sales are falling short of expectations.

Retail Stores

Inventory analysis is especially important for retail stores, because they usually don't have significant accounts receivables.

It doesn't matter whether a store sells clothing, electronics, or hardware—retail is about fad and fashion. Hot items come and go. Inventory levels increase when customers lose enthusiasm for the stores' wares. Inventories growing faster than sales is often your first clue that something is going wrong.

Most retail store sales are strongly seasonal. Retail store fiscal years typically end on January 31, and January quarter sales are usually double the next-highest quarter. Retailers stock up on holiday merchandise prior to Thanksgiving, so the October quarter's ending inventory levels are always the highest of the year.

Because retail sales are so strongly seasonal, it's best to use annual sales to iron out the seasonality factors. That works for looking at long-term trends and for comparing competitive chains. For instance, Table 12-6 lists the ending inventory expressed as a percentage of annual sales for major discount stores.

TABLE 12-6   End of Fiscal Year Inventory Percentage of Annual Sales for Discount Stores

	1/09	1/08	1/07	1/06	1/05	1/04	1/03	1/02	1/01	1/00
Costco°	7.0	7.6	7.6	7.6	7.6	7.8	8.1	7.9	7.7	8.1
Kohl's	17.1	17.3	16.5	16.6	16.6	15.4	17.8	16.0	16.3	17.4
Sears Holdings	18.8	19.6	18.7	18.3	16.5	13.9	16.4	17.0	17.0	19.8
Target	10.3	10.7	10.5	11.1	11.5	10.8	12.7	11.2	11.5	11.3
Wal-Mart	8.5	9.3	9.7	10.2	10.5	10.3	10.5	11.0	11.1	11.9

°Costco's fiscal year ends with August, so the year 1/09 actually reflects Costco's 8/08 FY.

Costco has been the most efficient operator over the 10 years, but Wal-Mart has shown the most improvement.

The stores listed in Table 12-6 are general-merchandise discount stores. What's normal in terms of inventory percentage of sales varies with the type of store. Table 12-7 shows the data for nominally full-price fashion department stores Macy's, Nordstrom, and West Coast chain Gottschalk's, which filed for bankruptcy early in 2009. Table 12-7 shows that Nordstrom is consistently better at managing its inventories than Macy's.

TABLE 12-7   End of Fiscal Year Inventory Percentage of Annual Sales for Fashion Department Stores

	1/09	1/08	1/07	1/06	1/05	1/04	1/03	1/02	1/01	1/00
Gottschalk's	23.5	24.5	23.8	23.3	23.7	24.3	23.3	27.4	23.5	
Macy's	19.2	19.2	19.7	24.4	19.8	20.9	21.8	21.6	21.8	22.4
Nordstrom	10.5	10.5	11.5	12.4	12.9	14.0	16.0	15.8	17.1	15.5

Table 12-8 shows the data for electronics superstores Best Buy and Circuit City, which filed for bankruptcy in November 2008. While Circuit City's numbers weren't terrible, Best Buy did a better job of managing its inventory.

TABLE 12-8   End of Fiscal Year Inventory Percentage of Annual Sales for Electronics Superstores

	1/09	1/08	1/07	1/06	1/05	1/04	1/03	1/02	1/01	1/00
Best Buy	10.6	11.8	11.2	10.8	10.4	10.6	9.9	10.6	11.6	9.5
Circuit City	13.4	13.2	14.7	14.0	15.4	14.0	13.0	13.7	13.3	13.8

Retail inventory levels generally run between 10 percent and 25 percent of annual sales. Retailers keep a tighter rein on inventory levels than manufacturing companies, so smaller changes constitute a danger signal or red flag. If you're using annual sales, a 5 percent increase warrants investigation, and 10 percent is a solid red flag. Double those tolerances when you use quarterly sales figures.

Statement of Cash Flows

Cash flow is the cash that flowed into or out of a firm's bank accounts during the reporting period. Cash flow is a better profitability measure than earnings. Earnings reflect a variety of arbitrary accounting decisions, whereas cash flow reflects the actual change in bank balances.

Operating cash flow is the cash generated or used by the company's basic operations. Free cash is operating cash flow minus capital expenditures. Companies can, and frequently do, report positive earnings when, in fact, they've lost money on a cash basis.

Cash Flow Red Flags

Some companies, though cash-flow-positive annually, habitually burn cash during certain quarters. Therefore, it's best to look at trailing 12 months cash flow rather than just the last quarter. Doing that requires some extra effort, because the statement of cash flow shows year-to-date totals, rather than each quarter's results separately. So you have to subtract the previous quarter's totals to derive the latest quarter numbers. If you don't want to do the math, Morningstar displays the TTM operating and free cash flow totals in its Financials section.

Negative cash flow and negative free cash flow, although undesirable, do not by themselves signal creative accounting or earnings manipulation and are not necessarily red flags.

Table 12-9 shows the net income, operating cash flow, and free cash flows generated by a sampling of well-known companies in 2008.

TABLE 12-9   2008 Net Income, Operating Cash Flow, and Free Cash Flow for a Sampling of Well-Known Stocks (in Millions of Dollars)

	Net Income	Operating Cash Flow	Free Cash Flow
Amazon.com	645	1,697	1,364
Apollo Group	477	892	792
Cheesecake Factory	52	169	84
Chipotle Mexican Grill	178	199	46
Cisco Systems	8,052	12,089	10,821
Crocs	−185	73	17
eBay	1,780	2,882	2,316
GameStop	288	503	327
Gilead Sciences	2,011	2,205	2,090
Google	4,227	7,853	5,494
Green Mountain Coffee	22	2	−47
Hansen Natural	108	200	193
Intel	5,292	10,926	5,729

TABLE 12-9 Continued

	Net Income	Operating Cash Flow	Free Cash Flow
Intuitive Surgical	204	278	216
Microsoft	17,661	21,612	18,430
Netflix	83	284	240
Oracle	5,521	7,402	7,159
Panera Bread	67	156	93
P.F. Chang's	27	140	53
Symantec	464	1,819	1,545
Yahoo!	424	1,880	1,205

Comparing Operating Cash Flow to Net Income

Net income or after-tax income, the bottom line on the income statement, is the top line on the cash flow statement. Cash flow from operations is usually a larger number than net income, because depreciation and amortization subtract from net income but not from operating cash flow.

As shown in Table 12-9, that is the case for most of the companies listed. Generally, operating cash flow increases in proportion to net income.

As mentioned, accounts receivables and/or inventories increasing faster than sales are both red flags. If you recall the accounting math, increasing receivables and inventories also reduces operating cash flow. So less-than-expected operating cash flow could be a tip-off to accounting shenanigans.

As noted in Chapter 11, recent research found that operating cash flow less than net income warns of future share price underperformance. The combination of increasing net income and decreasing operating cash flow was found to be especially significant.

Table 12-10 lists a sampling of companies that recorded operating cash flow below net income in 2008.

TABLE 12-10   Companies Reporting Operating Cash Flow Less Than Net Income in 2008 (in Millions of Dollars)

	Net Income	Operating Cash Flow	Free Cash Flow
Alexanders	76	9	−125
Archer Daniels Midland	1,802	−3,204	−4,983
Astec Industries	63	10	−30
Blue Nile	12	−3	−5
Cephalon	223	−2	−78
Commercial Metals	232	−44	−399
Corinthian Colleges	21	14	−41
Dril-Quip	106	41	−10
EnerSys	60	4	−41
GT Solar	36	2	−3
Harley Davidson	655	−685	−917
Health Net	95	−159	−255
McDermott Intl.	429	−49	−305
NL Industries	33	1	−6
Sepracor	515	163	113
Smithfield Foods	129	10	−451
Sotheby's	28	−176	−200
Southwest Airlines	178	−1,521	−2,444
United Natural Foods	49	9	−42
United Stationers	98	−129	−161
Valmont Industries	132	53	2
Wright Medical	3	−4	−66

Comparing net income to operating cash flow is faster and easier than computing accounts receivables and inventory percentages of sales. It may not be as effective as analyzing receivables and inventories, but it's an efficient method of spotlighting stocks requiring detailed examination.

Specifically, the following two instances signal the need to analyze receivables and inventories in detail:

- Net income for the most recent 12-month period exceeded operating cash flow
- Net income grew significantly more than operating cash flow

Pension Plan Income

Most corporations establish retirement plans for employees. Newer companies set up 401(k) defined-contribution plans and expense their contributions annually.

However, older corporations maintain defined-benefits plans, meaning that the company funds the plans with cash that the plan invests in stocks and other assets. Theoretically, the plan's assets should approximate its future obligations—that is, the money it will be required to pay out to its retired employees.

The defined-benefits pension plan's assets depend, however, on the returns it receives from investing the assets. The assets total will not necessarily match the plan's liabilities at any given time. If assets exceed liabilities, the plan is said to be overfunded. It's underfunded if its assets fall short of liabilities.

If the plan is overfunded, the company can count the plan's annual returns (income less costs) on its income statement, thereby increasing reported income. These pension plan credits can be substantial. For instance, IBM added $1.3 billion to its reported income in 2000.

The SEC doesn't require firms to show pension plan credits as separate line items on their income statements, so they are frequently buried in other income. The SEC does require companies to detail pension plan benefits in their annual report footnotes, so you can find them by searching for the words "pension" or "retirement."

However, there is no real need to dig out that information. Income contributed by pension plans are accounting entries and do not contribute to cash flow. Thus, significant pension plan contributions would cause net income to grow faster than operating cash flow.

Getting back to the IBM example, net income increased to $8.1 billion in 2000, up from $7.7 billion in 1999. However, operating cash flow dropped to $9.8 billion from $10.1 billion. The divergence between reported net income and operating cash flow signaled earnings quality issues.

Yellow Flags

Yellow flags are danger signals warning of long-term problems, but not necessarily in the next quarter.

Capital Expenditures

Depreciation accounts for the deterioration and obsolescence of buildings and capital equipment. To remain viable, a company must continuously upgrade and replace its aging equipment.

You can tell if that's happening by comparing the depreciation credit in the operating cash flows section to the capital equipment expenditures listed in the investing section of the cash flow statement. At a minimum, capital expenditures should equal the depreciation charge, and ideally capital expenditures should exceed depreciation.

Table 12-11 shows how IBM and Xerox did in that category. You can see that IBM generally invests more than it depreciates, while Xerox habitually underinvests.

TABLE 12-11 Depreciation Charges Versus Capital Expenditure (in Millions of Dollars)

	2008	2007	2006	2005	2004
IBM					
Depreciation	4,140	4,038	3,907	4,197	3,959
Capital expenditures	4,171	4,630	4,362	3,842	4,368
Xerox					
Depreciation	669	656	636	641	686
Capital expenditures	206	236	215	181	204

Income Tax Rates

The income before taxes entry on the income statement reflects what the firm's profits would be if it paid no income taxes. Then the company subtracts income taxes to compute the bottom-line net income. The reported earnings per share that gets all the attention at report time is the bottom-line net income divided by the number of shares outstanding. Few analysts and even fewer individual investors notice the income tax line, but they should. Here's why: Most corporations pay income taxes in the range of 35 percent to 40 percent of before-tax earnings. Of course, since the goal of individuals and corporations alike is to minimize taxes, the rate can vary widely.

Here's a hypothetical example that illustrates the significance of income taxes on reported earnings. Assume that a company earned $1,000 before taxes and has 1,000 shares outstanding. Table 12-12 shows how the reported EPS varies with the income tax rate.

TABLE 12-12   Reported EPS Versus the Income Tax Rate

Before-Tax Income	1,000	1,000	1,000	1,000
Tax Rate	0%	20%	38%	40%
After-Tax Income	1,000	800	620	600
EPS	1.00	0.80	0.62	0.60

The tax rate has a huge impact on EPS. Even a small change can mean the difference between a positive or negative earnings surprise.

Table 12-13 shows some companies that paid a 20 percent or lower corporate income tax rate in 2008.

TABLE 12-13   Companies That Paid a Less Than 20 Percent Corporate Income Tax Rate in 2008

Company	Tax Rate
American Express Company	19.8
Telephone & Data Systems Inc.	19.7
Alpha Natural Resources Inc.	19.5
Black & Decker Corp.	19.5
Adobe Systems Inc.	19.2
Abbott Laboratories	19.2
Sealed Air Corp.	19.1
NetApp Inc.	19.1
eBay Inc.	18.5
Wells Fargo & Company	18.5
Noble Corp.	18.4
International Flavors & Fragrances Inc.	18.1

Company	Tax Rate
Tidewater Inc.	18.0
Baxter International Inc.	17.8
Ormat Technologies Inc.	17.7
QUALCOMM Inc.	17.4
Ensco International Inc.	17.3
Cognizant Technology Solutions Corp.	16.4
IDACORP Inc.	16.3
Millipore Corp.	16.1
Bunge Limited	15.9
E.I. du Pont de Nemours & Company	15.9
Peabody Energy Corp.	15.8
Foster Wheeler AG	15.6
Cleco Corp.	15.3
WABCO Holdings Inc.	15.2
Microchip Technology Inc.	15.2
Onyx Pharmaceuticals Inc.	15.1
Agilent Technologies Inc.	15.0
Celanese Corp.	14.5
Altera Corp.	14.2
WestAmerica Bancorp.	14.2
The Cooper Companies Inc.	14.1
Thermo Fisher Scientific Inc.	14.0
W.R. Berkley Corporation	13.8
Harman International Industries Inc./DE	13.8
National Instruments Corp.	13.6
Waters Corp.	13.4
Synopsys Inc.	13.2
Lexmark International Inc.	12.9
Itron Inc.	12.5
DreamWorks Animation SKG Inc.	12.5
United States Cellular Corp.	12.2
Atwood Oceanics Inc.	12.0
Affiliated Managers Group Inc.	11.8
Equity Residential	11.8
Western Digital Corp.	11.6
Rayonier Inc.	11.3
WebMD Health Corp.	10.1

If a company you're analyzing recently paid a lower than 30 percent income tax rate, you need to know why. Some firms always pay lower taxes because of conditions particular to the company and/or its industry. Others, however, may be enjoying a temporary tax break because of earlier losses, or for other reasons.

MSN Money (Financial Statement 10-Year Summary) and Morningstar (Profitability Report) both list tax rates going back 10 years for each stock with that much history. Morningstar also shows the tax rate for the last 12 months (TTM), so that may be the best place to start.

If a company has been paying the same low tax rate for most of those 10 years, chances are it will continue to enjoy that rate. However, if it's a new company that just recently turned profitable, or the recent tax rate is lower than earlier years, the rate will probably move back up. When it does, earnings will take a hit. In theory, since analysts usually forecast the earnings drop triggered by an expected income tax hike, it should be a nonevent. But in practice, the stock usually drops anyway.

For more information, read recent quarterly report press releases to see if management discussed the tax rate. Unless you get lucky with a Google search, download recent quarterly or annual SEC reports. The issue will undoubtedly be discussed there.

In my view, it's not worth the effort. The tax rate will eventually return to historical norms. When that happens, earnings will take a hit.

Summary

Detecting the red and yellow flags often is your first clue that a company's growth rate is peaking. Getting out before the news becomes common knowledge can help you avoid big losses. These red flags warn that a cut in sales and earnings forecasts may be on the way, or that the company may fall short at report time.

Red Flags

- Slowing sales growth
- Accounts receivables increasing faster than sales
- Inventory levels increasing faster than sales
- Reported net income increased by pension plan income

Yellow Flags

Watch out for these yellow flags warning of potential problems down the road, but not necessarily by the next earnings report:

- Capital expenditure lagging depreciation write-offs
- Temporarily low income tax rates

Nothing always works in the stock market. Hence, the existence of red or yellow flags doesn't guarantee that the offending company will disappoint the market when it next reports earnings. However, the existence of each flag signals added risk.

Many market experts advise that the key to making money in the market is to avoid disastrous losses. Reducing your risks by heeding these risk flags will help you achieve that goal.

13

Analysis Tool #10: Ownership Considerations

Examining the percentage of outstanding shares held by institutions and insiders can help you avoid risky stocks.

Institutional Ownership

Institutions are mutual funds, pension plans, trust funds, and other large investors, and they account for roughly 50 percent of all stockholdings. The presence of strong institutional sponsorship (large holdings) verifies that a stock is a viable growth candidate.

Institutional Percentage of Shares Outstanding

Institutional ownership is the percentage of outstanding shares held by institutions. Hedge funds are not required to report their holdings to the SEC and thus are not counted as institutional owners.

Institutions trade stocks frequently and in large quantities. By virtue of the large commissions that those trades generate, institutional money managers are more wired into the market than you and I can ever hope to be. Consequently, there is no way that you would discover a stock that institutional buyers haven't already examined.

High institutional sponsorship (ownership) means that these tuned-in investors have analyzed the company and liked what they saw. Conversely, low institutional ownership means that institutions have analyzed the company and passed on it.

Institutions must report their holdings to the SEC (Form 13F) no later than 45 days after the end of the March, June, September, and December quarters. Thus, an institution that bought a stock on April 1 could wait until as late as mid-July to notify the SEC. While the timeliness issue diminishes the value of institutional holdings data (shown in Figure 13-1), it is still worthwhile to evaluate the information, especially for growth investors.

Ownership Information		
Shares Outstanding		8.89 Bil
Institutional Ownership (%)		58.98
Top 10 Institutions (%)		21.00
Mutual Fund Ownership (%)		1.84
5%/Insider Ownership (%)		13.81
Float (%)		86.19
Ownership Activity		
Description	# of Holders	Shares
Total Positions	1,662	5,243,581,440
New Positions	130	0
Soldout Positions	320	0
Net Position Change	-474	-708,855,232
Buyers	711	396,036,128
Sellers	1,185	-1,104,891,392

Figure 13-1   A portion of MSN Money's Ownership report for Microsoft. The report also lists the top holders.

Institutions, particularly mutual funds, are most often growth investors. For "in-favor" growth stocks, institutions typically hold at least 40 percent of the outstanding shares, and usually more. In many instances, institutional ownership runs as high as 95 percent of the outstanding shares. Growth investors should view candidates with less than 40 percent institutional ownership with caution. It could very well be that institutional buyers are shunning the stock for good reason.

It's a different story for value candidates. Mutual funds and other institutional holders often dump a stock when it tanks because they don't want their quarterly reports to show big losers in their portfolios.

Thus, low institutional holdings should signal an out-of-favor value candidate. However, because of the reporting time lag, it could take four or five months for institutional selling to be reflected in the holdings data. Value investors should keep in mind that time lag when evaluating candidates that crashed only recently.

Judging a Stock by the Company It Keeps

Checking the names of the funds that hold large positions of a stock offers additional insight. Figure 13-2 shows Morningstar's Top Fund Owners report, listing the mutual funds that have the largest holdings of Microsoft. Many websites report similar information, but I prefer this one because it shows Morningstar's Star Rating of each fund. (Morningstar rates funds from one to five stars, where five is best.) That's good information, because I'd rather buy stocks held mostly by five-star funds than those owned mainly by two-star funds.

Top Fund Owners					
Fund Name	Star Rating	% of Shares Held	% of Fund Assets	Change (000) in Ownership	Date of Portfolio
BlackRock Large Cap Growth Retirement K	Not Rated	6.00	1.79	532951	07-31-08
American Funds Growth Fund of Amer A	★★★★	1.41	2.17	-200	12-31-08
American Funds Invt Co of Amer A	★★★★	0.86	2.94	-1074	12-31-08
Vanguard 500 Index Investor	★★★	0.81	1.87	-2570	12-31-08
Vanguard Total Stock Mkt Idx	★★★	0.78	1.65	4442	12-31-08
American Funds Capital World G/I A	★★★★★	0.63	1.70	-16931	12-31-08
American Funds New Perspective A	★★★★	0.54	2.91	0	12-31-08
American Funds American Balanced A	★★★★	0.54	2.23	6900	12-31-08
Vanguard Institutional Index	★★★	0.53	1.88	300	12-31-08
American Funds Fundamental Investors A	★★★★	0.37	2.10	2500	12-31-08
Templeton Growth A	★★★	0.35	3.56	0	12-31-07
American Funds Washington Mutual A	★★★	0.35	1.24	5750	12-31-08
Vanguard PRIMECAP	★★★★★	0.30	2.34	0	12-31-08
Davis NY Venture A	★★★	0.30	1.89	-4993	01-31-09
GMO U.S. Quality Equity III	★★★★★	0.29	5.85	1835	11-30-08
American Funds AMCAP A	★★★★	0.25	2.98	2241	12-31-08
Vanguard Growth Index	★★★	0.25	3.77	-123	12-31-08
Fidelity Growth Company	★★★★	0.22	1.52	0	02-28-09
T. Rowe Price Growth Stock	★★★★	0.21	2.46	-54	12-31-08
Fidelity Spartan U.S. Equity Index Inv	★★★	0.20	1.87	408	02-28-09

Figure 13-2 Morningstar's Top Fund Owners report shows the funds with the largest holdings in a company—in this case, Microsoft.

The investing style of the funds with large holdings is also significant. Stocks mostly held by momentum-style funds are riskier than those held mostly by buy-and-hold-style managers, because the momentum managers would dump their holdings at the first sign of trouble. You can tell which is which by looking up the fund's portfolio turnover on Morningstar's Portfolio report for the fund. Turnover measures the percentage of the fund's trading activity. A 100 percent turnover means that, on average, the fund replaces its entire portfolio every year. Buy-and-hold-style funds have turnovers below 40 percent, and momentum funds' turnovers typically run above 150 percent.

Insider Ownership

Insiders are key officers, members of the board, and others holding at least 10 percent of the outstanding shares.

Insider ownership is usually expressed as the percentage of the firm's outstanding shares held by insiders. Institutions holding 10 percent of a company's shares are considered insiders, so the total of insider plus institutional holdings can exceed 100 percent of outstanding shares.

The term "insider" has two meanings. The preceding paragraph defines insiders for the purpose of measuring "insider ownership." However, when referring to "insider trading," "insider" means anyone with access to nonpublic information relevant to a stock's outlook.

Float

Insider holdings (insider ownership definition) are not available for daily trading, because insiders are restricted as to when and how often they can trade their shares. Float is defined as the number of shares that *are* available for daily trading. In other words, the float is the number of shares *not* held by insiders.

Yahoo!'s Share Statistics report shows the total number of shares outstanding, the float, and the percentage of shares held by insiders and institutions for any stock.

Avoid Very High Ownership

In days past, market gurus advised avoiding stocks with low insider ownership. They reasoned that company executives holding big stakes had a stronger interest in seeing the share price increase than those that didn't have much "skin in the game."

Nowadays, however, almost all corporations couple their executives' compensation to share price performance one way or another, often via stock options. The realities of modern-day corporate life make insider ownership irrelevant in terms of executives' motivation to keep up the share price. Nevertheless, you should still check insider ownership. Here's why.

During the 2004–2007 timeframe, private equity firms were buying up publicly traded corporations, taking them private, loading them with debt, and then taking them public again. When they took them public again, the original private equity investors held onto big chunks of stock. But they are not long-term holders. Instead, they are waiting for an opportunity to sell their shares.

High insider ownership—say, 55 percent or more—signals risk that the insiders may be large investors who intend to dump their holdings. It's no fun owning a stock when every few weeks large shareholders dump a few million shares onto the market.

In other instances, high insider ownership may reflect holdings owned by the founding family or by descendants of the founder. These family owners may or may not see an advantage to higher share prices.

Bottom line: Avoid companies with 55 percent or more insider ownership without further researching these issues.

Insider Trading

Insider buying or selling can be a tip-off to which way key executives see their company's share price headed. But interpreting the information requires some care. Insiders often exercise stock options and then sell those shares on the same day. They do that because they need the cash, not necessarily because they think the share price is headed down.

If you track insider trading, focus on transactions by the chief executive officer and chief financial officer. They are the most informed about the firm's outlook. The only significant transactions are large open-market purchases or sales that are unrelated to option exercises.

The significance of a trade depends on the trade size compared to the insiders' total holdings, including unexercised stock options. Reuters Officers and Directors report lists unexercised stocks options for major officers.

It's insignificant if an insider sells 20,000 shares but still holds 2 million shares. It *is* significant, however, if the insider sells 1.5 million of his or her 2 million shares.

Often, an insider trade may not be as significant as it appears. In the past, some companies have loaned money to executives to finance purchasing the company's shares. In these instances, their buying reflects the deal they're getting, rather than their view of the stock's appreciation prospects. Also, key insiders, especially the CEO, often have rights to shares that do not appear on their listed holdings, including the Reuters options report. It may appear that they are selling all their holdings, but they actually control, or have rights to, millions of additional shares.

Insiders are supposed to report their trades by the 10th of the following month. So trades made on September 20, for instance, should be reported by October 10. However, trades made on October 9 need not be reported until November 10. Late reporting is common, and I'm unaware of an insider's ever going to jail for late reporting of his or her trades.

The financial news media, as well as investors, both professional and amateur, monitor the SEC insider trading reports. Knowing that, you can be sure that corporate attorneys have developed creative methods that allow company execs to sell shares without the transactions appearing on SEC reports.

Summary

Despite the timeliness issue, growth investors should be cautious about investing in stocks with less than 40 percent institutional ownership, because it's likely that the smart money is avoiding the stock. Use caution for stocks with very high insider ownership, because that signals that big shareholders may be waiting for the opportune time to reduce their holdings.

The close attention given to insider trading reports in recent years has made that data less significant as insiders learned how to game the insider trading reports.

14

Analysis Tool #11: Price Charts

Even if you do a thorough fundamental analysis, sometimes you'll be wrong. Perhaps bad news is brewing that insiders know about but haven't made public. Maybe your candidate is about to be blindsided by a competitor's superior product. It's possible that you've overlooked an economic trend, such as changing interest rates, which will adversely affect your candidate's market.

Whatever the reason, you can often avoid unnecessary losses by looking at a company's stock price chart before you buy. You don't have to be a charting maven to get useful information from a chart.

Trends

Stock prices tend to move in trends. A stock price moving ever higher is in an uptrend, as shown in Figure 14-1. Stocks moving relentlessly lower are in a downtrend, as shown in Figure 14-2. Stocks moving in a directionless pattern are in consolidation, or no trend.

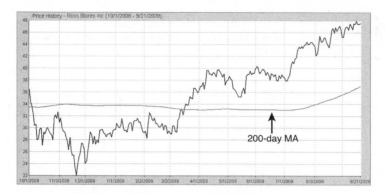

Figure 14-1 Ross Stores with a 200-day simple moving average. ROST moved above its 200-day moving average on March 16, 2009, and was still going strong on September 21, 2009, when I made this screenshot.

Source: MSN Money

Figure 14-2 Bank of America dropped below its 200-day simple moving average in March 2007 and stayed there until it started a new uptrend in July 2009.

Stocks in uptrends don't move up in price every single day. Instead they zigzag, some days moving up and other days moving lower. What identifies an uptrend is that each major up zigzag peak is higher than the previous peak, and each major low is higher than the previous low.

Downtrends have the opposite characteristics. Each major high is lower than the previous peak, and each major low is lower than the previous low.

If you can't see a pattern, the stock is probably consolidating, meaning that it's not trending up or down.

You can usually see which way a stock is moving by looking at a one- or two-year price chart. The stock is in an uptrend if the price on the right side of the chart is much higher than the price on the left. It's in a downtrend if the right side is lower than the left. These are generalizations, of course; a trend can end at any time.

Moving Averages

The moving average (MA) is the stock's average closing price over a specified period. For instance, the current value of the 200-day moving average is the stock's average closing price over the past 200 trading days.

The two types of moving averages are simple (SMA) and exponential (EMA). SMAs give equal weight to each day in the period averaged, while exponential averages put more emphasis on the most recent closing prices. Each version has its advocates, but I've found little advantage in using one over the other, and I usually use the SMA.

A stock is considered in an uptrend if it's above its moving average. The distance between the stock price and its moving average indicates the trend strength. That is, the higher a stock is above its average, the stronger the trend. A stock is in a consolidation pattern if it's crisscrossing its moving average.

Value Investors

If you are a value investor, your target price analysis gives you better buy and sell points than the price charts. Nevertheless, you should still look at the price chart before buying. The best value candidates will be trading below or near their 200-day moving average and, in any case, not more than 10 percent above the average. For instance, the maximum buy price would be $22 if the moving average was $20. Don't buy if your candidate is in a steep downtrend. On the other hand, you're too late to the party if your candidate has already started a significant move up. That means that the stock has already been discovered.

Growth Investors

Growth investors must pay closer attention to the charts than value investors. The best time to buy is at the beginning of an uptrend. That usually happens when the stock has been consolidating (no trend) for some time and then starts reaching new highs, as shown in Figure 14-3.

Source: MSN Money

Figure 14-3   AutoZone had been consolidating since August 2007 before breaking out to the upside in January 2009. The frequent crossings over and under its 200-day moving average are known as "whipsaws" and indicate a consolidation pattern.

The second-best time to buy a growth stock is when it's in an established uptrend but hasn't moved into a high-risk zone (see "The Risk Zone" later in this chapter).

It's okay to buy a stock when it's consolidating, but only when you're confident about your fundamental analysis and you're sure that its next move is up.

Avoid Downtrends

No matter what, *never* buy a stock when it's in a downtrend. A downtrend signals that the stock is likely to move lower rather than higher. The only exception is when the downtrend is induced by events unrelated to the company, such as an overall market overreaction to an external event, such as the September 11 attacks.

Don't be in a rush to jump on downtrending stocks when you think you've spotted a reversal. Most stocks consolidate for months before recovering from a significant downtrend, so you usually have plenty of time.

Compare Short- and Long-Term Moving Averages

Another way to determine a stock's overall direction is by comparing its current price to its 200-day and 50-day moving averages, as shown in Figure 14-4.

Source: MSN Money

Figure 14-4   Netflix moved above both its 50-day and 200-day moving averages in January 2009, a tough month for most stocks.

The 200-day moving average gives you a longer-term perspective than the 50-day moving average. The stock is probably in an uptrend if it's trading above both MAs.

If it's above its 200-day MA but below its 50-day MA, it's probably in a short-term downtrend of a long-term uptrend—in other words, a dip. Conversely, consider it a short-term spike if it's above its 50-day MA but below its 200-day MA.

Some chartists consider it especially significant when the 50-day MA crosses the 200-day MA. For them, it's a buy signal when the 50-day MA crosses above the 200-day MA, and a sell when the 50-day MA drops below the 200-day MA. As you can see from Figure 14-4, you would have missed part of Netflix's move up if you had waited for the 50-day MA to cross above the 200-day MA.

Don't use the moving averages to override what you can see by visually inspecting the chart. In other words, don't interpret a stock above both of its moving averages as being in an uptrend if a visual inspection of the chart clearly shows that it's heading down.

The Risk Zone

If you're a growth investor, you probably won't be the first to discover a hot prospect. Growth stocks often experience strong price run-ups and then falter, often retracing much of their recent progress. Jumping on a fast-moving stock after it has already made a big move adds risk.

I've settled on an unscientific rule of thumb for determining when a stock is in that condition. I measure the difference between the stock's closing price and its 200-day moving average. It's in the risk zone when the stock price is 50 percent or more higher than its moving average. For example, a stock would be in the risk zone if it was trading at \$80 per share, but its moving average was at 50 (the stock is 60 percent above its MA).

Being in the risk zone doesn't mean that the stock isn't going higher, just that it's a riskier bet than stocks that are trading closer to their 200-day MA. Qualcomm moved into the risk zone when it crossed \$10 in March 1999, on its way to \$180.

I haven't found a website that displays that ratio directly, but it's easy to compute. Yahoo! displays the current value of the 200-day MA in the Stock Price History section of its Key Statistics report. Divide the stock price by the MA to get the ratio. If it's 1.5 or higher, the stock is in the risk zone.

Chart Types

Many websites offer the option of viewing a price chart in two formats: line or bar chart. A line chart consists of a line connecting the closing prices.

A bar chart, as shown in Figure 14-5, uses a vertical line (bar) to represent one period. The bar period is typically a day, week, or month, depending on the time span covered. The top of the bar is the highest price for the period, and the bottom is the low. A horizontal extension to the left represents the opening price, and an extension to the right shows the closing price for the period.

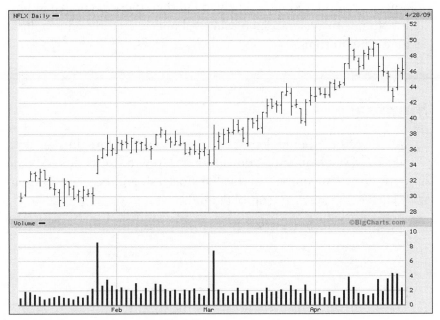

Source: www.bigcharts.com

Figure 14-5   Netflix bar chart including daily trading volume. Each bar represents one day.

Line charts are best for viewing long-term trends, while bar charts give detailed information useful for interpreting short-term movements.

Trading Volume

Most websites offer the option of displaying trading volume at the bottom of a price chart. Volume is the number of shares traded during the period. A stock is said to have high volume if the current level is at least 50 percent higher than the volume over the past 10 or 20 periods. A stock is said to have low volume when the volume looks like it's petering out.

Many charting experts consider volume an important factor when a stock starts a new uptrend after consolidating. New uptrends on low volume are considered more likely to fail than those accompanied by high volume. In general, increasing volume is considered a bullish factor during uptrends.

Summary

All investors should look at a price chart before buying and should avoid stocks in strong downtrends. Growth stocks should be in an uptrend when you buy, and value stocks should be close to their 200-day moving average (consolidating).

Part III

The Analysis Process

15

Quick Prequalify

There's no point in wasting time analyzing stocks that don't fit your investing strategy. In this chapter, you'll learn how to rule out bad ideas early.

Concentrate on the Strongest Candidates

The best way to analyze stocks is to start with a large group of candidates and then eliminate the weakest contenders as soon as possible. This "survival of the fittest" strategy allows you to spend your time more efficiently by focusing on the strongest candidates.

In this chapter, you'll learn how to weed out the obvious misfits early. They may be firms that are mostly hype and don't have real sales and earnings, or they simply may not fit your requirements. You should be able to eliminate most bad ideas in less than five minutes once you get the hang of it.

You'll probably end up eliminating 15 out of every 20 candidates if they originated from tips from TV pundits, magazines, friends, and so forth. The survival rate will likely be higher for candidates turned up by your own screens.

You could use many financial websites to do the analysis. I'll demonstrate using Morningstar to analyze Buffalo Wild Wings. While Morningstar's website has sections that require a subscription, everything I describe here is free.

Company Overview

Begin by determining the company's line of business. Keep in mind that this is just a quick look, not a detailed analysis.

Morningstar's Company Profile, found on its Snapshot page, gives you a quick overview, as shown in Figure 15-1.

Company Profile | More

What Does This Company Do?
Based in Minneapolis, Buffalo Wild Wings is a casual dining restaurant chain that specializes in serving its guests chicken wings spun in one of the firm's 14 original sauces, alcohol, and sports. The company owns, operates and franchises nearly 560 restaurants in 38 states. Each restaurant has an open layout and an extensive multimedia system, including approximately 40 televisions and 7 projection screens, providing different forms of entertainment to all customers.

Employees	12,000
Direct Investment	No
Dividend Reinvestment	No

Address:
1600 Utica Avenue
Suite 700
Minneapolis, MN 55416

Phone: 1 952 593-9943

Visit Company Website

Figure 15-1   Morningstar Company Profile for Buffalo Wild Wings

From Morningstar, you know that Buffalo is a casual restaurant chain. Moreover, its restaurants are basically sports bars with a limited menu emphasizing chicken wings.

Morningstar's profiles usually include a link to the company's website. Always check out those links. Five minutes on a company's website will give you a better perspective on its business than you could get from Morningstar or any other analyst. Buffalo's website makes it clear that Buffalo takes "casual" to the limit and is as much about the experience as the food.

Currently, with the economy in the dumps, low-priced restaurants are outperforming the overall market. Thus, considering only its market sector and current conditions, Buffalo would be of interest to growth investors who find its business plan appealing. Keep your personal feelings out of the equation. Whether or not you like chicken wings or watching sports on TV doesn't matter.

Since Buffalo's concept is in sync with current fashions and economic conditions, it would not make a very good value candidate. However, consumer tastes can turn on a dime. Remember the Atkins diet? Should the country take off on a low-calorie or healthy-eating craze, Buffalo, with its menu of wings, burgers, and ribs, would suffer. Then, it would be a potential value play.

At this point, discard candidates that don't interest you based on industry sector or business plan.

While on the Snapshot report, also check market capitalization, which is how most investors gauge company size.

Market Capitalization

Market capitalization is how much you'd have to shell out to buy all the outstanding shares. You could compute it by multiplying the number of shares outstanding by the current share price. But you don't have to do the calculation, because most websites list market cap.

Market capitalization categorizes a company as micro-cap, small-cap, mid-cap, or large-cap. No hard-and-fast rule defines those categories, but here are my rules of thumb:

- **Large-cap**: $8 billion plus
- **Mid-cap**: $2 billion to $8 billion
- **Small-cap**: $200 million to $2 billion
- **Micro-cap**: Below $200 million

To put the numbers in perspective, Table 15-1 lists some familiar names in each category.

TABLE 15-1   Market Caps of Well-Known Stocks

Company	Market Cap (in Billions of Dollars)
Large-Cap	
Exxon Mobil Corp.	330.2
Wal-Mart Stores Inc.	189.7
Microsoft Corp.	177.4
AT&T Inc.	151.3
Procter & Gamble Co.	145.6
International Business Machines (IBM)	134.7
Chevron Corp.	132.3
General Electric Co.	126.7
Google Inc.	121.1
Cisco Systems Inc.	109.0
Oracle Corp.	98.4

TABLE 15-1   Continued

Company	Market Cap (in Billions of Dollars)
Large-Cap	
Coca-Cola Co.	97.8
Pfizer Inc.	90.3
Verizon Communications Inc.	88.0
Hewlett-Packard Co.	84.9
Intel Corp.	84.0
Home Depot Inc.	44.2
NIKE Inc.	26.9
Dell Inc.	21.2
eBay Inc.	20.8
Costco Wholesale Corp.	20.4
Applied Materials Inc.	15.2
Mid-Cap	
Bed Bath & Beyond Inc.	7.9
Coca-Cola Enterprises Inc.	7.8
Intuit Inc.	7.4
Analog Devices Inc.	6.0
McAfee Inc.	5.7
Macy's Inc.	5.3
Southwest Airlines Co.	5.1
H&R Block Inc.	5.0
Humana Inc.	4.9
Harley-Davidson Inc.	4.6
JM Smucker Co.	4.5
Maxim Integrated Products Inc.	4.1
Hasbro Inc.	3.9
Host Hotels & Resorts	3.7
Seagate Technology	3.4
SanDisk Corp.	3.4
Whirlpool Corp.	3.0
PetSmart Inc.	2.9
Whole Foods Market Inc.	2.7
Netflix Inc.	2.7
Marvel Entertainment Inc.	2.3
Burger King Holdings Inc.	2.3
Aeropostale Inc.	2.2

Company	Market Cap (in Billions of Dollars)
Small-Cap	
Panera Bread Co.	1.9
Weight Watchers International Inc.	1.9
Jabil Circuit Inc.	1.6
Barnes & Noble Inc.	1.5
Under Armour Inc.	1.2
Rambus Inc.	1.2
JDS Uniphase Corp.	1.1
Men's Wearhouse Inc.	0.9
EarthLink Inc.	0.8
Take Two Interactive Software Inc.	0.7
Saks Inc.	0.6
Steven Madden Ltd.	0.5
NutriSystem Inc.	0.4
TASER International Inc.	0.3
Micro-Cap	
K-Tron International Inc.	0.2
Movie Gallery Inc.	0.1

Morningstar listed Buffalo's market cap at $686 million, putting it in the small-cap category.

There are no good and bad market caps. Large-caps generally are the safest category because they've usually been in business for years, are financially solid, and have already survived a variety of economic ups and downs.

Micro-caps and small-caps typically have the greatest growth potential because they are mostly emerging companies introducing new products or entering new markets. On the downside, micro-caps are too small to interest mutual funds and other institutional investors. Consequently, they don't have much analyst coverage, making them difficult to research.

Which market caps have the best price appreciation prospects? Putting risk aside, the smaller the company, the greater the appreciation potential. However, you can't put aside risk. In my experience, once you get below $500 million or so in terms of market cap, you are more likely to lose big than you are to score a big gain.

At this point, eliminate candidates that don't fit your requirements in terms of market cap.

Valuation Ratios

Valuation ratios tell you whether the market is pricing your candidate as a value, growth, or momentum stock. Value stocks are usually former growth stocks that fumbled and are now out of favor with most market players. Growth stocks, which most investors prefer, are stocks expected to grow sales and earnings at least 15 percent annually, and often much higher. Momentum stocks are the subset of growth stocks that are the most in favor. They have already moved up in price substantially and have probably outrun their fundamentals. Thus, they are higher risk than other growth stocks. Nevertheless, they will likely continue to move up until something goes wrong.

Morningstar displays three valuation ratios—price/earnings (P/E), price/sales (P/S), and price/book (P/B)—on its Snapshot page. Each ratio has its pluses and minuses. However, at this point, your goal is to determine whether the stock you're evaluating is being priced in the value, growth, or momentum category by the overall market. For that, the price/sales ratio is your best bet.

Here are my rules of thumb for using the price/sales ratio to determine the value/growth/momentum category:

P/S	Category
Less than 2.0	Value
2.5 to 8	Growth
9+	Momentum

Use these guidelines to rule out stocks that don't fit your investing style. Since my guidelines are arbitrary, use them to avoid obvious misfits, not as a final arbiter of value. For instance, a value investor shouldn't automatically reject a stock because its P/S is 2.1. However, it would be unusual to find a worthwhile value candidate with a P/S ratio of, say, 4.

Conversely, it's unlikely that a growth investor would find a stock with a P/S of 0.5 that would survive the growth analysis. Growth investors will often find momentum-priced stocks almost irresistible, but caution is advised.

Consider current market conditions when applying these guidelines. In a bull market, all categories would be trading at higher price/sales ratios, and vice versa.

Morningstar listed Buffalo's price/sales ratio at 1.7. Normally, a ratio that low would disqualify a potential growth candidate. But not when I researched this chapter in April 2009. Then, most stocks were trading at half their usual valuation ratios, if not lower.

Trading Volume

Trading volume, also referred to as liquidity, is the average number of shares traded daily. For trading volumes, higher is usually better. Lightly traded stocks—say, those trading less than 40,000 shares daily—often make big moves because of the actions of a single buyer or seller. Also, rumors posted on stock message boards can move lightly traded stocks.

Mutual funds and other institutional players who trade in big numbers cannot establish or unload meaningful positions in lightly traded stocks without disrupting the market. Consequently, they avoid those stocks. That's an important consideration, because institutional buying pressure frequently moves up share prices.

At this point, rule out candidates with average daily trading volumes below 50,000 shares.

According to Morningstar, Buffalo, trading 608,000 shares daily, easily passed that test.

Float

Like so many other things, stock prices are subject to the laws of supply and demand. Stock prices move up when buyers want to buy more shares than sellers want to sell, and vice versa. Ideally, when good news hits the wires for a stock you own, you'd like to see buying demand overwhelm supply. Thus, in terms of supply, smaller is better, at least up to a point.

The supply side of the equation starts with the number of shares issued by the corporation. These are the number of shares outstanding. However, not all of the shares outstanding are available for trading.

Insiders, such as key executives, directors, and other large share-holders, can't freely trade their shares. They can trade at only certain times, they must notify the SEC of their trades, and they have other limitations on their trading. Consequently, the insiders' holdings are unavailable for daily trading. The *float* is the number of shares that are available for trading. It's the total shares outstanding minus the insiders' holdings.

Generally speaking, the smaller the float, the more upside potential when good news happens and buyers scramble for shares. However, a too-small float would dissuade institutional investors. As a rule of thumb, below 5 million shares is too small, and a 10 million to 25 million-share float is ideal. When I checked, more than 400 widely traded stocks met that criterion.

Buffalo's 16.5 million-share float puts it in the sweet spot by that definition (data from Yahoo!'s Key Statistics report).

At this point, eliminate candidates with floats that don't meet your requirements.

Cash Flow

Operating cash flow is the amount of cash moving into or out of a company's bank account generated by its basic business. Very fast-growing companies often burn cash (negative cash flow) in their early stages. However, companies growing sales less than 25 percent annually should be generating positive cash flow. Growth investors should require positive operating cash flow for candidates growing annual sales less than 25 percent and would be well served by avoiding cash burners.

Value investors need candidates with a solid track record of producing strong cash flows, but they may not be doing so now, due to current problems. Therefore, value investors would not eliminate cash burners at this stage.

Morningstar's 10-year Cash Flow report showed that Buffalo has generated positive operating cash flow every year since its 2002 IPO.

At this point, rule out candidates that do not meet your cash flow requirements.

Real Revenues + Real Earnings + Real Growth = Real Stock

Many stocks have great stories to tell. That may have a cure for cancer, faster Internet connections, more efficient solar panels—you name it. Sad to say, in most cases, those stories will never translate to meaningful revenues and earnings.

Your best bets are stocks that already have a track record of producing meaningful revenues and earnings, along with consistent growth in both departments.

Morningstar's 5-Yr Restated and Growth Rates reports give you the information you need to make that assessment. The 5-Yr Restated report is shown in Figure 15-2.

	2004	2005	2006	2007	2008	TTM
Sales $Mil	171	210	278	330	422	422
Operating Income $Mil	11	13	21	26	35	35
Income Tax $Mil	4	5	8	9	12	12
Net Income $Mil	7	9	16	20	24	24
Earnings/Share $	0.42	0.51	0.92	1.10	1.36	1.36

Figure 15-2   A portion of Morningstar's 5-Yr Restated report for Buffalo Wild Wings. Access the report from the Financial Statements menu.

Revenues and Earnings

The 5-Yr Restated report shows, among other items, revenues (sales) and earnings per share for each of the past five fiscal years. Use this data to confirm that you are researching a real company with real revenues and real earnings.

Avoid companies with revenues of less than $40 million over the past 12 months (TTM). Since it's unlikely that consistent money losers will survive your detailed analysis, check the earnings-per-share figures, and disqualify firms showing more unprofitable years than profitable years.

Buffalo Wild Wings, with TTM revenue of $422 million, and profitable during the last 12 months, as well as in every one of the five years listed, easily met those requirements.

At this point, disqualify stocks with insufficient revenues. Growth investors should also rule out candidates lacking a consistent earnings history.

Growth Rates

Next, check historical growth. Morningstar's Growth Rates report, shown in Figure 15-3, lists year-over-year and three-, five-, and 10-year average annual growth rates for revenues, operating income, and earnings per share. You can access the report from Morningstar's Key Ratios menu.

Buffalo Wild Wings, Inc. BWLD

| Profitability | **Growth Rates** | Cash Flow | Financial Health | Efficiency Ratios |

Growth

	1999	2000	2001	2002	2003	2004	2005	2006	2007	2008	latest Qtr
Revenue Growth											
Year over Year	---	---	---	---	31.6%	35.2%	22.6%	32.7%	18.5%	28.1%	32.6%
3-Year Average	---	---	---	---	---	---	29.7%	30.0%	24.5%	26.3%	---
5-Year Average	---	---	---	---	---	---	---	---	28.0%	27.3%	---
10-Year Average	---	---	---	---	---	---	---	---	---	---	---
Operating Income											
Year over Year	---	---	---	---	19.0%	49.5%	21.9%	65.6%	19.1%	38.2%	55.7%
3-Year Average	---	---	---	---	---	---	29.4%	44.5%	34.0%	39.7%	---
5-Year Average	---	---	---	---	---	---	---	---	33.7%	37.8%	---
10-Year Average	---	---	---	---	---	---	---	---	---	---	---
EPS											
Year over Year	---	---	---	---	1.9%	52.7%	21.4%	81.4%	18.9%	23.6%	72.0%
3-Year Average	---	---	---	---	---	---	23.6%	49.8%	37.8%	38.7%	---
5-Year Average	---	---	---	---	---	---	---	---	32.4%	37.7%	---
10-Year Average	---	---	---	---	---	---	---	---	---	---	---

Figure 15-3   Morningstar's Growth Rates report for Buffalo Wild Wings

If you're a growth investor, look for a minimum 15 percent year-over-year revenue growth in recent years; higher is better. Buffalo Wild Wings' 28 percent year-over-year revenue growth for 2008 would get any growth investor's attention. The 33 percent most recent quarter's growth signals that growth might be accelerating. High 20 percent and accelerating revenue growth is about as good as it gets for growth investors these days.

Buffalo's EPS growth is reasonably consistent with revenue growth, signaling that Buffalo is a well-managed company.

As good as Buffalo might look to growth investors, value investors would find nothing of interest here. For them, a busted growth stock such as laser vision correction center operator LCA-Vision would be of more interest (see Figures 15-4 and 15-5).

	2004	2005	2006	2007	2008	TTM
Sales $Mil	127	177	239	293	205	174
Operating Income $Mil	18	35	41	46	-8	-23
Income Tax $Mil	-12	16	19	19	-3	-9
Net Income $Mil	32	23	28	33	-7	-16
Earnings/Share $	1.53	1.07	1.34	1.64	-0.36	-0.88

Figure 15-4   A portion of Morningstar's 5-Yr Restated Report for LCA-Vision

LCA-Vision, Inc. LCAV

Profitability	**Growth Rates**	Cash Flow	Financial Health	Efficiency Ratios

Growth

	1999	2000	2001	2002	2003	2004	2005	2006	2007	2008	latest Qtr
Revenue Growth											
Year over Year	63.0%	10.6%	7.3%	(9.2%)	31.7%	56.1%	51.4%	33.5%	13.9%	(29.9%)	(51.2%)
3-Year Average	61.0%	53.4%	24.6%	2.5%	8.7%	23.1%	46.0%	46.7%	32.0%	2.2%	---
5-Year Average	---	35.9%	37.7%	28.6%	18.3%	17.2%	24.8%	30.4%	36.5%	20.3%	---
10-Year Average	---	---	---	---	---	---	30.2%	34.0%	32.5%	19.3%	---
Operating Income											
Year over Year	---	---	---	---	---	238.4%	102.2%	16.5%	(20.0%)	---	(263.9%)
3-Year Average	---	---	---	---	---	---	---	99.7%	23.5%	---	---
5-Year Average	---	---	---	---	---	44.7%	---	---	---	---	---
10-Year Average	---	---	---	---	---	---	18.9%	---	---	---	---
EPS											
Year over Year	---	---	---	---	---	250.0%	(4.6%)	22.5%	(8.9%)	---	---
3-Year Average	---	---	---	---	---	---	---	59.9%	2.1%	---	---
5-Year Average	---	---	---	---	---	22.4%	---	---	---	---	---
10-Year Average	---	---	---	---	---	---	49.3%	---	---	---	---

Figure 15-5   Morningstar's Growth Rates Report for LCA-Vision

LCA-Vision got off to a slow start in 2000–2002, but growth took off in 2003, peaking at 50 percent year-over-year growth in the mid-2000s. From there, revenue growth and earnings slowly deteriorated until everything went wrong in 2008. However, 2008 was the year the entire economy nearly imploded. Thus, LCA-Vision would be worth a look as a value candidate.

At this point, rule out candidates with revenue and earnings growth histories that don't meet your requirements.

Check the Buzz

There's no point in digging into financial statements and calculating target prices if the competition just announced a new widget that obsoletes one of your candidates' major products, a rating service just downgraded its bonds to junk status, or the FBI is investigating the company for Medicare fraud.

On the other hand, you'd probably redouble your research efforts if you knew that your candidate has a hot new product that is stealing market share from the competition.

Finding out the buzz could determine how you analyze a company and should be an early step in your research.

News Websites

Yahoo! Finance is the best website for recent company news. It displays headlines from a large variety of sources, but it keeps most of them in its database for only a couple of months. Clicking a headline brings up the entire story, but depending on the source, you may need to subscribe to the website to see the entire story.

MarketWatch has fewer sources, but it keeps headlines generated by MarketWatch writers in its database forever. However, once you go back a couple of years, only a small percentage of MarketWatch-authored headlines are clickable. Still, MarketWatch is your best free resource for researching old news on companies.

StreetInsider.com is a good resource for news going as far back as 2006 about a specific company's earnings reports, guidance changes, and analysts' reactions to those actions.

The Archives option on Google News (not Google Finance) is also a worthwhile resource for looking up old news on a specific company.

If you want to research a specific company's old press releases, the company may maintain several years of press release archives on its own website.

At this point, if you're a growth investor, disqualify stocks with significant recent bad news. On the other hand, value investors should discard candidates reporting a preponderance of recent good news.

Summary

Your time is your most valuable asset. Don't waste it analyzing stocks that aren't qualified candidates. Concentrate on your strongest candidates by eliminating bad ideas as soon as possible. This chapter described a few simple checks. You'll probably add some of your own ideas as you gain experience.

16 ————————————————

The Value Investing Process

Value investing is a strategy for investors willing to take a contrarian position and buy stocks that most investors are selling.

Concentrate on the Strongest Candidates

By March 2001, the market, especially for tech stocks, was in the pits. But graphics chip maker Nvidia was riding high. Microsoft had selected the new Nvidia chip for its Xbox video game machine, which was expected to be a blockbuster. Nvidia had just penetrated the Mac market for the first time. Nvidia reported January quarter sales up 70 percent, and its January fiscal year earnings had soared 137 percent.

Much of Nvidia's success had come at the expense of competitor ATI Technologies. Although it was still outselling Nvidia, ATI's sales slumped 15 percent in its November 2000 quarter, and the company expected to report a stunning 40 percent drop in its February 2001 quarter. ATI was losing money and wasn't expected to turn a profit anytime soon. By mid-March 2001, its shares were trading in the low $4 range, an all-time low.

Nvidia was cleaning ATI's clock, so picking the winner between those two was a no-brainer. Nvidia's investors were richly rewarded for their astute stock picking. Nvidia returned 39 percent between mid-March 2001 and mid-March 2002. But ATI was the Cinderella of this story. Thanks to new products that users perceived to be better than Nvidia's, ATI shareholders enjoyed a 200 percent return in the same period.

Here's a more recent story.

2007 was not a great year for teen apparel retailers. Category leader Abercrombie & Fitch's stock price ended the year at breakeven. Thanks to a series of merchandising missteps, and despite opening 21 new stores, bringing the count to 847, competitor Hot Topic suffered a 3 percent sales drop in 2007. The market noticed, sending its share price down 70 percent for the year.

But Hot Topic was still profitable. Its net income rose 18 percent in 2007 (technically fiscal year February 2008). Cash flow for the year totaled $52 million, and Hot Topic carried no long-term debt. As bad as things went in 2007, in the world of fashion, especially teen fashion, what's in and what's out can turn on a dime. Table 16-1 shows how the market valued the top three teen fashion retailers on December 31, 2007, using the price/sales ratio as a gauge.

TABLE 16-1   December 31, 2007 Price/Sales Ratio for Teen Retailers

	P/S
Abercrombie & Fitch	2.0
American Eagle Outfitters	1.7
Hot Topic	0.3

So, how did investors holding those stocks fare in 2008? Table 16-2 tells the story.

TABLE 16-2   2008 Share Price Appreciation for Teen Retailers

	2008 Return
Abercrombie & Fitch	–71%
American Eagle Outfitters	–54%
Hot Topic	59%

Value investing works because the market overreacts to news. Good news drives stock prices into the stratosphere, creating valuations far surpassing underlying fundamentals. Conversely, a temporary setback or an adverse economic cycle can drive a good company's share price into the ground.

However, a beaten-down stock price per se doesn't equate to a worthwhile value candidate. For that, value investors must understand how the company can recover from the setback that drove it into the value category.

A stock could not be a viable growth and value candidate at the same time. Value candidates report sinking profit margins—growth investors prefer healthy and rising margins. Value candidates' earnings are down or nonexistent—growth investors look for accelerating earnings growth. A value candidate's last earnings report probably disappointed the market—growth investors seek out companies with recent positive surprises.

Cycles

Value investors view the economy and all industries as cyclical. They know that there are times when each industry shines and analysts predict continuing strong growth for the foreseeable future. Then, as sure as night follows day, the industry overexpands, growth falters, profit margins contract, and stock prices plunge. Eventually weaker players drop out, the excess capacity is absorbed, demand picks up, and the cycle repeats.

Value investors don't try to predict the timing of these cycles. They don't know whether the market is heading up or down. They don't know which way interest rates are heading, and they don't follow analysts' buy/sell advice. They don't know if all the bad news is already priced into a stock price, or if further disappointments will drive the share price down even more.

Rather than trying to predict the unpredictable, value investors employ a target price strategy to time their trades. They calculate sell target prices and buy when and if the shares trade sufficiently below the sell targets to justify the risk. They close their positions when the price moves up into the sell range. They don't know when that will happen, and they're prepared to hold as long as it takes, typically two to five years.

Normalizing

The bad news that dropped a stock into the value category probably also killed its profit margins, profitability ratios, and bottom-line earnings. Consequently, value investors must look beyond current problems and evaluate a company's likely performance after its underlying problems are fixed. You do that by analyzing historical patterns.

The process of using historical performance to look beyond current difficulties is termed *normalizing*. A normalized operating margin, for instance, is the expected margin when the company has recovered—say, two or three years down the road.

Normalizing requires reasonably consistent historical performance, and you need at least five years of history. Companies with erratic historical earnings and cash flows, or ones that haven't been operating for at least five years, don't lend themselves to the process.

The Value Analysis Process

Although different in their details, the value and growth analysis processes follow the same 11 steps:

1. Analyze analysts' data.
2. Examine the current valuation.
3. Set target prices.
4. Evaluate the industry.
5. Analyze the business plan.
6. Assess management quality.
7. Gauge financial health.
8. Analyze profitability and growth trends.
9. Search for red flags.
10. Examine ownership.
11. Check the price chart.

Each step employs a corresponding analysis tool explained in detail in Part II of this book. The procedures described in this chapter assume that you're already familiar with those analysis tools.

This chapter concludes by describing when to sell, a key decision for value investors.

Start with at least 10 and preferably 20 candidates so that you can compare them and eliminate the weakest contenders as you progress through the analysis steps. Be sure to run your candidates through the quick prequalify analysis (see Chapter 15) so that you don't waste time analyzing bad ideas.

Eliminate a stock as soon as it flunks any one of these tests so that you can focus on the strongest candidates.

Step 1: Analysts' Ratings and Forecasts

Start by analyzing the analysts' ratings and forecasts.

Sentiment Index

The sentiment index measures the market's enthusiasm by comparing the number of strong buy ratings to the number of holds, sells, and strong sells. Negative sentiment scores mean that most analysts are recommending selling, and these make the best value candidates. Boeing, for instance, trading in the $30 range, hit sentiment scores as low as −14 in late 1999 before starting its run to $70.

Stocks scoring as high as 1 or 2 could also be value candidates, but scores of 3 and above reflect too much positive sentiment for value stocks.

Table 16-3 shows the distribution of analysts' forecasts and the resulting Sentiment score for nine potential value candidates.

Calculate the sentiment score by adding 1 point for each strong buy and subtracting 1 point for each hold, sell, or strong sell recommendation. Don't count buy recommendations.

TABLE 16-3   Distribution of Analysts' Buy/Sell Recommendations for Potential Value Candidates

Company	Strong Buy	Buy	Hold	Sell	Strong Sell	Sentiment Score
American Capital Strategies	0	0	11	3	0	−14
American Ecology	3	2	2	0	0	1
American Public Education	4	6	1	0	0	3
BJ Services	3	2	9	5	0	−11
Coach	5	5	8	2	0	−5
Federal Express	4	0	15	2	1	−14
FMC Technologies	2	5	6	2	0	−6
General Electric	2	2	11	0	1	−10
Paychex	4	0	10	1	1	−8

With most Sentiment scores solidly in negative territory, only American Public Education would be automatically ruled out by this test.

Earnings Growth Forecasts and Trends

Analysts' earnings growth forecasts and recent forecast changes will help you rule out bad value candidate ideas.

Forecast Earnings Growth

Require negative or, at most, flat earnings growth expectations, reflecting the event that propelled them into value territory. Look at the current and next fiscal year earnings growth forecasts. Year-over-year growth forecasts higher than 5 percent for either year disqualify a value candidate. Table 16-4 shows the numbers.

TABLE 16-4   Analysts' Year-Over-Year Earnings Growth Forecasts for the Current Fiscal Year and the Next Fiscal Year

Company	Current FY	Next FY
American Capital Strategies	–58%	–22%
American Ecology	–17%	18%
BJ Services	–62%	–33%
Coach	–8%	–5%
Federal Express	–37%	–10%
FMC Technologies	–20%	–11%
General Electric	–45%	–4%
Paychex	–4%	–3%

American Ecology's 18 percent next fiscal year growth forecast disqualifies it as a value candidate.

Earnings Forecast Trends

Analysts change their forecasts when they receive new information. The best value candidates show a negative earnings forecast trend. A flat trend—that is, less than a $0.02 change in either direction—is okay. Positive forecast trends signal improving sentiment, meaning that the market is pricing a recovery into the stock price, and it's too late for value investors. For this check, the trend is the difference between the current and "90 days ago" forecast for either the current or next fiscal year. A positive $0.05 trend means that the current forecast is $0.05 above the consensus forecast from 90 days ago. Table 16-5 shows the numbers for the surviving candidates.

TABLE 16-5   Earnings Trend: the Difference Between the Current and 90 Days Ago Earnings Forecasts for the Current and Next Fiscal Years

Company	CFY Trend	NFY Trend
American Capital Strategies	–$1.23	–$1.35
BJ Services	–$0.52	–$0.58
Coach	$0.02	$0.05
Federal Express	–$0.41	–$1.12
FMC Technologies	–$0.26	–$0.51
General Electric	–$0.29	–$0.40
Paychex	$0.00	–$0.11

Coach, with a positive $0.05 next fiscal year earnings trend, flunked this test.

Surprise History

Value candidates' recent earnings surprises are likely to be negative. However, surprise history is not used in the value analysis process.

Revenue Forecasts

By the time you find a value candidate, analysts will have cut revenue growth forecasts down to flat or negative. As is the case with surprise history, revenue forecasts are not used in the value analysis process.

Analysts Research Reports

If you've done a good job of picking value candidates, most analyst research reports will have a negative tone. Still, they contain relevant background and industry information that would otherwise be hard to come by. Read all the analysts' reports that you can find for the information they contain, but ignore the buy/sell recommendations.

Step 2: Valuation

Gauging the expectations built into a stock's current price and determining buy and sell target prices are the linchpins of value investing. The GARP (growth at a reasonable price) strategy does not apply to the value analysis.

Implied Growth

Table 5-1 in Chapter 5 lists the long-term earnings growth rate implied by a stock's P/E ratio. Stick with value candidates trading at least 50 percent below their normalized growth rates.

For example, suppose that you've identified a candidate that you expect to resume its earlier 15 percent average annual earnings growth rate when it recovers. In that instance, the current price should reflect no more than half the 15 percent normalized growth rate—that is, 7.5 percent.

Using the Price/Sales Ratio to Estimate Implied Growth

Since many value candidates will report losses, not earnings, you can't use the P/E ratio to look up implied growth. Nevertheless, your candidates will still record sales. Thus, you can use the price/sales (P/S) ratio instead of P/E. Here's how.

P/E and P/S are related mathematically by the firm's net profit margin (net income/sales). Specifically:

$$P/E = P/S \text{ / profit margin}$$

Use the current price/sales ratio, but use the expected profit margin when the company recovers (normalized profit margin). You can estimate the normalized margin by reviewing historical margins.

You can see historical profit margins on MSN Money or Morningstar's Key Ratios reports. Table 16-6 shows historical annual profit margins for each of the remaining candidates, along with my estimated normalized profit margin. LFY stands for last fiscal year, LFY-1 stands for one year prior, and so on.

TABLE 16-6 Historical and Estimated Profit Margins

Company	LFY	LFY-1	LFY-2	LFY-3	LFY-4	LFY-5	LFY-6	LFY-7	Estimated Margin
American Capital Strategies	Loss	57%	104%	66%	84%	57%	14%	18%	65%
BJ Services	11%	16%	18%	14%	14%	9%	10%	16%	15%
Federal Express	3%	6%	6%	5%	3%	4%	4%	3%	5%
FMC Technologies	8%	7%	6%	4%	4%	3%	3%	2%	6%
General Electric	10%	13%	13%	13%	12%	12%	12%	11%	12%
Paychex	28%	27%	28%	26%	23%	27%	29%	29%	27%

Normally, you should give more weight to recent years than to earlier years. However, in this case, General Electric is an exception to that rule. GE's credit unit, which was its biggest profit contributor in recent years, will probably never return to its former glory.

You can find the current P/S ratio on most financial websites. Use the current P/S and your estimated normalized margin to compute the P/E that you need to look up the implied growth in Table 5-1. Call it the "implied P/E." Here's the formula:

$$\text{implied P/E} = \text{P/S} / \text{normalized profit margin}$$

When you calculate the implied P/E, use the decimal version of the profit margin, not the percentage (such as 0.18, not 18%). Table 16-7 lists the implied P/Es for the remaining value candidates.

TABLE 16-7   Implied P/Es for the Remaining Value Candidates

Company	Normalized Margin	P/S	Implied P/E
American Capital Strategies	0.65	0.8	1
BJ Services	0.15	0.9	6
Federal Express	0.05	0.5	10
FMC Technologies	0.06	1.0	17
General Electric	0.12	0.8	7
Paychex	0.27	4.6	17

In May 2009, according to the Financial Forecast Center (www.forecasts.org), the AAA corporate bond rate was 5.5 percent. Table 16-8 shows the relevant portion of Table 5-1. It lists the implied growth for values of P/E and corporate bond rates. For instance, the table shows that the implied growth rate corresponding to a 20 P/E and 5 percent bond rate is 7 percent.

The May 2009 5.5 percent bond rate required averaging the 5 percent and 6 percent implied growth numbers. For example, for a 20 P/E, the implied growth was 8 percent.

TABLE 16-8 A Portion of Table 5-1 Showing Growth Implied by P/E Ratios of 10, 15, and 20 for 5 and 6 Percent AAA-Rated Corporate Bond Rates

	Bond Rates	
P/E	5%	6%
10	1%	2%
15	2%	6%
20	7%	9%

Table 16-9 shows the implied annual growth figures for the remaining value candidates.

TABLE 16-9 Implied Annual Earnings Growth Rates

Company	P/E	Implied Annual Earnings Growth
American Capital Strategies	1	0.2%
BJ Services	6	0.9%
Federal Express	10	1.5%
FMC Technologies	17	6.8%
General Electric	7	0.8%
Paychex	17	6.8%

Using rounded numbers, the market was pricing FMC Technologies and Paychex at 7 percent annual earnings growth. Qualified value candidates should currently be trading at prices equating to implied growth rates no higher than 50 percent of the growth rate you expect when the company recovers. Thus, to qualify, you would have to forecast that FMC Technology and Paychex will grow earnings at least 14 percent annually when they recover.

The same thing is true for the other candidates, only their benchmarks are a lot lower. For instance, you'd only need to expect Federal Express to grow earnings 3 percent annually to qualify.

Price/Sales Valuation Check

Value candidates, by definition, must be trading at low valuations compared to historical levels. You can see historical valuation ratios going back 10 years on Morningstar's 10-Year Valuation report (available from the Valuation Ratios menu) and on MSN Money's Key Ratios 10-Year Summary report. Table 16-10 shows historical price/sales ratios for the candidates using data from Morningstar's report.

TABLE 16-10   Historical Average Price/Sales Ratios by Fiscal Year

Company	LFY	LFY-1	LFY-2	LFY-3	LFY-4	LFY-5	LFY-6	LFY-7	Current
American Capital Strategies	0.6	4.7	7.4	6.6	7.7	7.9	5.9	8.7	0.8
BJ Services	1.0	1.6	2.2	3.7	3.3	2.6	2.2	1.3	0.9
Federal Express	0.8	1.0	1.1	0.9	0.9	0.9	0.8	0.6	0.5
FMC Technologies	0.7	2.1	1.5	1.3	1.3	0.7	0.7	0.6	1.0
General Electric	0.9	2.2	2.6	2.7	2.8	2.8	1.9	3.2	0.8
Paychex	6.2	8.2	8.4	7.6	11.0	10.5	13.7	16.7	4.6

American Capital Strategies, BJ Services, General Electric, and Paychex were trading comfortably below historical valuations. Federal Express was also trading below historical valuations, but not by as wide a margin. FMC Technologies was trading more or less within its historical range. So there is no point in further analyzing FMC.

Step 3: Target Prices

The implied growth and price/sales valuation analysis qualified five stocks as worth further evaluation. Now it's time to get down to brass tacks and establish maximum buy prices and target sell price ranges.

Calculating target prices starts with the assumption that the company will return to profitability at some point. Call that the target year. Then calculate target prices for the date when the target year's results are reported, and call that the target date. For instance, the target date would be early 2011 if you think the company will return to profitability in its fiscal year ending December 2010. It's not a disaster if the company recovers a year later than you expect. That event pushes back the date when you can take profits, but it doesn't materially affect the result.

The target price calculation involves forecasting future revenue growth using historical revenue data. It does not use analysts' forecasts.

Developing the target sell price range consists of five steps:

1. Estimate sales in the target year.
2. Estimate the number of shares outstanding at the end of the target year.
3. Use the results from steps 1 and 2 to compute estimated target-year sales per share.
4. Estimate expected target date range of price/sales ratios.
5. Use steps 3 and 4 to compute the estimated low and high target prices (target price range).

Your maximum buy price is 50 percent of the average of the low and high target prices.

You can use this procedure to forecast target prices any number of years ahead. The target price date is always the day after the company reports its target year results.

I'll demonstrate the process using Paychex. Its fiscal year ends in May, and I'll use its 2011 fiscal year as my target year. Paychex will probably report its May 2011 fiscal-year results in June or July 2011.

You can use MSN's Key Ratios 10-Year Summary and Financial Statements 10-Year Summary reports, or Morningstar's 10-Year Income report (available from the Financial Statements menu) to do the analysis. You'll find that the analysis goes faster if you print the appropriate reports before you start.

Step 1: Target Year Sales

Start by reviewing recent fiscal year revenues. It's not necessary to go back 10 years. Usually, the last five or six are enough. Table 16-11 shows the numbers for Paychex.

TABLE 16-11   Paychex Historical Revenues

Year	Revenues (in Millions of Dollars)
FY 5/03	1,099
FY 5/04	1,240
FY 5/05	1,385
FY 5/06	1,574
FY 5/07	1,753
FY 5/08	1,935

Next, compute the year-over-year revenue growth in dollars, not percentage, for each year. Table 16-12 shows the results.

TABLE 16-12   Paychex Historical Revenues and Year-Over-Year Dollar Growth

Year	Revenues (in Millions of Dollars)	YOY Growth (in Millions of Dollars)
FY 5/03	1,099	
FY 5/04	1,240	141
FY 5/05	1,385	145
FY 5/06	1,574	189
FY 5/07	1,753	179
FY 5/08	1,935	182

Paychex had grown revenues $167 million per year, on average, over the previous five years. However, in the more recent years, the numbers hovered more in low $180 million range, so I used $180 million for my estimate. Table 16-13 shows the revenue growth table with those forecasts added.

TABLE 16-13   Paychex Historical Revenues and Year-Over-Year Dollar Growth, with Forward Estimates Added

Year	Revenues (in Millions of Dollars)	YOY Growth (in Millions of Dollars)
FY 5/03	1,099	
FY 5/04	1,240	141
FY 5/05	1,385	145

Year	Revenues (in Millions of Dollars)	YOY Growth (in Millions of Dollars)
FY 5/06	1,574	189
FY 5/07	1,753	179
FY 5/08	1,935	182
FY 5/09	2,115 estimated	180 estimated
FY 5/10	2,295 estimated	180 estimated
FY 5/11	2,475 estimated	180 estimated

Thus, Paychex's target year FY 5/11 revenues were $2,475 million.

These estimates assume that recent growth trends will continue. Of course, that's not always the case. Modify your sales estimates if you have better information.

Step 2: Shares Outstanding

Next, estimate the total shares outstanding at the end of the target year. Many companies consistently increase shares outstanding because they issue stock to raise cash, make acquisitions, or allocate shares for employee stock options. As with revenues, use history as your guide. Table 16-14 show the historical data.

TABLE 16-14   Paychex Historical Shares Outstanding Data

Year	Shares Outstanding (in Millions of Dollars)	YOY Growth (in Millions of Dollars)
FY 5/03	376.7	
FY 5/04	378.0	1.3
FY 5/05	378.6	0.6
FY 5/06	380.3	1.7
FY 5/07	382.2	1.9
FY 5/08	360.5	–21.2

Paychex was adding around 1.5 million shares annually, but then it spent $1 billion to buy back shares in FY 5/08. It's unknown whether Paychex would do another buyback. I assumed that its share count would remain constant over the next three years. Table 16-15 shows the historical data with my estimates added.

TABLE 16-15   Paychex Historical and Estimated Shares Outstanding

Year	Shares Outstanding (in Millions of Dollars)	YOY Growth (in Millions of Dollars)
FY 5/03	376.7	
FY 5/04	378.0	1.3
FY 5/05	378.6	0.6
FY 5/06	380.3	1.7
FY 5/07	382.2	1.9
FY 5/08	360.5	−21.2
FY 5/09	360.5 estimated	0.0 estimated
FY 5/10	360.5 estimated	0.0 estimated
FY 5/11	360.5 estimated	0.0 estimated

Step 3: Sales Per Share

Just as earnings per share is annual earnings divided by the number of shares outstanding, sales per share is annual revenues divided by the number of shares outstanding.

I estimated Paychex's target-year revenues of $2,475 million and shares outstanding at 360.5 million. So my estimated target year sales are $6.87 per share.

Step 4: Price/Sales Ratios

Research has found that comparing a firm's valuation to its own historical ranges works better for forecasting future prices than comparing to competing companies or to the overall stock market.

Although P/E is the most watched valuation gauge, it's too volatile for our purposes. Also, P/E isn't useful when earnings are very low or negative. Instead, we'll use the more stable price/sales ratio. Table 16-16 shows Paychex's historical P/S ratios.

TABLE 16-16   Paychex Historical P/S Ratios

Company	LFY	LFY-1	LFY-2	LFY-3	LFY-4	LFY-5	LFY-6	LFY-7	Current
Paychex	6.2	8.2	8.4	7.6	11.0	10.5	13.7	16.7	4.6

Recent years are usually more relevant than earlier years. When doing the analysis, ignore outlying numbers (those out of normal range).

In the most recent four years, Paychex's P/S ratios stayed within a relatively narrow range of 6.2 to 8.4. Before that, the ratios were much higher. While I normally would have looked at the most recent five years, given the abrupt drop from LFY-4 to LFY-3, I doubted that Paychex would trade at double-digit ratios in the future.

Thus, I estimated Paychex's target year P/S range at 6.2 to 8.4.

Step 5: Compute the Target Price Range

The price/sales ratio is share price divided by annual sales. However, it can also be stated this way:

$$\text{share price} = \text{per-share sales} \times \text{P/S}$$

For instance, a stock would be trading at $20 if its sales per share were $10 and the P/S ratio was 2.

So the target price formula is

$$\text{target price} = \text{target year per-share sales} \times \text{target year P/S}$$

In steps 3 and 4, I estimated target year sales at $6.87 per share and a target year price/sales range of 6.2 to 8.4.

Rounding to the nearest dollar, Paychex's target year price range is $43 to $58, and the average target price is $50.50.

Paychex's maximum buy price is 50 percent of the average target price, which is $25.25 per share. When I did the analysis, Paychex was changing hands at around $27 per share. Thus, based on the target price calculation, Paychex was trading above its maximum buy price.

Given those numbers, you would wait for Paychex to trade at $25.25 or below before buying.

Step 4: Industry Analysis

Value investing, unlike growth, is not about picking the strongest player in hot industries. Instead, value analysis focuses primarily on the candidate, rather than its industry. Even so, some aspects of industry analysis require the attention of value investors.

Industry Growth

According to MSN Money's Earnings Growth Rate report, Paychex is in the computer services industry. Analysts were forecasting 16 percent annual earnings growth for that industry in April 2009. Discounting the forecast industry earnings growth by 30 percent yielded a moderate 11 percent expected average annual revenue growth, which, according to Table 7-1 in Chapter 7, is the sweet spot for value candidates.

Higher expected industry growth forecasts—say, 15 percent—imply high expectations, the bane of value investing. Nevertheless, high forecast industry growth is not a disqualifying factor. The only disqualifying industry growth factor is too-slow growth—namely, less than 3 percent.

Industry Concentration

Concentration refers to the number of companies competing in the same industry sector. Industries with few major competitors are said to be concentrated, as opposed to fragmented industries with many competitors. Companies in concentrated industries are usually more profitable than players in fragmented industries.

Using Yahoo!'s Business Summary (Profile) report, Reuters' Company Profile, and information on Paychex's own website, I found that Paychex mainly provides payroll and employee benefits outsourcing services for small businesses. While other corporations offer similar services, Paychex was the only nationwide company targeting small business. Targeted customer size aside, only a handful of players offer payroll services. Thus, Paychex's industry would be described as concentrated.

Industry Scuttlebutt

Surveying trade publication websites, Google, and Google News turned up nothing significant about Paychex.

Step 5: Business Plan Analysis

The business model analysis evaluates the characteristics of a company's business plan that are likely to influence its success. Use the business plan scorecard to tabulate the scores for each category. Score each category 1, –1, or 0, corresponding to business plan advantage, disadvantage, or not applicable, respectively. Chapter 8 describes how to do a business plan analysis.

Brand Identity

Paychex, being the only payroll services provider focusing on small businesses, is relatively well known within its target customer base. However, small owner-run businesses are price-sensitive. The Paychex brand is probably not strong enough to overcome price competition from local sources. Thus, Paychex has no brand identity advantage. Score = 0.

Other Barriers to Entry

Paychex, with more than 100 offices around the country, would be a formidable competitor to new players attempting to penetrate the market. I rated the barriers to entry high. Score = 1.

Distribution Model/Access to Distribution

Paychex uses its own sales force to market directly to potential small-business customers. Distribution is not an issue. Score = 0.

Product Useful Life/Product Price

Product life is irrelevant to service providers. Score = 0.

Access to Supply/Number of Suppliers

Obtaining needed products and materials is not an issue for most service providers. Score = 0.

Predictable Revenue Stream

Small businesses are unlikely to switch payroll service providers unless something goes wrong. Paychex's revenue stream is very predictable. Score = 1.

Number of Customers

Paychex provides payroll services to more than 500,000 small businesses. Score = 1.

Product Cycle

Product cycle is irrelevant to most service providers. Score = 0.

Product and Market Diversification

Paychex's payroll and benefits services, in theory, are a single product. However, its market comprises many different business sectors, so it meets the diversification requirement. Score = 1.

Organic Growth Versus Acquisition Growth

Paychex has grown both organically and by acquisition. Score = 0.

Business Model Score

Paychex's business model score was 4, which is good. However, business model scores are best used to help you decide between competing value candidates.

Step 6: Management Quality

Key Executive and Board Quality

Jonathon Judge had been Paychex's CEO since 2004. Before that, he was CEO of an information management software company. Board Chairman Thomas Golisano founded Paychex in 1971. Most of the outside Board members were investment managers rather than working in businesses related to Paychex's operations. In all, I ranked Paychex's management quality as acceptable.

Clean Accounting/Earnings Growth Stability

The clean accounting test totals one-time charges or nonrecurring charges found on annual income statements and compares that total to annual sales. The test judges accounting as clean if the nonrecurring charges' percentage of sales averaged less than 3 percent over the past five years.

Nonrecurring charges are labeled "Unusual Expense (Income)" on Reuters and MSN Money income statements. Consistent nonrecurring percentage of revenues of 4 percent or higher, although not automatically a red flag, warrants your attention.

Paychex showed no one-time or nonrecurring charges on its income statements, qualifying its accounting as clean.

The earnings growth stability test requires a visual inspection of Paychex's quarterly earnings history to gauge earnings volatility. You can find the EPS data on Earnings.com (www.earnings.com). It's easier to assess earnings volatility if you organize the EPS data into a table resembling Table 16-17.

TABLE 16-17   Paychex Quarterly Earnings Per Share

	FY 5/09	FY 5/08	FY 5/07	FY 5/06	FY 5/05
1st quarter	$0.41	$0.40	$0.35	$0.30	$0.23
2nd quarter	$0.39	$0.40	$0.35	$0.30	$0.23
3rd quarter	$0.36	$0.39	$0.35	$0.30	$0.24
4th quarter		$0.38	$0.36	$0.32	$0.27
Totals		$1.57	$1.41	$1.22	$0.97

Considering the hit that the global economy took in 2008 and 2009, Paychex's quarterly earnings growth was remarkably stable. I rated Paychex "excellent" in this category.

Stock Ownership

According to Yahoo!'s Insider Roster, Paychex CEO Jonathan Judge held 105,000 shares, and CFO John Morphy held 58,000 shares. Founder and Board Chair Tom Golisano held 73,000 shares. In addition, Reuters' Officers and Directors report showed that Judge held options for 900,000 additional shares and Morphy held options for 103,000 shares.

Ideally, you'd like to see the CEO and CFO holding millions of shares. CEO Judge comes close, but the CFO falls short by that measure. Still, I ranked Paychex "good" in the Stock Ownership category.

Step 7: Financial Fitness

The purpose of evaluating financial fitness is to determine whether the company has the financial strength to survive the problems that made it a value candidate.

Firms generally run into financial difficulties for one of two reasons:

- They are a busted cash burner, meaning that they are burning cash and are in danger of running out.
- They are overburdened debtors—typically formerly profitable firms that, due to current difficulties, can't service their debt.

Value candidates are more likely to be potential overburdened debtors than potential busted cash burners.

Potential busted cash burners can be evaluated using the Busted Cash Burners analysis, while potential overburdened debtors require the Detailed Fiscal Fitness Exam.

Use the leverage ratio (total assets divided by shareholders' equity), which you can look up on many financial websites, including MSN Money, to determine the most appropriate test for your candidate:

Leverage Ratio	Suggested Analysis
Negative equity	Detailed Fiscal Fitness Exam
Less than 2.5	Busted Cash Burners
2.5 or greater	Detailed Fiscal Fitness Exam

Paychex's balance sheet showed no long-term debt. Both its total and long-term debt/equity ratios are 0. However, Paychex's balance sheet listed roughly $3.9 billion for "client fund obligations" in the current liabilities category. Consequently, despite having no long-term debt, Paychex's leverage ratio was 4.3, which called for the Detailed Fiscal Fitness Exam.

Detailed Fiscal Fitness Exam

Chapter 10 describes how to run the Detailed Fiscal Fitness Exam, so I'll only describe the results here:

1. Net income positive: Paychex scored 1 point in this category, which requires that the last 12 months' net income be a positive number. Paychex's 12 months' net income was $576 million.

2. Operating cash flow positive: Paychex's $725 million cash flow earned it 1 point.

3. Net income growth: Paychex's 12 percent net income growth exceeded its –15 percent net asset growth, earning it 1 point in this category.

4. Operating cash flow: Operating cash flow exceeded net income, so Paychex scored 1 point.

5. Asset growth: Assets shrank 15 percent versus a 4 percent drop in total liabilities. Paychex scored 0 points here because total asset growth did not exceed total liability growth.

6. Current ratio: This test requires that the ending current ratio must be equal to or greater than the year-ago figure. Paychex's 1.1 current ratio was the same for both periods, earning it 1 point in this category.

7. Shares outstanding: Paychex's number of shares outstanding dropped versus year ago, easily meeting the requirement that the total shares outstanding must not have increased more than 2 percent. Score 1 point.

8. Gross margins: Paychex's gross margins were the same for the current and year-ago periods, flunking this test, which requires that gross margin increase. Score 0 points.

9. Sales growth: Sales grew 9 percent while total assets shrank 15 percent, meeting the requirement that sales growth exceed asset growth. Score 1 point.

10. Total liabilities/EBITDA: Paychex's $4,113 million total liabilities were 5.2 times its $796 million EBITDA, over the 5.0 maximum ratio required to score a point in this category. Score 0 points.

11. Total liabilities versus operating cash flow: Paychex total liabilities were 5.7 times its $725 million cash flow, above the 4.0 ratio required to earn 1 point in this category. Score 0 points.

Paychex's 7-point score qualified it as fiscally fit.

Step 8: Profitability Analysis

The value strategy requires buying when the numbers look bad. Margins may be down, sales growth may have stalled or even become negative, and earnings may have turned to losses. The value investing strategy is based on the principle of reverting to the mean.

Reverting to the mean suggests that abnormally high numbers will come down, and unusually low numbers will move back up to historic values. For example, companies reporting unusually high operating margins, compared to their own historical values or industry averages, will likely see those margins come down in future quarters, and vice versa. Where growth investors see above-average or rising margins as good, value players interpret them as a potential sell signal.

Value investing is usually about buying formerly profitable stocks performing below historical ranges. Avoid companies with histories of negative cash flow, erratic operating and profit margins, or abnormally low long-term ROAs (less than 5 percent).

However, as shown in Table 16-18, the market downturn of 2008–2009 presented unusual opportunities for value investors. Although Paychex's share price had dropped with the market, and growth stalled, its profitability metrics, except for its net profit margins, remained within historical norms.

TABLE 16-18   Key Operating Figures for Paychex

	Q 2/09	Q 11/08	Q 8/08	FY 5/08	FY 5/07	FY 5/06	FY 5/05
YOY Sales Growth	−0.7	3.2	5.3	10.4	11.4	13.6	11.7
Gross Margin	70.1	69.0	72.2	71.0	70.4	70.4	82.8
Operating Margin	35.3	38.1	38.7	36.0	32.4	34.9	34.2
Net Profit Margin	25.5	27.8	29.2	29.8	29.4	29.5	26.6
SG&A % of Sales	30.6	28.1	28.2	29.8	32.5	29.5	42.0

Table 16-19 shows that Paychex's profitability, as measured by return on assets, cash flow, and EBITDA, was inline with historical figures. The negative cash flow for its November 2008 quarter was better than the year-ago −$148.2 million figure and reflected seasonal factors.

TABLE 16-19   Paychex Profitability, Operating Cash Flow, and EBITDA

	Q 2/09	Q 11/08	Q 8/08	FY 5/08	FY 5/07	FY 5/06	FY 5/05
ROA	9.1	11.0	11.4	10.8	8.3	8.4	8.4
Operating Cash Flow	121.1	−100.8	80.3	724.7	631.2	569.2	467.9
EBITDA	202.5	206.6	224.6	796.1	664.4	643.2	565.2

Note: Quarterly ROA figures are annualized.

Operating cash flow is an especially important consideration for value investors. Look for firms with a solid record of generating positive operating cash flows, even though the current numbers could be negative.

Although net profit margins were down, Paychex was hardly a basket case. In step 3 of the price target calculation, I estimated fiscal year May 2011 sales at $2,475 million. Assuming that Paychex's net margin moves back up to 29.8 percent, which was its FY 2008 number, Paychex's net income would total $737.5 million, equating to $2.04 per share, based on my estimated 361 million shares outstanding.

Step 9: Red Flags

For value investors, there is no need to look for red flags pointing to an earnings shortfall, because in most cases, earnings are already down. However, one earnings quality issue still needs to be assessed.

Capital Expenses Versus Depreciation

Savvy managers know that they must continue to invest in new capital equipment, even when times are tough. Generally, capital expenditures should at least equal depreciation charges.

You can find the depreciation and capital expenditure numbers on the cash flow statement. Some websites combine depreciation and amortization into a single figure. Don't use those. You need depreciation alone. Both MSN Money and Reuters show depreciation separately. Table 16-20 shows the Paychex numbers.

TABLE 16-20 Paychex Depreciation and Capital Expenses (in Millions of Dollars)

	FY 5/08	FY 5/07	FY 5/06	FY 5/05
Depreciation	80.6	73.4	66.5	82.0
Capital Expenditures	82.3	79.0	81.1	70.7

This data shows that Paychex continued to invest in new capital equipment. Be wary of companies that habitually spend less on capital equipment than they depreciate.

Step 10: Ownership

Total insider holdings is the most significant ownership factor for value investors.

Insider ownership levels exceeding 55 percent of shares outstanding signals potential problems. Yahoo!'s Key Statistics report showed Paychex's insider ownership at 11 percent.

Large stock purchases by key insiders such as the CEO or CFO after a big sell-off in a stock may indicate that these insiders have confidence in the company's future. However, insider buying is a secondary signal and is not as relevant as other factors.

Institutional ownership data's lack of timeliness limits its usefulness. Institutional ownership generally is less than 50 percent of outstanding shares if the company has been in the market's doghouse for several months. However, at best, the institutional ownership data will only confirm what you've already determined.

Step 11: Charts

Pay attention to the relationship between the share price and the 200-day moving average. The best value candidates are trading below or near their 200-day MA. Be wary of stocks trading more than 10 percent above their 200-day MAs. This usually means that you are too late to the party.

When I checked, Paychex was trading close to its 200-day moving average.

When to Sell

Deciding when to sell is just as important as analyzing buy candidates. Here are suggested selling rules for value investors.

The Target Price Is Achieved

A stock trading within your sell target range is your best sell signal. This often happens much sooner than expected, especially if the firm hires a new CEO or the market finds other reasons to get excited about its prospects.

If that happens, take the money and run. Don't wait for the fundamentals to recover. The share price will drop when the market realizes that the recovery won't happen overnight.

If the fundamentals do recover and all goes as planned, you will be selling when analysts are increasing earnings and sales growth forecasts and growth investors are buying.

You Realize That Your Estimates Won't Happen

Unfortunately, not all value stocks return to their former glory. Sell when you realize that the recovery you expected won't happen.

Acquisitions

Sell if your company acquires another business that is at least 25 percent (sales or market capitalization) as large as your company. Also, sell if your company makes a series of smaller acquisitions that, taken together, add up to 25 percent of its original size.

Deteriorating Fundamentals

Sell if the ROA, operating cash flow, and/or operating margins continue to deteriorate two or three quarters after you've bought the stock.

Earlier Financials Are Restated

Restating previously reported results increases the likelihood of future problems. Unless your stock has new management at the helm, sell when it significantly reduces previously reported sales or earnings.

Increased Borrowings

Ballooning debt signals that the company is generating insufficient cash flow to solve its problems. Sell if your company significantly increases borrowings. This doesn't apply if it is using new borrowings to pay off existing debt.

The Share Price Is 50 Percent Above the 200-Day Moving Average

Stocks in this territory have already made a big move in a relatively short time. It's time for you to move on. In this instance, don't wait for the stock to hit your sell target.

Red Flags

Our buy analysis didn't check for red flags because most value stocks' financial statements are in disarray when you find them. Don't worry about revenue growth, but check for inventory and receivables red flags in quarterly reports after the company stabilizes. You can expect the company to pay lower income tax rates if it suffered earlier losses, but be wary of how future tax rate increases could depress net income.

Summary

Value investing is about picking stocks left for dead by the growth crowd. If you've picked the right stocks, sell when they are trading within your target sell range. If something goes wrong, sell as soon as you realize that the recovery you expected won't happen. Don't procrastinate. Waiting for more information in the face of solid sell signals will likely diminish your profits or turn small losses into big ones.

17

The Growth Investing Process

Most investors look for growth stocks because they offer potentially higher gains than value plays. However, since almost all hot growth stocks eventually stumble, growth investors must constantly check for clues of an impending problem, and be prepared to react quickly.

Concentrate on the Strongest Candidates

Every generation has its success stories: the Microsofts, Googles, Hansen Naturals, and Intuitive Surgicals that seemingly came out of nowhere to score massive price gains that made their shareholders rich.

For many growth investors, finding the next Google is the Holy Grail. But you don't have to find the next Google to be a successful growth investor.

In the end, share prices follow earnings. If you spot a company growing earnings (and hence share price) 15 percent annually, you'll turn $1,000 into more than $4,000 in 10 years. Find a stock growing 20 percent annually, and you'll grow $1,000 into more than $6,000; 25 percent annual growth turns $1,000 into more than $9,000 in 10 years.

Despite the massive 2008–2009 downturn in the economy, as of mid-2009, 262 U.S. listed stocks had averaged more than 15 percent compounded average annual earnings growth over 10 years, 133 firms grew their earnings more than 20 percent annually, and 69 exceeded

25 percent average annual earnings growth. Looking back five years, 177 firms grew their annual earnings faster than 20 percent annually, and 109 exceeded 25 percent average annual earnings growth.

> ### Note
>
> This counts only stocks trading at a $5 minimum and with minimum $100 million market caps as of May 14, 2009.

Growth investing is about finding companies with exciting new products and services that are capable of growing at above-average rates. You don't need to find a single company that will sustain above-average growth for years. You can start with one stock and switch to another when your first pick's growth falters. But to pull that off, you have to detect sputtering growth early and switch horses before it becomes common knowledge and sinks the share price.

In the 1990s, growth was synonymous with tech investing, but now, as shown in Table 17-1, growth is everywhere.

TABLE 17-1   A Sampling of Stocks Recording 25 Percent or Higher Average Annual Share Price Appreciation Over Five Years (Returns Do Not Include Dividends, if Any)

Company	Industry	5-Year Average Annual Return
Monsanto Company	Agrochemical	42
Terra Industries Inc.	Agrochemical	46
Terra Nitrogen Company L.P.	Agrochemical	87
The Mosaic Co.	Agrochemical	34
Precision Castparts Corp.	Aircraft parts	29
Green Mountain Coffee Roasters	Beverage	66
Hansen Natural Corp.	Beverage manufacturing	76
Alexion Pharmaceuticals Inc.	Biotechnology	26
Gilead Sciences Inc.	Biotechnology	26
Illumina Inc.	Biotechnology	61
Myriad Genetics Inc.	Biotechnology	31
Vertex Pharmaceuticals	Biotechnology	28
FTI Consulting Inc.	Business consulting	28

Company	Industry	5-Year Average Annual Return
Quality Systems Inc.	Business software	44
Apple Inc.	Consumer electronics manufacturing	55
Seaboard Corp.	Food producer	25
Publix Supermarkets Inc.	Groceries	71
Valmont Industries Inc.	Industrial products	26
Greenhill & Co. Inc.	Investment banking	32
Flowserve Corp.	Machinery	28
NuVasive Inc.	Medical equipment	26
Intuitive Surgical Inc.	Medical equipment	56
General Cable Corp.	Metal products	38
Compass Minerals International	Mining	28
Arena Resources Inc.	Oil/gas	49
BP Prudhoe Bay Royalty Trust	Oil/gas	31
Oceaneering International	Oil/gas drilling services	27
Range Resources Corp.	Oil/gas exploration and production	41
Southwestern Energy Co.	Oil/gas exploration and production	65
Core Laboratories N.V.	Oil/gas services	32
Diamond Offshore Drilling Inc.	Oil/gas services	33
Dril-Quip Inc.	Oil/gas services	37
Priceline.com Inc.	Online travel agency	34
Express Scripts	Pharmaceutical benefit manager	26
Buckle Inc.	Retail clothing	30
Allegheny Technologies Corp.	Steel/iron	29
Nucor Corp.	Steel/iron	26
Stifel Financial Corp.	Stockbroker/ investment bank	28
Clean Harbors Inc.	Waste management	45

Different industries will probably dominate a similar list two, three, or five years down the road. And that's the point.

Growth investors enjoy the process. They relish the excitement of spotting the next high flyer ahead of the crowd. Some follow a top-down strategy. In other words, they try to pinpoint a strong industry and then pick the best candidates from the leading players in the group. Others follow a bottom-up approach, searching out fast growers regardless of industry. It doesn't matter, as long as your approach turns up interesting candidates.

Growth Candidates

For growth investors, the ideal candidates are members of emerging, fast-growing industries. The rewards can be enormous if you can pinpoint the eventual winner in a still-fragmented industry, such as early investors in Dell Computer, Microsoft, and Wal-Mart were able to do.

Unfortunately, those opportunities are hard to find, and the next-best growth candidates are firms offering unique products or services to existing markets, with a history of consistent earnings growth and expanding profit margins.

The worst growth candidates are those selling into markets where price is the main differentiator between competitors' products. Next-worst after those are firms that are not the number one or number two players in their market.

Growth investing is not about buying low. Your best prospects will likely be well off their lows when you discover them. Growth stocks often rise to values unsupported by fundamentals. While an analyst downgrade can trigger a temporary dip, strong growth stocks rarely suffer sustained losses simply because they're overvalued. They crash when something goes wrong, usually word of slowing growth. Thus, spotting the red flags pointing to slowing growth before the crowd notices is crucial to successful growth investing.

The Process

The growth analysis process consists of 11 steps:

1. Analyze analysts' data.
2. Examine the current valuation.

3. Set target prices.
4. Evaluate the industry.
5. Analyze the business plan.
6. Assess management quality.
7. Gauge financial health.
8. Analyze profitability and growth trends.
9. Search for red flags.
10. Examine ownership.
11. Check the price chart.

Each step employs a corresponding analysis tool explained in detail in Part II of this book. The procedures described in this chapter assume that you're already familiar with those tools.

The chapter concludes by discussing how to spot clues that it's time to sell, which for many is the most difficult step of the investing process.

You'll get the best results if you research several stocks at the same time. The process of comparing competing candidates forces you to be more analytical and to make better decisions. That said, don't waste time analyzing stocks that have no chance of surviving your analysis. Run your candidates through the quick prequalify analysis (see Chapter 15) to eliminate the obvious misfits before you begin this process.

Concentrate on the strongest candidates. Rule out bad ideas as soon as you identify them so that you can spend your time researching your best prospects.

Step 1: Analysts' Ratings and Forecasts

Growth investing works best when you find stocks attracting increasing interest from the market. Analysts' buy/sell ratings and earnings forecasts are a key indicator of market enthusiasm.

Sentiment Index

The Sentiment Index tells you how the market views your candidate. Highly negative scores, such as 4 or lower, identify out-of-favor stocks, usually better value plays than growth candidates. However, don't overlook otherwise-qualified growth candidates with slightly negative sentiment scores. They can score good gains when they surprise the market with better-than-expected results. Mining equipment maker Joy Global, for instance, had a –3 sentiment score in April 2005, when it was trading for $20 per share. By November of that year, with three better-than-expected earnings reports under its belt, the stock was changing hands at $29, a sweet 45 percent gain.

Generally, you'll find the most reliable growth candidates in the 0 to +4 sentiment score range. Aircraft parts maker Precision Castparts, for example, had a +4 score in March 2006 when its shares were going for $53 or so. Precision's share price peaked at $150 in October 2007, a 180 percent gain.

Increasing sentiment scores, even though relatively low, signal growing enthusiasm, which equates to higher risk. Once you get up to scores of 9 or more, you're in high expectation territory, which equates to high risk.

I'll use two stocks, casual restaurant operator Buffalo Wild Wings and adult educator Strayer Education, to demonstrate the growth analysis process.

When I did the analysis, five analysts were rating Buffalo Wild Wings "strong buy" and eight were advising "hold," giving it a –3 sentiment score. Strayer Education scored +3 for sentiment. Usually, Buffalo's –3 would be marginal for a growth candidate (notwithstanding the Joy Global example), but in mid-2009 analysts were more pessimistic than usual, so both Buffalo and Strayer looked good in terms of sentiment.

Earnings Forecasts and Trends

Analysts' earnings growth forecasts—more specifically, changes in earnings forecasts—are the primary driver of growth stock prices and consequently should be weighted accordingly in your analysis.

For instance, in May 2006, Precision Castparts reported March quarter earnings of $0.74 per share, 42 percent above the year-ago quarter and 4 cents above analysts' forecasts,. This motivated analysts to raise forecasts for future quarters. Table 17-2 shows Precision's analysts' consensus forecast history (fiscal years only) as of mid-May 2006.

TABLE 17-2   Consensus Earnings Forecast History for Precision Castparts in May 2006

	Current Year: March 2007	Next Year: March 2008
Current estimate	3.18	3.73
7 days ago	3.14	3.63
30 days ago	3.14	3.63
60 days ago	2.55	3.06
90 days ago	2.49	3.00

Although Precision beat year-ago earnings by 42 percent, it was much more significant that Precision beat forecasts. While the 4-cent beat amounted to only 6 percent of forecast earnings, the market pays more attention to the number of cents than to the percentage. Anything above 3 cents on the upside is significant. On the downside, even a 1-cent miss would be enough to motivate analysts to cut forecasts, which in turn would drive the share price down.

Evaluating Forecast Trends

Table 17-2 shows that Precision's fiscal year March 2007 earnings forecasts had already moved up to $3.14 per share from $2.49 two months earlier (90 days ago), before it reported March quarter results. That's not unusual. Rising earnings forecasts frequently forecast a positive earnings surprise at report time.

The momentum triggered by an earnings beat continues for some time. Table 17-3 shows what Precision's forecast history looked like a month later, in mid-June. Current-year forecasts had moved up $0.10, and the next fiscal year's forecast gained $0.16.

TABLE 17-3   Precision Castparts Analysts' Consensus Forecast History as of Mid-June 2006

	Current Year: March 2007	Next Year: March 2008
Current estimate	3.28	3.89
7 days ago	3.28	3.89
30 days ago	3.18	3.73
60 days ago	3.14	3.63
90 days ago	3.06	3.49

Precision's strong positive earnings trend signaled a strong June quarter report. Precision did just that, reporting earnings 48 percent above year-ago and, more important, in terms of share price action, 12 cents above forecasts.

Tables 17-4 and 17-5 show what Buffalo Wild Wings and Strayer Education's forecast trends looked like in May 2009.

TABLE 17-4   Buffalo Wild Wings Analysts' Consensus Forecast History

	Current Year: December 2009	Next Year: December 2010
Current estimate	1.69	2.06
7 days ago	1.69	2.06
30 days ago	1.67	2.03
60 days ago	1.67	2.03
90 days ago	1.67	2.03

TABLE 17-5   Strayer Education Analysts' Consensus Forecast History

	Current Year: December 2009	Next Year: December 2010
Current estimate	7.27	8.93
7 days ago	7.25	8.89
30 days ago	6.99	8.62
60 days ago	6.99	8.63
90 days ago	6.99	8.61

Based only on earnings forecast trends, Strayer looked like the stronger candidate, but Buffalo's more-or-less flat trend wouldn't disqualify the sports bar operator.

When evaluating forecast trends, focus on fiscal year numbers, and ignore less than 2-cent changes in forecasts. Rule out candidates with forecasts trending down, because the negative trend is likely to continue and could lead to a negative surprise at report time.

Although positive forecast trends are best, don't eliminate companies with flat trends at this point. If, in the end, it comes down to choosing between two otherwise equal companies, pick the company with the stronger positive forecast trend.

Evaluating Forecast Growth

Usually, stocks with the highest year-over-year growth forecasts get the most attention and hence have the most appreciation potential. That doesn't apply, however, if the year-ago annual earnings figure is very small—say, 25 cents or less.

Although earnings growth in the 10 to 15 percent range technically qualifies for the growth category, you'll do best sticking with companies growing earnings at least 20 percent annually, and higher is better, up to a point. Forecast annual earnings growth rates much above 40 percent are not sustainable.

Growth Red Flags

Avoid stocks with forecast revenue growth below historical rates, even if the forecast growth is still substantial. For instance, say that a stock that had been growing revenues 50 percent annually is now expected to grow at a 25 percent rate. Even though 25 percent growth is strong per se, the market had been valuing the stock for 50 percent growth. The share price will invariably get hit when the slowdown becomes evident.

Compare the earnings and sales growth forecasts for the same period. Use caution if fiscal year forecast revenue growth is down from year-ago but forecast earnings growth isn't. This could mean that the earnings forecasts assume improving profit margins, which may not happen.

Table 17-6 shows the March 2007 and March 2008 fiscal year earnings and revenues year-over-year growth forecasts for Precision Castparts as of early March 2007.

TABLE 17-6 Precision Castparts Analysts' Consensus Earnings and Revenue Growth Forecasts in March 2007

	Current Year: March 2007	Next Year: March 2008
Forecast Earnings Growth	66%	24%
Forecast Revenue Growth	52%	17%

Forecast earnings growth for fiscal year March 2007 was higher than forecast revenue growth, but not unreasonably so. However, in the following year, analysts expected a substantial revenue growth slowdown. That 67 percent slowdown (from 52 percent to 17 percent) is a red flag. Many investors don't notice the revenue forecasts. The share price would undoubtedly get hit when the company reports a revenue growth slowdown of that magnitude.

Smaller forecast growth slowdowns, such as from 25 percent to 20 percent, would not be a red flag early in the fiscal year. Analysts typically raise next year's forecasts when a company surprises on the upside. If they don't, even a slowdown from 25 percent to 20 percent would be a cause for concern as the next fiscal year approaches.

Tables 17-7 and 17-8 show what the numbers looked like for Buffalo and Strayer.

TABLE 17-7   Buffalo Wild Wings Analysts' Consensus Earnings and Revenue Growth Forecasts

	Current Year: December 2009	Next Year: December 2010
Forecast Earnings Growth	22%	22%
Forecast Revenue Growth	30%	20%

TABLE 17-8   Strayer Education Analysts' Consensus Earnings and Revenue Growth Forecasts

	Current Year: December 2009	Next Year: December 2010
Forecast Earnings Growth	28%	23%
Forecast Revenue Growth	26%	21%

Buffalo had typically grown revenues 20 percent annually, so the expected 30 percent growth in 2009 may have been an anomaly, possibly triggered by an acquisition. Since I did the analysis in May, Strayer's 19 percent falloff in expected growth (21 percent versus 26 percent) would not be a deal killer this early in the current fiscal year.

Surprise History

Recent earnings surprise history often predicts the future. Companies with a recent history of positive surprises often continue to surprise on the upside, and vice versa.

Avoid companies with recent negative surprises. The amount doesn't matter. A 1-cent negative surprise is just as significant as a 50-cent shortfall.

The positive surprise amount, however, is significant. Most firms manage earnings expectations so that if all goes as planned, they will report a positive 1- or 2-cent surprise. Thus, 1 or 2 cents on the upside is not a surprise. It would be a surprise if a company with a history of positive 2-cent surprises reports earnings even with forecasts. That event would likely drive its share price down.

A consistent history of large surprises, such as 15 cents or higher, can be dangerous, because the market expects more of the same. In such instances, even a positive 5-cent surprise might disappoint the market.

The optimum surprise history is a consistent string of 4- to 9-cent positive surprises. Those are sufficient to move up the stock price on report day without creating abnormal expectations. A history of small (0.01 or 0.02) positive surprises or no surprises is okay. If the last four quarters' surprise history is mixed, pay the most attention to the latest quarter.

Table 17-9 shows Precision's surprise history as of February 2007.

TABLE 17-9   Precision Earnings Surprise History

	March 2006	June 2006	September 2006	December 2006
Estimate	0.70	0.74	0.91	0.98
Actual	0.74	0.86	1.03	1.15
Surprise	0.04	0.12	0.12	0.17

With that positive and accelerating surprise record, it's no wonder that Precision's share price gained 51 percent in 2006.

Tables 17-10 and 17-11 show how Buffalo and Strayer looked in May 2009.

TABLE 17-10   Buffalo Wild Wings Earnings Surprise History

	June 2008	September 2008	December 2008	March 2009
Estimate	0.27	0.31	0.39	0.46
Actual	0.31	0.25	0.43	0.47
Surprise	0.04	–0.06	0.04	0.01

TABLE 17-11   Strayer Education Earnings Surprise History

	June 2008	September 2008	December 2008	March 2009
Estimate	1.47	0.81	1.70	1.97
Actual	1.50	0.83	1.71	2.07
Surprise	0.03	0.02	0.01	0.10

Strayer, with a recent $0.10 surprise, looked the most promising. However, Buffalo's record, even including a negative surprise three quarters back, still fell into the acceptable range for growth candidates.

Disqualify stocks with two or more negative surprises in the last four quarters, or with a negative surprise in the most recent quarter. The amount doesn't matter.

Research Reports

Analysts' research reports contain valuable background information about a company and its industry. Try to find at least two research reports for each candidate. Sometimes you'll find that the information detailed in the report contradicts the analysts' buy/sell rating.

Step 2: Valuation

Growth investors don't spend nearly as much time worrying about valuation as do value investors. That's not as ridiculous as it sounds, because growth stocks often trade at levels unjustified by their fundamentals, especially when they are in their fast growth phase. It's usually slowing growth, not overvaluation, which sinks the share price.

For example, in July 2005, Innovative Solutions & Support, a maker of specialized display systems for airplanes, was trading at $24 and change, which equated to a 24 P/E and 5.9 price/sales ratio. Considering that it had just reported June quarter year-over-year sales and earnings growth of 39 percent and 50 percent, respectively, Innovative was hardly overvalued. Yet Innovative's share price dropped 22 percent the day after it reported those numbers, mainly because its new order rate warned that growth was slowing.

All that said, eventually share prices reflect the fundamentals, even for growth stocks. Thus, as a growth investor, you need to know how the market is valuing your candidate.

Growth at a Reasonable Price (GARP)

Most growth investors rely on GARP, which compares a stock's price/earnings ratio to its historical or expected earnings growth to determine if it's fairly valued. The ratio of P/E to the forecast growth rate is called the PEG ratio. In normal markets, a stock is considered fairly valued when its growth rate equals its P/E (PEG = 1). It's overvalued when the P/E exceeds the P/E, and vice versa.

In early 2006, Precision Castparts was trading at an 18 P/E based on its fiscal year March 2007 expected earnings. At the time, analysts were forecasting 20 percent average annual long-term earnings growth. Thus, Precision was trading at a slightly undervalued 0.9 PEG.

In May 2009, based on forecast current-year earnings, Buffalo Wild Wings was trading at 20.5 P/E. Based on analysts' 22 percent forecast year-over-year growth, Buffalo's PEG was 0.9 (20.5 PE divided by 22). Strayer, with a 26 P/E and 29 percent forecast current fiscal year growth, was also trading at a 0.9 PEG.

Both Buffalo and Strayer were trading slightly below fair value, an unusual situation for stocks with apparently solid growth prospects. The sour economy held down valuations. In normal markets, stocks with PEGs in the 1.1 to 1.4 range outperform stocks with PEGs below 1.0.

Implied Growth

Implied growth gives you another way of looking at a stock's valuation.

The implied growth rate table (see Table 5-1 in Chapter 5) uses Benjamin Graham's intrinsic value formula to determine the long-term average annual earnings growth rate implied by a stock's P/E. The only variable is the current corporate AAA-rated bond interest rate, which you can find at the Financial Forecast Center (www. neatideas.com/aaabonds.htm).

The bond rates were hovering around 5.5 percent in March 2007. Based on Table 5-1, Precision Castparts 18 P/E corresponded to a low 5 percent or so implied growth.

Coincidentally, AAA-rated corporate bond rates were also 5.5 percent when I analyzed Buffalo and Strayer. Table 5-1 shows that Buffalo Wild Wings' 21 P/E equated to 9 percent implied annual earnings growth, and Strayer Education's 26 P/E equated to 12 percent implied growth.

Since both Buffalo and Strayer were growing much faster than the rates implied by their P/Es, both appeared reasonably valued when measured by both GARP and implied growth.

Step 3: Target Prices

It's more work, but calculating a target price range gives you further insight into a stock's valuation. The calculation, described in detail in Chapter 6, involves choosing a target fiscal year, estimating target year sales and the number of shares outstanding at the end of that year, and then using those figures to estimate target year sales per share. Finally, you use that number plus historical price/sales ratio ranges to determine high and low target prices for the day after the company announces target year results.

Since most investors don't hold growth stocks much longer than a year or so, I ran the calculations in May 2009 and defined 2010 as the target year for both Buffalo Wild Wings and Strayer Education. Thus, I calculated the target price as of early February 2011, when both are likely to report fiscal year 2010 results.

Step 1: Target Year Sales

Tables 17-12 and 17-13 list the historical sales figures and my sales estimates for 2009 and 2010 for Buffalo and Strayer.

TABLE 17-12   Buffalo Wild Wings Historical and Estimated Annual Sales and Sales Growth

Year	Revenues (in Millions of Dollars)	YOY Growth (in Millions of Dollars)
FY 12/04	171.1	
FY 12/05	209.7	38.6
FY 12/06	278.2	68.5
FY 12/07	329.7	51.5
FY 12/08	422.4	92.7
FY 12/09	493.4 estimated	71.0 estimated
FY 12/10	573.4 estimated	80.0 estimated

TABLE 17-13   Strayer Education Historical and Estimated Annual Sales and Sales Growth

Year	Revenues (in Millions of Dollars)	YOY Growth (in Millions of Dollars)
FY 12/04	183.2	
FY 12/05	220.5	37.3
FY 12/06	263.7	43.2
FY 12/07	318.0	78.3
FY 12/09	403.0 estimated	85.0 estimated
FY 12/10	498.0 estimated	95.0 estimated

Both Buffalo and Strayer were growing sales, but Strayer's growth looked more consistent and robust in recent years than Buffalo's. I assumed that Strayer's growth would accelerate in 2009 and again in 2010. Buffalo's 2008 growth looked abnormally high, so I assumed that it would drop back a bit in 2009 and accelerate modestly in 2010.

Step 2: Target Year Shares Outstanding

Tables 17-14 and 17-15 list the historical shares outstanding fig-ures and my 2009 and 2010 forecasts for Buffalo and Strayer.

TABLE 17-14   Buffalo Wild Wings Historical and Estimated Shares Outstanding

Year	Shares Outstanding (in Millions of Dollars)	YOY Growth (in Millions of Dollars)
FY 12/04	16.9	
FY 12/05	17.0	0.1
FY 12/06	17.3	0.3
FY 12/07	17.7	0.4
FY 12/08	17.9	0.2
FY 12/09	18.2 estimated	0.3 estimated
FY 12/10	18.5 estimated	0.3 estimated

TABLE 17-15   Strayer Education Historical and Estimated Shares Outstanding

Year	Shares Outstanding (in Millions of Dollars)	YOY Growth (in Millions of Dollars)
FY 12/04	14.7	
FY 12/05	14.3	–0.4
FY 12/06	14.3	0
FY 12/07	14.4	0.1
FY 12/09	14.4 estimated	0 estimated
FY 12/10	14.4 estimated	0 estimated

Buffalo averaged 0.3 million annual share inflation, while Strayer kept its share count more or less stable in recent years.

Step 3: Target Year Sales Per Share

I estimated Buffalo's 2010 target year sales at $573.4 million and its shares outstanding at 18.5 million, resulting in per-share sales of $30.99.

Strayer's estimated $498.0 million target year sales and 14.4 million target year shares outstanding resulted in target year sales per share of $34.58.

Step 4: Price Sales Ratios

Tables 17-16 and 17-17 list each stock's historical average price/sales ratios for recent years.

TABLE 17-16   Buffalo Wild Wings Historical Average Price/Sales Ratios

Year	Average P/S
FY 12/04	1.7
FY 12/05	1.4
FY 12/06	1.7
FY 12/07	1.3
FY 12/08	1.1

Buffalo Wild Wings' estimated target year price/sales range is 1.3 to 1.7.

TABLE 17-17   Strayer Education Historical Average Price/Sales Ratios

Year	Average P/S
FY 12/04	9.0
FY 12/05	6.3
FY 12/06	5.8
FY 12/07	7.8
FY 12/08	7.7

Strayer Education's estimated target year price/sales range is 6.0 to 7.8.

Buffalo typically trades at a lower price/sales ratio than Strayer. Its lower-than-usual 2008 ratio probably reflected negative sentiment about restaurant stocks triggered by the weak economy. I assumed that Buffalo wouldn't trade that low when the economy recovered. Strayer didn't suffer the same fate as Buffalo in 2008 because education stocks were thought to be recession-proof. Strayer's 2006 ratio looked unusually low compared to other recent years, so I set the probable low P/S at 6.0 rather than 5.8. By the same token, I didn't think that a 9 price/sales ratio would be in the cards for some time, so I set the high P/S at 7.8.

Step 5: Target Price Estimates

The target price is estimated per share sales multiplied by the price/sales ratio.

For Buffalo:

Low target price: $30.99 multiplied by 1.3 is $40.29.

High target price: $30.99 multiplied by 1.7 is $52.68.

For Strayer Education:

Low target price: $34.58 multiplied by 6.0 is $207.48.

High target price: $34.58 multiplied by 7.8 is $269.72.

Buffalo was trading at $35 when I ran the calculation. Thus, its theoretical price appreciation potential ranged from 15 percent to 51 percent.

Strayer was trading at $193. So its appreciation potential ranged from 8 percent to 40 percent.

Step 4: Industry Analysis

Understanding your candidate's industry prospects and competitive position is an important part of the growth stock analysis process.

The Industry

Using information from its own website and Morningstar's Company Profile, I learned that Buffalo Wild Wings is a casual dining restaurant chain with a sports bar atmosphere that specializes in serving chicken wings and other casual items along with alcoholic beverages. About two-thirds of Buffalo's 500-plus restaurants are franchises, and the balance are company-owned.

Strayer provides education programs to working adults. It focuses on business administration, accounting, information technology, healthcare, public administration, and education both online and via physical campuses in 15 states.

Industry Growth

MSN Money's Earnings Growth Rate report noted that Buffalo Wild Wings is in the restaurant industry, which analysts expect to average 15 percent annual long-term earnings growth. Strayer Education is in the schools industry, which is expected to grow earnings around 24 percent annually.

Discounting the analysts' earnings growth projections by 30 percent yielded 11 percent annual sales growth for restaurants and 17 percent for schools.

Table 7-1 in Chapter 7 defines the restaurant industry's 11 percent growth rate as "moderate," which ranks as only "fair" in terms of suitability for growth candidates. It classified the school industry's 17 percent forecast growth rate as "fast," a good category for growth candidates.

Industry Concentration

The restaurant industry is very competitive, with many players. Buffalo, however, has defined a unique niche. There are few other national sports bar chains. Buffalo competes mostly with locally owned sports bar operations. However, in a broader sense, Buffalo competes for the dining dollar with numerous casual-restaurant chains.

Strayer faces several major competitors, including Apollo Group, DeVry, ITT Educational Services, Capella Education, and more.

Picking Industry Winners

Buffalo Wild Wings operates in a mature industry with many larger, better established, and more diversified players. However, Buffalo is strictly a niche player. It will continue to grow until it

saturates its narrowly defined market or makes operational missteps
that trigger an unexpected growth slowdown.

Strayer, by contrast, is competing against similar companies all
targeting the same customers. Table 17-18 shows how Strayer stacks
up against the competition based on the characteristics defined in
Chapter 7.

TABLE 17-18   Key Performance Measures for Strayer Education

Company	Annual Revenue (in Millions of Dollars)	Revenue Growth	Operating Margin	SG&A % Sales
Strayer Education	$396	25%	32.0%	35.0%
Apollo Group	$3,141	15%	23.9%	32.5%
Capella Education	$272	20%	14.7%	41.1%
Career Education	$1,075	–2%	4.6%	52.1%
Corinthian College	$1,069	16%	4.2%	36.7%
DeVry	$1,092	17%	14.9%	38.7%
ITT Education	$1,015	17%	32.3%	29.9%
Lincoln Education	$377	15%	9.4%	49.8%

In terms of market share, Apollo Group is the industry leader,
and Strayer is one of the smallest players. Strayer, however, is the
fastest grower. All else equal, the fastest grower is usually the best
growth candidate.

Operating margins define profitability before income taxes and
certain interest charges are deducted. Here, Strayer is second only to
ITT Educational Services and is substantially more profitable than
the other players.

"SG&A % of Sales" measures overhead, and, in this case, lower is
better. By this measure, Strayer is better than competitors with similar revenues, but not as efficient as Apollo Group and ITT Educational Services, which have much larger sales bases to absorb
overhead costs.

Industry Scuttlebutt

Buffalo Wild Wings is a sports bar with lots of TVs, spicy food, and a variety of beers—nothing more. Most online reviews gave Buffalo high marks, although service can be spotty. I found no significant complaints from franchise holders.

It was a similar story for Strayer Education. Other than occasional complaints from students about actions of their instructors, I found nothing that signaled problems brewing at Strayer.

Industry Summary

Buffalo Wild Wings is a niche player in a mature industry with many well-established competitors. However, in its niche, Buffalo's main competition comes mainly from locally owned restaurants.

Strayer battles much larger competitors for the same customers. However, Strayer is growing faster and is more profitable than its competitors.

Step 5: Business Plan Analysis

Business Plan Scorecard

The business model analysis evaluates qualities of a company's business plan that are likely to influence its success. Use the business plan scorecard to tabulate the scores for each category. Score each category 1, –1, or 0, corresponding to advantage, business plan disadvantage, or not applicable, respectively.

Brand Identity

Buffalo Wild Wings has strong and generally positive brand identity in the markets it serves. Score = 1.

Strayer Education is not particularly well known and is not necessarily perceived as better quality than the competition. On the other hand, none of Strayer's competitors enjoys strong brand identity either. Score = 0.

Other Barriers to Entry

Any of the large, publicly traded restaurant operators could emulate Buffalo's concept, should they choose. Thus, Buffalo enjoys no barriers to entry to prevent competitors from entering its markets. On the other hand, Buffalo faces no barriers that would prevent it from entering new market areas. Score = 0.

Strayer Education also enjoys no particular barriers to prevent competitors from invading its markets. But, as was the case for Buffalo, Strayer faces no barriers that would prevent it from entering new markets. Score = 0.

Distribution Model/Access to Distribution

Access to distribution is not an issue for Buffalo. Score = 0.

Similarly, access to distribution is not an issue for Strayer. Score = 0.

Product Useful Life/Product Price

Buffalo's products are inexpensive and last only until its customers get hungry again. Thus, its products have a very short product life. Score = 1.

Once they've completed a course of study, Strayer's students probably won't return, at least for the same courses. Strayer's products have a very long life, but they are not considered discretionary purchases in the same sense as automobiles or entertainment centers. Score = 0.

Access to Supply/Number of Suppliers

Obtaining the food and other products necessary to run its business is not an issue for Buffalo. Score = 0.

Access to supply is also not an issue for Strayer. Score = 0.

Predictable Revenue Stream

Buffalo's products and services are in effect fashion items, and its revenue is unpredictable. Score = –1.

Strayer does not enjoy a predictable revenue stream. Score = –1.

Number of Customers

Buffalo serves thousands of customers daily and thus is not dependent on a few large customers. Score = 1.

Strayer also serves thousands of students. Score = 1.

Product Cycle

Buffalo's spicy chicken wings are unlikely to become obsolete anytime soon. Score = 1.

Strayer also sells long life-cycle products. Score = 1.

Product and Market Diversification

Buffalo sells a variety of casual food items and could easily develop different products should spicy wings go out of style. However, in another sense, Buffalo serves a single market segment (sports bars). Score = 0.

For Strayer, product and market diversification is not an issue. Score = 0.

Organic Growth Versus Acquisition Growth

Although it has made some acquisitions, Buffalo grows primarily by opening new restaurants. Goodwill plus intangibles accounts for only 4 percent of total assets. Score = 1.

Strayer has made no significant acquisitions, and its goodwill plus intangibles represents 0 percent of total assets. Score = 1.

Business Model Score

Buffalo Wild Wings' business model score of 4 is above average, while Strayer's score of 2 is more or less average. Use the Business Model Scores to compare candidates you are evaluating.

Step 6: Management Quality

Key Executive and Board Quality

Buffalo's CEO, although she had no previous restaurant experience, has been running the company since 1996 and is credited with inventing the business model that led to Buffalo's expansion. She also serves on the board of the National Restaurant Association. Buffalo's Senior Vice President, Franchise and Development, the only other officer with restaurant experience, previously served in various executive positions at Denny's and, before that, at Burger King. None of Buffalo's board members are in the restaurant industry. I ranked Buffalo's key executive and board quality as fair.

Strayer's CEO has held that position since 2001 but had no prior experience in the education industry. Only one Strayer top executive, the Executive Vice President and Chief Administrative Officer, had prior significant experience in the for-profit education industry. However, two board members are professional educators. I ranked Strayer's key executive and board quality as fair.

Clean Accounting/Earnings Growth Stability

The clean accounting test totals a firm's one-time charges found on annual income statements and compares that total to annual sales. Persistent one-time charges exceeding 3 percent of sales define a firm's accounting practices as unclean.

Buffalo's total one-time charges versus sales totaled 0.5 percent of sales in 2008, 0.3 percent of sales in 2007, 0.4 percent of sales in 2006, and 0.9 percent of sales in 2005. Those numbers qualified Buffalo's accounting as "clean."

Strayer's total one-time charges totaled 0 in all years checked. Thus, Strayer's accounting also qualified as "clean."

The earnings growth stability test entails a visual look at quarterly earnings history to gauge earnings volatility. Table 17-19 shows Buffalo's recent quarterly earnings history using data from Smart Money's financial statements. To avoid seasonal distortions, always compare the same quarter of each year, such as March 2009 to March 2008.

TABLE 17-19 Buffalo Wild Wings Quarterly Earnings Per Share

Quarter	2006	2007	2008	2009
March	0.20	0.32	0.36	0.47
June	0.14	0.22	0.31	
September	0.20	0.24	0.25	
December	0.39	0.33	0.43	

Buffalo's earnings were reasonably consistent. There were no negative quarters, and December 2007 was the only quarter that did not beat year-ago numbers. Notice that December is always the biggest quarter, in terms of earnings, for each year.

Table 17-20 shows the quarterly earnings numbers for Strayer.

TABLE 17-20 Strayer Education Quarterly Earnings Per Share

Quarter	2006	2007	2008	2009
March	1.10	1.30	1.64	2.07
June	0.97	1.20	1.50	
September	0.44	0.64	0.83	
December	1.11	1.34	1.70	

Strayer's numbers were even more consistent than Buffalo's. There were no losing quarters, and every quarter beat the year-ago number. Notice the seasonality. December is always the best quarter, and September the worst.

Stock Ownership

Buffalo's CEO held 123,000 shares and options for another 65,000 shares. The CFO held 90,000 shares and options for another 42,000 shares. No other key officers held shares and/or options totaling at least 100,000 shares.

Strayer's CEO held 190,000 shares and options for another 500,000 shares. Strayer's CFO held only 14,000 shares plus options for another 110,000 shares.

Both Buffalo's and Strayer's two key officers, the CEO and CFO, had enough skin in the game to care about the share price.

Summary

I judged both Buffalo's and Strayer's key executive and board quality as only fair. But both showed clean accounting and excellent earnings stability. In both cases, the CEO and CFO held significant stock and/or stock options.

Step 7: Financial Health

Ensuring that your candidate is not a bankruptcy candidate is an important part of your analysis. Different financial health tests are required, depending on whether your candidate is a low- or high-debt firm.

Use the financial leverage ratio found on MSN Money, Morningstar, or Forbes to determine whether the Busted Cash Burner analysis is sufficient or whether the Detailed Fiscal Fitness exam is required.

Negative leverage ratios, or ratios of 2.5 or greater, require the Detailed Fiscal Fitness Exam. Otherwise, the Busted Cash Burner exam is sufficient.

Buffalo Wild Wings' financial leverage ratio was 1.4, and Strayer's ratio was 2.1. So both qualified for the Buster Cash Burner test.

Busted Cash Burners

The first step evaluates each stock's operating cash flow history.

Figure 17-1 shows the pertinent portions of Morningstar's 5-Yr Restated report for Buffalo Wild Wings. Buffalo generated positive operating cash flow for each of the years shown, and its last 12 months cash flow totaled $69 million. Based on those numbers, you can assume that, barring unexpected events, Buffalo will continue generating positive cash flow for some time.

Cash Flow $Mil

Fiscal year-end: 12

	2006	2007	2008	TTM = Trailing 12 Months TTM
Operating Cash Flow	33	44	66	69
- Capital Spending	24	41	67	76
= Free Cash Flow	9	2	-1	-7

Balance Sheet

Assets	$Mil	Liabilities and Equity	$Mil
Cash	7.0	Current Liabilities	38.2
Other Current Assets	55.0	Long-Term Liabilities	32.6
Long-Term Assets	190.0	Shareholders' Equity	180.7
Total	251.5	Total	251.5

Figure 17-1   A portion of Morningstar's 5-Yr Restated Report for Buffalo Wild Wings (May 2009)

Buffalo's cash plus other current assets totaled $62 million compared to current liabilities of $38.2 million. So, Buffalo's working capital totaled $23.8 million.

Consequently, Buffalo Wild Wings, with the ideal combination of positive cash flow and positive operating cash flow, passes the cash burner test and qualifies as fiscally fit.

Figure 17-2 shows a portion of Morningstar's 5-Yr Restated report for Strayer Education.

Cash Flow $Mil

Fiscal year-end: 12

	2006	2007	2008	TTM = Trailing 12 Months TTM
Operating Cash Flow	62	81	89	101
- Capital Spending	13	15	21	22
= Free Cash Flow	49	66	68	79

Balance Sheet

Assets	$Mil	Liabilities and Equity	$Mil
Cash	32.0	Current Liabilities	148.2
Other Current Assets	192.0	Long-Term Liabilities	11.5
Long-Term Assets	78.0	Shareholders' Equity	143.7
Total	303.4	Total	303.4

Figure 17-2   A portion of Morningstar's 5-Yr Restated Report for Strayer Education

Strayer also was operating cash-flow-positive in the last 12 months as well as in the three fiscal years displayed. Since its working capital was a positive $75.8 million ($32.0 + $192.0 − $148.2), Strayer also passed the test and qualified as fiscally fit.

Step 8: Profitability

Successful growth investing hinges on identifying candidates that will meet, and ideally beat, the market's growth expectations. Step 7 checked working capital and cash flows to ensure that your candidate is financially sound. In this step, you analyze factors that will help you assess your candidate's earnings prospects.

By the time you discover a stock, everything about its past performance has already been factored into earnings growth expectations. Those expectations are wrong! Your job is to figure out which way. If the expectations were too low, the share price will probably rise while you own the stock. Conversely, you'll undoubtedly lose if the expectations were too high.

Make the Trend Your Friend

Analyzing profitability at a single point in time won't tell you much about the future. Instead, you must analyze everything in terms of trends. Are the factors that affect profitability trending in a direction that signals improving or deteriorating future results?

Sales Growth

Assuming steady profit margins, sales growth translates directly into earnings growth, which is what moves share prices. In practice, as shown in Table 11-1 in Chapter 11, that relationship usually holds up reasonably well.

For instance, Bed Bath & Beyond's 18 percent average annual sales growth over the past 10 years translated into 17 percent annual earnings growth. Cognizant Technology grew both sales and earnings 47 percent, on average, annually, over the past 10 years. Exelon's 10-year annual sales and earnings growth both averaged 14 percent.

Normally, earnings growth triggers similar share price growth. However, with the market 43 percent off its October 2007 high when I tabulated the figures in May 2009, none of the three stocks mentioned achieved share price growth as high as the earnings growth numbers quoted.

In any case, the point is that picking good growth stocks starts with pinpointing stocks that have strong sales growth potential.

Tables 17-21 and 17-22 show Buffalo Wild Wings' and Strayer Education's recent sales numbers.

TABLE 17-21   Buffalo Wild Wings Fiscal Year Sales and Year-Over-Year Sales Growth

	FY 2005	FY 2006	FY 2007	FY 2008
FY Sales (in Millions of Dollars)	209.7	278.2	329.7	422.4
YOY Sales Growth	23%	33%	19%	28%

TABLE 17-22   Strayer Education Fiscal Year Sales and Year-Over-Year Sales Growth

	FY 2005	FY 2006	FY 2007	FY 2008
FY Sales (in Millions of Dollars)	220.5	263.6	318.0	396.3
YOY Sales Growth	20%	20%	21%	25%

Both candidates' historical revenue figures qualify them as strong growth candidates. Of the two, Strayer looks better because its revenue growth accelerated in 2007 and even more in 2008. Buffalo's growth was spottier, which probably triggered stock sell-offs in the down years.

Next, we'll examine recent quarterly sales numbers to determine whether the long-term trends are faltering (bad), continuing (okay), or accelerating (best).

Table 17-23 shows the recent quarterly sales figures for Buffalo.

TABLE 17-23   Buffalo Wild Wings Quarterly Sales (in Millions of Dollars)

Quarter	2006	2007	2008	2009
March	64.3	79.9	97.3	131.6
June	62.3	76.0	97.9	
September	68.4	82.4	106.1	
December	83.3	91.4	121.2	

The sales numbers by themselves are difficult to interpret. You can tell more by converting the figures to year-over-year percentage sales growth, as shown in Table 17-24.

TABLE 17-24   Buffalo Wild Wings Quarterly Year-Over-Year Percentage Sales Growth

Quarter	2007	2008	2009
March	24%	22%	35%
June	22%	29%	
September	20%	29%	
December	10%	33%	

Tables 17-25 and 17-26 show the same information for Strayer Education.

TABLE 17-25   Strayer Education Quarterly Sales (in Millions of Dollars)

Quarter	2006	2007	2008	2009
March	67.1	80.2	97.1	124.5
June	65.6	78.9	97.9	
September	56.7	69.8	87.0	
December	74.3	89.1	114.3	

TABLE 17-26   Strayer Education Quarterly Year-Over-Year Percentage Sales Growth

Quarter	2007	2008	2009
March	20%	21%	28%
June	20%	24%	
September	23%	25%	
December	20%	28%	

Buffalo's December 2007 trip-up makes you wonder if its December 2008 quarter growth looked good only because the year-ago number was weak. However, its strong March 2009 showing at least partly mitigated that fear, especially since the economy was in the dumpster in early 2009.

The numbers show that revenue growth is accelerating for both Buffalo and Strayer. Already-strong and accelerating revenue growth is about as good as it gets for growth investors.

Margin Analysis

Deteriorating margins can trigger a negative surprise, even if the company meets sales growth expectations. Conversely, improving margins lead to positive surprises. Analyzing margin and overhead (SG&A) trends can help you determine if margins are more likely to improve or deteriorate in upcoming quarters.

Table 17-27 shows Buffalo's recent gross margin, operating margin, and SG&A percentage of sales history, and Table 17-28 shows the same data for Strayer.

TABLE 17-27   Buffalo Wild Wings Gross Margins, Operating Margins, and SG&A Percentage of Sales

	FY 2007	FY 2008	Q 3/08	Q 3/09
Gross Margin	25.4%	25.8%	N/A*	26.0%
Operating Margin	8.1%	8.9%	9.8%	9.8%
SG&A % of Sales	12.2%	11.4%	10.8%	10.5%

*Buffalo's March 2008 gross margin was unavailable. Its March 2007 gross margin was 25.7 percent.

TABLE 17-28   Strayer Education Gross Margins, Operating Margins, and SG&A Percentage of Sales

	FY 2007	FY 2008	Q 3/08	Q 3/09
Gross Margin	68.4%	66.8%	69.7%	71.1%
Operating Margin	30.7%	29.3%	36.6%	38.2%
SG&A % of Sales	35.1%	35.0%	30.8%	30.4%

Operating margin is the most important of the three because it includes the effects of gross margin and SG&A changes. Seasonality factors affect margins, so compare the most recent quarter to the year-ago quarter, not to fiscal-year data.

Buffalo's operating margin rose in 2008 versus 2007, but its March 2009 quarter was flat compared to March 2008. Buffalo's overhead (SG&A) was trending down, showing that management was doing a good job of controlling costs.

Strayer's operating margin dropped 5 percent in 2008 (29.3 versus 30.7) but moved up in its March 2009 quarter.

Increasing margins signal the possibility of positive earnings surprises at report time. Flat margins are okay, but avoid companies with significant declining margins. As a rule of thumb, consider a 5 percent decline (such as 9.5 down from 10.0) significant when you're comparing annual operating margins. A 10 percent decline (such as 9.0 down from 10.0) is significant when you're comparing quarterly figures.

Return on Assets

The profitability analysis we've done so far compares a company's recent performance to its own history. Return on assets measures profitability in absolute terms.

Use the annual ROAs, because the quarterly figures are too volatile. Table 17-29 shows recent fiscal year ROA data for Buffalo and Strayer.

TABLE 17-29 Annual ROA for Buffalo Wild Wings and Strayer Education

Company	2006	2007	2008
Buffalo	10.1%	10.0%	10.0%
Strayer	19.3%	18.9%	24.9%

Buffalo's consistent 10 percent or so ROA is better than average. Strayer's 19 percent 2006–2007 ROA was already better than most growth stocks. Its surge to 25 percent in 2008 was just icing on the cake.

In summary, both stocks qualified as growth stock candidates in terms of profitability.

Cash Flows

Because it must be reconciled to actual bank balances, many money managers consider operating cash flow the best earnings measure. It is the cash generated by a firm's main operations. Free cash flow is operating cash flow minus funds used for acquisitions and capital expenditures. Free cash flow is surplus cash over and above the amount needed to run or expand the existing business.

Table 17-30 shows the annual operating and free cash flow numbers for Buffalo, and Table 17-31 lists the same information for Strayer.

TABLE 17-30   Annual Operating Cash Flow, Cash Used for Acquisitions, Cash Used for Capital Expenditures, and Free Cash Flow for Buffalo Wild Wings (in Millions of Dollars)

	2006	2007	2008
Operating Cash Flow	33.0	43.6	66.1
Acquisitions			23.1*
Capital Expenses	23.8	41.4	67.4
Free Cash Flow	9.2	2.2	−24.4

*Acquisition of franchised restaurants

TABLE 17-31   Cash Flow Figures for Strayer Education (in Millions of Dollars)

	2006	2007	2008
Operating Cash Flow	61.8	80.8	88.6
Acquisitions			
Capital Expenses	13.2	14.9	20.7
Free Cash Flow	48.6	65.9	67.9

Buffalo had been spending almost all of its available cash to fund expansion, which is typical for companies in fast-growth mode. Buffalo went in the hole in 2008 to acquire franchised restaurants. It will have to raise cash by borrowing or selling more shares if it continues to acquire franchised restaurants.

Strayer's strong free cash flow tells you that it is generating more cash than it can spend, which is good. It can use the excess cash to acquire new businesses, pay dividends, or for other purposes that could enhance shareholder value.

Step 9: Red Flags

Now it's time to check for red flags signaling a potential earnings shortfall in the current or next quarter and for yellow flags warning of longer-term problems. At your option, you can compare net income to operating cash flow and, if your candidate passes that test, skip the accounts receivables and inventory tests.

Sales Growth

A slowdown in historical sales growth rates is a red flag, but if it existed, you would have discovered it in Step 8. In this step, you compare forecast sales growth rates to historical trends. It's a red flag if the forecast sales growth rates are significantly below historical levels.

Tables 17-32 and 17-33 show the annual sales and year-over-year sales growth figures from step 8 with the consensus analyst forecasts for 2009 and 2010 added.

TABLE 17-32   Buffalo Wild Wings Historical Fiscal Year Sales and Year-Over-Year Sales Growth with Analysts' Forecasts for 2009 and 2010 Added

	FY 2005	FY 2006	FY 2007	FY 2008	FY 2009*	FY 2010*
FY Sales (in Millions of Dollars)	209.7	278.2	329.7	422.4	547.7	658.1
YOY Sales Growth	23%	33%	19%	28%	30%	20%

*Figures for 2009 and 2010 are consensus analyst forecasts.

TABLE 17-33 Strayer Education Historical Fiscal Year Sales and Year-Over-Year Sales Growth with Analysts' Forecasts for 2009 and 2010 Added

	FY 2005	FY 2006	FY 2007	FY 2008	FY 2009*	FY 2010*
FY Sales (in Millions of Dollars)	220.5	263.6	318.0	396.3	501.0	607.7
YOY Sales Growth	20%	20%	21%	25%	26%	21%

*Figures for 2009 and 2010 are consensus analyst forecasts.

Analysts expect Buffalo's growth to continue at a 30 percent pace in 2009, consistent with the growth in 2008. However, they are forecasting only 20 percent sales growth in 2010. That's a 33 percent slowdown (20 percent versus 30 percent). I did this analysis in May 2009. Analysts typically raise the next fiscal year's forecasts when a company reports strong current-year numbers. Thus, Buffalo's forecast 20 percent 2010 growth, although not a red flag in May, would be cause for concern toward the end of its fiscal year.

For Strayer, analysts are forecasting 2009 growth consistent with 2008. The 21 percent growth figure for 2010 will probably increase to 25 percent or so as the year progresses.

After the September results are announced, consider an expected 25 percent falloff in sales growth (such as 20 percent versus 25 percent) a red flag warning of future problems.

Net Income Versus Operating Cash Flow

Net income or after-tax income, the bottom line on the income statement, is the top line on the cash flow statement. Cash flow from operations would normally be a larger number than net income because depreciation and amortization subtract from net income but not from operating cash flow. Operating cash flow should increase in proportion to net income.

Tables 17-34 and 17-35 show the recent net income and operating cash flow numbers for Buffalo and Strayer.

TABLE 17-34   Fiscal Year Net Income and Operating Cash Flow for Buffalo Wild Wings (in Millions of Dollars)

	2005	2006	2007	2008
Net Income	8.9	16.3	19.7	24.4
Operating Cash Flow	24.6	33.0	43.6	66.1

TABLE 17-35   Fiscal Year Net Income and Operating Cash Flow for Strayer Education (in Millions of Dollars)

	2005	2006	2007	2008
Net Income	48.1	52.3	64.9	80.8
Operating Cash Flow	55.1	61.8	80.8	88.6

Both Buffalo and Strayer consistently reported operating cash flow greater than net income. However, in 2008, Strayer's operating cash flow grew by only 10 percent compared to 24 percent net income growth. Though not a red flag at this point, it bears watching.

If operating cash flow exceeds net income, consider the following receivables and inventory analyses optional. However, those analyses are required when net income exceeds operating cash flow.

Accounts Receivables/Inventories

These checks compare growth in receivables and inventories to sales growth. Normally, receivables and inventories more or less track sales.

It's a red flag if either receivables or inventories grew significantly faster than sales over the past 12 months. The easiest way to determine if that happened is to compute the ratios of receivables to sales and of inventory to sales. Express the ratios as percentages of sales. For instance, if the receivables were $100 and the sales $1,000, the receivables were 10 percent of sales.

Comparing the latest ratios to year-ago figures tells you if receivables and/or inventories increased faster then sales.

Table 17-36 compares March 2008 and March 2009 quarter sales, accounts receivable, and inventory numbers for Buffalo. Table 17-37 shows the same information for Strayer.

TABLE 17-36   Receivables and Inventory Analysis for Buffalo Wild Wings

	Q 3/08	Q 3/09
Sales	97.3	131.6
Receivables	7.7	9.0
Receivables % of Sales	7.9%	6.8%
Inventory	2.6	3.5
Inventory % of Sales	2.7%	2.7%

TABLE 17-37   Receivables and Inventory Analysis for Strayer

	Q 3/08	Q 3/09
Sales	97.1	124.5
Receivables	103.5	134.3
Receivables % of Sales	106.6%	107.9%
Inventory	0	0

Neither Buffalo nor Strayer holds significant inventory, and Buffalo carries very small accounts receivables on its books.

Strayer, however, does carry significant accounts receivables. Its receivables expressed as a percentage of sales increased by 1 percent (107.9 versus 106.6) in March 2009 versus a year ago.

The receivables and/or inventory ratios must increase by at least 10 percent (such as from 50 percent to 55 percent) to be of concern. Calculate the percentage change by dividing the latest number by the year-ago figure. For instance, the ratio increased 14 percent if the latest ratio is 40 percent compared to a year-ago 35 percent number (40 divided by 35).

The numbers showed no red flags for either Buffalo or Strayer.

Pension Plan Income

Both Buffalo and Strayer, being relatively new firms, offer employees 401(k) defined-contribution plans. Thus, there is no potential for creative accounting related to pension plan income.

Yellow Flags

The next two items are potential yellow flags. They could signal long-term problems, but they're not necessarily issues that would trigger a negative surprise as soon as the next earnings report.

Capital Expenditures Versus Depreciation

A company must keep investing in its business to remain viable. Capital expenditures measure the amount that the company is investing in new plants and equipment, while depreciation tells you how fast it's writing off its existing capital equipment. It's a yellow flag if the company's depreciation consistently exceeds its capital expenditures. You can find both items on the cash flow statement. Use annual figures, because capital expenditures come in discrete increments, and you'll see too much volatility in the quarterly numbers.

Tables 17-38 and 17-39 show the relevant numbers for Buffalo and Strayer.

TABLE 17-38   Annual Depreciation and Capital Expenditures for Buffalo Wild Wings (in Millions of Dollars)

	2005	2006	2007	2008
Depreciation	11.8	14.5	17.0	23.4
Capital Expenditures	21.9	23.8	41.4	67.4

TABLE 17-39   Annual Depreciation and Capital Expenditures for Strayer Education (in Millions of Dollars)

	2005	2006	2007	2008
Depreciation	6.6	7.1	8.5	10.8
Capital Expenditures	12.3	13.2	14.9	20.7

Both Buffalo and Strayer are rapidly expanding and spending much more for capital expenditures than they are depreciating, so there are no depreciation/capital expenditure yellow flags.

Income Tax Rate

Most corporations pay federal income taxes amounting to 35 to 40 percent of pretax income. Unusually low income tax rates can temporarily boost reported earnings.

Table 17-40 shows recent annual corporate income tax rates for Buffalo and Strayer.

TABLE 17-40   Corporate Income Tax Rates for Buffalo Wild Wings and Strayer Education

Company	2004	2005	2006	2007	2008
Buffalo	36%	38%	32%	31%	33%
Strayer	39%	38%	38%	38%	38%

Strayer pays higher taxes, but both firms' recent tax rates were within historical norms. Rates normally vary somewhat from year to year. Consider it a yellow flag if the recent rate is 15 percent or more below historical rates (such as 29 percent versus 35 percent).

Consult the management's discussion in the annual report if the tax rate is abnormally low. It's not a problem if management expects rates to remain low.

Step 10: Ownership

The percentage of shares outstanding owned by institutions and by insiders are both important factors for growth investors to consider.

Institutional Ownership

Strong institutional ownership means that wired-in investors have analyzed your candidate and liked what they saw. Low institutional ownership signals that they saw something they didn't like. Stocks with institutional ownership exceeding 40 percent of outstanding shares are your best bet. Avoid stocks if institutions hold less than 30 percent.

In May 2009, institutional ownership amounted to 77 percent of shares outstanding for Buffalo and 95 percent for Strayer.

Insider Ownership

Insider ownership levels exceeding 55 percent of shares outstanding could indicate that investors with significant holdings are waiting for the opportunity to sell their shares. If insiders hold more than 55 percent, use MSN Money's Ownership report to see who holds the shares.

It may not be a problem if company founders hold most of the shares. It *is* a problem if private equity investors are major holders.

In May 2009, insiders held 7 percent of Buffalo's outstanding shares and 5 percent of Strayer's shares outstanding.

Step 11: Price Chart

Check the price chart before you buy. Growth stocks should be in an uptrend, meaning that the current price should be above both its 50-day and 200-day moving averages. According to some charting mavens, the ideal buy point is when the 50-day MA has recently moved above the 200-day MA. There is added risk if the stock has already made a big move up—that is, if the share price is more than 50 percent above its 200-day MA. You can see the MA data on Yahoo!'s Key Statistics report.

When I did the analysis, Buffalo, at $34.50, was trading 9 percent below its 50-day MA but 19 percent above its 200-day MA.

Strayer, at $193.00, was trading 7 percent above its 50-day MA but 2 percent below its 200-day MA.

Summary

Based on this analysis, both Buffalo Wild Wings and Strayer Education qualify as viable growth stock candidates. However, with Buffalo trading below its 50-day MA, and Strayer flirting with its 200-day MA, it would be wise to wait until their price charts look stronger before buying.

When to Sell

Growth stocks can drop quickly, and your first loss is often your best loss. Develop strict sell guidelines, and don't procrastinate when one of these guidelines is triggered.

Target Prices or the PEG Limit Are Exceeded

Review your target price assumptions before taking action. It may be that your original sales or price/sales range assumptions are out of date and can be revised.

Exceeding your target price means that the stock has entered a higher-risk zone, not that it won't go much higher. Growth stocks often develop strong momentum and go far beyond levels justified by fundamental analysis. You should have a profit at that point. Sell some or all of your position, depending on your risk tolerance and your ability to track the stock on a daily basis.

Any Red Flag

Fast-moving growth stocks crash and burn in response to any disappointment. You won't have time to react when it happens. Analyze the company after each quarterly report the same as if it were a new candidate, and sell on any red flag.

Lowered Sales or Earnings Forecasts

Sales or earnings forecasts reductions lead to lower share prices and are usually followed by more of the same. Your stock will already be down on this news, but it will probably head still lower. Don't procrastinate. Sell on any significant forecast reduction.

A Competitor Reduces Guidance or Misses a Forecast

When a company warns that it will miss forecasts, analysts usually advise that the problem is company-specific. But they are almost always wrong. All industry competitors face the same market conditions. If you own a competitor, consider it a gift that your stock wasn't hit first. Sell immediately.

Consecutive Negative Surprises

Two negative surprises in a row constitute a trend, regardless of their magnitude. Sell immediately. Things will only get worse.

Acquisitions

Sell if your company acquires another business that is at least 25 percent (sales or market capitalization) as large as the acquiring company. Also sell if the company makes a series of smaller acquisitions that, taken together, add up to 25 percent of the company's original size. In this instance, there's no rush to sell. It will take months before the market realizes that the acquisition was a big mistake.

Deteriorating Fundamentals

Sell if ROA, operating cash flow, or operating margins deteriorate significantly in two sequential quarters.

Restating Earlier Financials

Restating previously reported results downward is a red flag signaling future problems. Sell when a company significantly restates downward previously reported sales or earnings unless new management has taken over since the original misstatement.

Same-Store Sales Growth Declines

Same-store sales applies to retail stores and restaurants. It measures year-over-year sales growth at locations that have been operating for at least one year. Sales at newer locations don't count. For successful operators, same-store sales usually grow in the mid-single-digit range, but sometimes much higher. Negative same-store sales growth warns of future earnings misses. Sell retail stores or restaurants if same-store sales drop by any amount for two quarters in a row.

Sequential Large One-Time Charges

Repeated instances of significant nonrecurring charges tell you that management is scrambling to meet forecasts, and disaster looms. Sell the second time the company takes significant one-time (nonrecurring) charges.

Summary

As the saying "Trees don't grow to the sky" suggests, almost all growth stocks eventually fall short of expectations, triggering a 25 to 50 percent sell-off before you can react. Successful growth investors must learn to recognize the danger signals and sell before the news hits the street.

18

Analysis Scorecards

The value and growth analysis scorecards follow the same steps as the corresponding analysis chapters. Use the scorecards to document your conclusions while you are analyzing a candidate. You'll find both in this chapter, suitable for photocopying.

A single analysis step could involve multiple scorecard entries. For instance, Scorecard Step 4, Industry Analysis, includes two tests described in Chapter 7: Industry Growth and Industry Concentration.

The scorecards award points for desirable characteristics and subtract them for undesirable characteristics. Each test is worth a single point. But some tests can add or subtract a point, others can only add a point, and still others can only deduct a point. Some tests can disqualify a candidate from further consideration.

Generally, positive totals reflect strong candidates. But use the scorecard as a guide, not the final answer. It can't cover all the nuances of your research. Common sense should prevail over numeric scores.

After you've analyzed a firm, examine where your candidate lost points, and try to find similar companies without those weaknesses. For instance, look for a prospect with clean accounting if your candidate lost points in that area.

Save the scorecards whether or not you decide to buy the stock. You'll be amazed at how much you'll learn by reviewing your scorecards months later in light of the company's subsequent stock price performance.

Value Stock Analysis Scorecard

I'll use Paychex, the same company I used to illustrate the value analysis process, to describe how to score a value candidate.

Step 1: Analysts' Ratings and Forecasts

The best value prospects are stocks that stock analysts don't like much. The Sentiment Index reflects analysts' buy/sell ratings, and the scorecard rewards low sentiment scores. Paychex's Sentiment score was –8, which earned it 1 point on the scorecard.

The scorecard penalizes value candidates with high earnings growth forecasts and/or positive earnings growth forecast trends. Paychex's negative current year's earning growth forecast avoided a penalty point in that category. So Paychex scored 0 for earnings growth.

Since its current fiscal year earnings forecast trend was flat, Paychex also avoided an earnings growth forecast trend penalty point. Paychex scored 0 for earnings forecast trend.

So, Paychex earned 1 point for negative sentiment and avoided potential earnings forecast penalty points.

Step 2: Valuation

Value candidates' share prices should reflect low growth expectations. The scorecard rewards candidates with implied average annual earnings growth below 5 percent and penalizes those with implied growth exceeding 10 percent.

Paychex's 7 percent implied growth scored 0.

Step 3: Target Price

Buying at the right price is critical for successful value investing. The target price formula establishes a maximum buy price. But this is not a pass/fail test. If a stock is trading above its maximum buy, continue with the analysis. But don't buy the stock until it trades below its maximum buy price.

Paychex was trading above its maximum buy price when I did the target price analysis.

Step 4: Industry Analysis

Although high growth is okay, the best value candidates are in moderate-growth (9 percent to 14 percent) industries. Stagnant or declining industries are bad news. The scorecard penalizes firms in industries growing less than 3 percent annually and rewards firms in moderate-growth industries.

Paychex is in the computer services industry, which is expected to grow sales around 11 percent annually. Thus, Paychex scores 1 point for industry growth.

The scorecard also awards 1 point for candidates in concentrated industries. I evaluated Paychex's payroll-processing industry, having only a few players, as concentrated. Thus, Paychex also scores 1 point for this category.

Step 5: Business Plan

Transfer the business plan score computed during your analysis, up to a maximum of plus or minus 4 points, to the scorecard. Paychex's business plan score totaled +4. Thus, Paychex earned 4 points for business plan. If its business plan score were higher than 4, it would still score only 4 points.

Step 6: Management Quality

The right management can make a good company great, so the scorecard rewards companies with key executive and board quality that you graded as very good or excellent. Ineffective management's results will show up in other performance measures, and the scorecard doesn't deduct for low grades. I rated Paychex's management as acceptable, so it didn't earn a point for this test.

Most firms do have clean accounting and show reasonable earnings growth stability, so the scorecard penalizes those that don't pass these tests, but it doesn't reward those that do.

I rated Paychex's accounting as clean, and its earnings growth stability as excellent, so it didn't lose any points.

Step 7: Financial Health

Failing the appropriate financial health test disqualifies a candidate. I used the Detailed Fiscal Fitness Exam to analyze Paychex, and it passed. No points are associated with this test.

Step 8: Profitability

The best value candidates were highly profitable before they stumbled and can be expected to return to previous profitability levels. The scorecard rewards firms with expected return on assets above 14 percent and penalizes those below 6 percent.

Paychex's recent ROAs in were in the 10 percent range, above the 8 percent historical norm. I assumed that Paychex would continue to generate ROAs in the 8 to 10 percent range, so Paychex scored no points in this category.

Step 9: Red Flags

Since value candidates, by definition, are underperforming, the existence of balance sheet or revenue growth red flags does not affect the score.

But the depreciation versus capital expenditures yellow flag test does apply. Deduct 1 point if a stock fails this test. Paychex passed, so it scored 0 points for red flags.

Step 10: Ownership

Very high insider ownership spells risk, and this test penalizes firms in that category. Paychex's 11 percent insider ownership was far below the 55 percent limit, so Paychex wasn't penalized.

Step 11: Price Chart

A strong price chart indicates that your candidate's recovery prospects have already been recognized and it's probably too late to buy. This step penalizes firms with share prices 10 percent or more above their 200-day moving average.

Paychex was trading close to its 200-day MA when I did the analysis, so it wasn't penalized.

Summary

Paychex scored 7 points. Use these scores to compare candidates you are evaluating.

Value Stock Analysis Scorecard

Company_____ Date: _____

Step 1. Analysts' Ratings and Forecasts

Sentiment Index _____

Add 1 point for a Sentiment Index score below –3.

Subtract 1 point if the SI score is greater than 2.

Earnings Growth _____

Subtract 1 point for forecast YOY earnings growth over 4 %.

Earnings Forecast Trend _____

Subtract 1 point if EPS forecasts are up more than $0.01 in the last 90 days.

Step 2. Valuation

Implied Growth _____

Add 1 point for implied growth below 5%.

Subtract 1 point for implied growth above 10%.

Step 3. Target Price

Current Price Versus Target Buy Price

Do not buy if the current price is above the target buy price.

Step 4. Industry Analysis

Industry Growth _____

Add 1 point for an industry sales growth rate of 9%–14%.

Subtract 1 point if the industry growth rate is below 3%.

Industry Concentration _____

Add 1 point if the industry has less than five major competitors.

Step 5. Business Plan

Business Plan Score _____

Record the business plan score (maximum –4 to +4).

Step 6. Management Quality

Key Executive and Board Quality   _____

Add 1 point for quality rated very good or excellent.

Clean Accounting/Earnings Growth Stability   _____

Subtract 1 point for nonrecurring more than 3% of sales or poor earnings growth stability.

Step 7. Financial Health

Disqualify candidates that fail the appropriate test.

Step 8. Profitability

Expected Return on Assets   _____

Add 1 point for expected ROA over 14%.

Subtract 1 point for ROA below 6%.

Step 9. Red Flags

Historical Capital Expenses Versus Depreciation   _____

Subtract 1 point for a depreciation /capital expenditures yellow flag.

Step 10. Ownership

Total Insider Ownership   _____

Subtract 1 point if insider ownership is above 55%.

Step 11. Price Chart

Share Price Versus Moving Average   _____

Subtract 1 point if the share price is more than 10% above the 200-day MA.

Total   _____

Growth Stock Analysis Scorecard

I'll use restaurant operator Buffalo Wild Wings to describe how to fill out the growth stock scorecard.

Step 1: Analysts' Ratings and Forecasts

The best growth candidates have relatively moderate sentiment scores and strong earnings growth prospects.

The scorecard rewards firms with sentiment scores in the 0 to +4 range and penalizes stocks with scores below –3 (too weak) and above 8 (too strong).

The scorecard also penalizes companies with forecast annual earnings growth below 15 percent.

Negative earnings forecast trends or a history of negative earnings surprises automatically disqualify growth candidates.

Buffalo's –3 sentiment score earned it 0 points in that category. Its 26 percent forecast current fiscal year earnings growth was sufficient to avoid a growth penalty point.

Buffalo's earnings forecasts were trending up, and its surprise history was acceptable. Thus, Buffalo passed the earnings forecast trend and earnings surprise checks.

Step 2: Valuation

In the growth stock world, moderately overvalued stocks tend to outperform undervalued stocks. That said, momentum often pushes growth stocks up to unrealistic valuations.

This test rewards stocks trading at PEGs of 1.1 to 1.4 with 1 point and penalizes stocks 1 point that are trading at PEGs above 2.0.

Buffalo's 0.9 PEG earned it 0 points.

Step 3: Target Price

Growth stocks often trade at prices not justified by fundamentals. This test penalizes stocks 1 point when they are trading within or above their target sell price range.

Buffalo was trading below its low target sell price. Thus, it was not penalized and scored 0 points for this test.

Step 4: Industry Analysis

Good growth candidates are often found in fast-growing, concentrated industries. This test rewards firms in industries growing faster than 20 percent and penalizes those in industries growing less than 10 percent annually. Firms in concentrated industries earn another point, but since most industries don't fit that description, firms in fragmented industries aren't penalized.

I estimated Buffalo's restaurant industry growth at 11 percent, so it did not earn or lose a point in that category.

Since Buffalo operates in a fragmented industry, it also earned 0 points in that category.

Step 5: Business Plan

Transfer the business plan score computed during your analysis, up to a maximum plus or minus 4 points, to the scorecard.

Buffalo's business plan score of 4 earned it 4 points in this category.

Step 6: Management Quality

Growth and value investors alike benefit by picking firms with quality management. The scorecard rewards companies with key executive and board quality that you graded as very good or excellent. It does not deduct points for poor management.

I rated Buffalo's management and board quality as fair, so Buffalo did not earn a point for management quality.

Since clean accounting and reasonable, stable earnings growth are the norm, the scorecard deducts 1 point for companies that fail this test. Firms that pass get 0.

I rated Buffalo's accounting as clean, and its earnings growth was consistent, so it wasn't penalized.

Step 7: Financial Health

Failing the appropriate financial health test disqualifies a candidate. Buffalo qualified for the busted cash burners test and passed.

Step 8: Profitability

Strong sales growth and profit margins are hallmarks of promising growth candidates. The sales growth test rewards firms with growth exceeding 25 percent and penalizes those growing slower than 15 percent.

Similarly, the return-on-assets test rewards firms with ROA above 14 percent and penalizes those with ROA below 6 percent.

Deteriorating operating margins warn of future problems. Significant margin declines disqualify candidates. By the same token, persistent cash burners are riskier investments than cash generators and are also disqualified.

Buffalo's recent 30 percent year-over-year sales growth earned it 1 point in that category.

Buffalo's operating margin had been trending up, not down. Since Buffalo consistently generated positive cash flow, it passed both the operating margin and cash flow tests and hence was not disqualified.

Buffalo's consistent 10 percent return on assets fell short of the number needed to earn a point in the profitability category.

Step 9: Red Flags

Red flags warn of a future growth slowdown, which is bad news for growth stocks. Hence, any red flag disqualifies a growth candidate.

Yellow flags pointing to longer-term problems signify added risk but don't necessarily disqualify a stock. Subtract 1 point for each yellow flag found.

My analysis revealed no red flags for Buffalo, so it was not disqualified.

Similarly, I also found no yellow flags for Buffalo, so it did not lose any points in this category.

Step 10: Ownership

Institutional buyers, such a mutual funds, usually load up on growth stocks. It's a danger sign if they don't.

The institutional ownership test disqualifies growth candidates with less than 30 percent institutional ownership.

Very high insider ownership may be a tip-off that big shareholders are waiting for an opportunity to unload their holdings. The scorecard penalizes firms 1 point if they have more than 55 percent insider ownership.

When I checked, since institutions owned 77 percent of Buffalo's shares, it passed the institutional ownership test and wasn't disqualified.

Since insider ownership totaled 7 percent of shares outstanding, Buffalo did not lose a point in that category.

Step 11: Price Chart

Growth stocks should be moving up in price, not down. Nevertheless, stocks trading far above their 200-day moving averages are riskier than stocks that have just begun their move.

To avoid weak stocks, the scorecard penalizes stocks 1 point if they are trading below their 200-day moving average.

To avoid stocks that may have moved up too fast, the scorecard also penalizes stocks 1 point if they are trading more than 50 percent above their 200-day MA.

When I checked, Buffalo was trading 19 percent above its 200-day moving average, so it passed both checks and was not penalized.

Summary

Buffalo's score totaled 5 points, but the score by itself has little meaning. Instead, these scores are meant to help you compare various candidates you are evaluating.

Growth Stock Analysis Scorecard

Company_____ Date: _____

Step 1. Analysts' Ratings and Forecasts

Sentiment Score   _____

Add 1 point for score 0 to 4. Subtract 1 point for score below –3 or above 8.

Earnings Growth   _____

Subtract 1 point if forecast YOY EPS growth is below 15%.

Earnings Forecast Trend

Disqualify if the current FY EPS trend is down $0.03 or more.

Earnings Surprise History

Disqualify if two of the last four earnings surprises negative.

Step 2. Valuation   _____

Add 1 point for PEG 1.1 to 1.4. Subtract 1 point for PEG above 2.0.

Step 3. Target Price   _____

Subtract 1 point if the current price exceeds the low target buy price.

Step 4. Industry Analysis

Industry Growth   _____

Add 1 point if the growth rate exceeds 20%.

Subtract 1 point if less than 10%.

Industry Concentration   _____

Add 1 point if the industry has fewer than five major competitors.

Step 5. Business Plan   _____

Record the business plan score (maximum: –4 to +4).

Step 6. Management Quality

Key Executive and Board Quality   _____

Add 1 point if key executive and board quality are rated very good or excellent.

Clean Accounting/Earnings Growth Stability   _____

Subtract 1 point if nonrecurring exceeds 3% of sales or poor EPS stability.

Step 7. Financial Health

Disqualify candidates that fail an appropriate test.

Step 8. Profitability

Sales Growth _____

Add 1 point if YOY sales growth exceeds 25%.

Subtract 1 point if below 15%.

Operating Margins

Disqualify candidate if operating margins are deteriorating.

Return on Assets _____

Add 1 point if ROA exceeds 14%.

Subtract 1 point if ROA is below 6%.

Operating Cash Flow

Disqualify if OCF was negative in two of the last three fiscal years.

Step 9. Red Flags

Red Flags

Disqualify if any red flags are detected.

Yellow Flags _____

Subtract 1 point for each yellow flag.

Step 10. Ownership

Institutional Ownership

Disqualify if institutional ownership is below 30%.

Insider Ownership _____

Subtract 1 point if insider ownership is above 55%.

Step 11. Price Chart

Share Price Versus Moving Average _____

Subtract 1 point if price is below 200-day MA or more than 50% above.

Total _____

Part IV

Appendixes

Appendix A _____

Industry Information

Analyzing a stock requires staying on top of trends in that industry and figuring out where the company fits into the big picture. Here are some websites where you can find that info:

ABA Banking Online (www.banking.com/aba), published by the American Bankers Association, offers news on and analysis of banking industry trends.

Access Control & Security Systems (www.securitysolutions. com) covers the security industry, including access control, identification, and intrusion detection systems. The site features dozens of recent news stories and feature articles that may give you some good investing ideas. You can also find companies active in a particular sector, such as facial recognition systems. Do that by selecting Research & Tools, clicking Supplier Directory, and selecting Security.

Advertising Age (www.adage.com), although ostensibly about the advertising business, keeps you tuned into the buzz about many industries.

American Printer (www.americanprinter.com) covers the traditional printing and quick-print industries.

Apparel (www.apparelmag.com) focuses on business and technology issues affecting the clothing industry.

Biotech (www.biospace.com) is the place to go for biotech industry news. Especially interesting in that regard is the Clinical Development News, accessed from the Investors section. Pay most attention to the Phase III section. The approval cycle for new drugs can drag on for years. News coming out of Phase III trials (the final phase) can signal big stock moves in either direction.

Byte and Switch (www.byteandswitch.com) contains news about the storage networking industry.

Capital Link Shipping (http://shipping.capitallink.com) is a good place to find profiles of and news headlines for all types of ocean shipping companies, including dry-bulk, LNG/LNG, tanker, and container shippers. It shows current and historical charter day rates for dry-bulk and crude oil tankers. Check the Industry Reports section for analysis reports that I haven't seen anywhere else.

Chain Drug Review (www.chaindrugreview.com) is where you can keep up with the drugstore industry.

Chain Store Age (www.chainstoreage.com) is a good place to research trends in retailing, as well as firms that supply hardware, such as computers and checkout systems, to retail stores.

Dental Economics (http://de.pennet.com) is where you can learn about new products aimed at dentists.

DrugTopics.com (www.drugtopics.com) is the online version of *Drug Topics* magazine. Although targeted toward pharmacists, it's a good, easy-to-understand source of news about the pharmaceutical industry.

Edmunds AutoObserver (www.autoobserver.com) is the place to keep up with news about the global auto industry.

Energy Information Administration (www.eia.doe.gov), a U.S. government agency site, has all sorts of data about petroleum, natural gas, and electricity production, supplies, and usage. Check here for current and historical prices for coal, crude oil, gasoline, and heating oil. You also can find crude oil price forecasts, as well as historical and forecast energy consumption figures through 2030.

Energy Pulse (www.energypulse.net/centers) is dedicated to providing commentary on the global power industry. Very good!

Farm Industry News (www.farmindustrynews.com) contains news and views on farming and, more importantly, farm equipment suppliers.

Food Navigator.com (www.foodnavigator-usa.com) is the best source of news about food and beverage development. Its strongest point is its coverage of the science and nutrition aspects of food development, which is where all the industry action is these days.

Food Processing Magazine (www.foodprocessing.com) contains news and feature articles about food makers and grocery stores.

Health Data Management (www.healthdatamanagement.com) covers how the healthcare industry is rapidly embracing information systems to reduce paperwork and improve patient care. New systems allow a consulting doctor anywhere in the world to view a patient's medical history, lab results, current condition, and treatment plans. HDM is written for healthcare executives responsible for implementing these types of systems. It's a good resource for investors interested in companies serving this market.

Insurance Journal (www.insurancejournal.com) covers the insurance industry and its suppliers.

Light Reading (www.lightreading.com) contains optical networking news and analysis. This website is good at explaining the various technologies and, even better, naming the important players in each sector.

Modern Healthcare (www.modernhealthcare.com) is a good resource for investors interested in the healthcare field, including medical equipment makers. Covers hospitals, clinics, drugstores, and their suppliers.

National Real Estate Investor (www.nreionline.com) contains news and analysis about commercial real estate, including multifamily and real estate investment trusts (REITs).

Nation's Restaurant News (www.nrn.com) provides excellent coverage of the restaurant industry, especially from an investor's perspective.

News Directory (www.newsdirectory.com) is a good resource for finding trade magazines. Select Browse Magazines and click Industry Trade Publications to see a list of more than 70 U.S.-based trade magazines.

North American Windpower (www.nawindpower.com) contains news and analysis about the wind power industry, focusing on North America.

Oil & Gas Investor (www.oilandgasinvestor.com) is primarily a subscription magazine, but it offers a considerable amount of free information.

Oil & Gas Journal (http://ogj.pennnet.com) is full of news and research about all facets of the oil and gas industry, including exploration, drilling, production, and processing.

Outsourcing Center (www.outsourcing-center.com) monitors outsourcing—the practice of reducing costs by farming out tasks such as manufacturing and customer support call centers to third parties. This website covers both sides of outsourcing—the third-party contractors as well as the firms that farm out the work. Outsourcing is one of the fastest-growing business trends. As an investor, you can benefit by spotting companies that are improving their competitive position by outsourcing as well as by pinpointing publicly traded contractors benefiting from the trend.

The Register (www.theregister.co.uk) is a U.K.-based site. Its logo, "Biting the hand that feeds it," describes its intentionally provocative approach. The Register covers technology with mostly original stories. It's not a techie magazine; it focuses on the business side of the industry. The Register is always interesting, but sometimes it gets things wrong.

Retail Traffic Magazine (www.retailtrafficmag.com) covers trends affecting retail chains and large shopping malls. RTM's focus on interpreting rather than just presenting news makes it especially useful for investors interested in shopping center REITs (real estate investment trusts).

RFID Journal (www.rfidjournal.com) describes RFID (radio frequency identification), a new technology that may someday replace the ubiquitous barcode system. This free magazine has everything you'd want to know about RFID, including the scoop on what all the industry players are doing.

SolarBuzz (www.solarbuzz.com) is the place for news and commentary about the solar energy industry.

SteelGuru (www.steelguru.com), although targeted mostly toward people working in the steel industry, is a good source of industry news.

TechNewsWorld.com (www.technewsworld.com) is a good resource for analysis of happenings in the tech world.

Tech Web (www.techweb.com) contains news and features covering a wide range of computer and communications sectors.

Telecommunications Online (www.telecommagazine.com) is oriented toward industry professionals, sometimes going into more detail than you want to know.

TortoWheaton Research (http://tortowheatonresearch.com) is a research outfit specializing in office and industrial real estate. Most of its reports cost big bucks, but TWR's weekly About Real Estate column is free and very informative.

Transport Topics (www.ttnews.com) is the place to keep up with happenings in the trucking industry.

VerticalNet (www.verticalnet.com) contains links to more than 60 separate sites, each covering a different industry. The thrust here is facilitating e-commerce between industry players, but the sites are a good source of industry news. Each offers a free e-mail newsletter.

Yahoo!'s Industry Center (http://finance.yahoo.com) is a good place to start your industry analysis. For each major industry, Yahoo! lists the top 10 companies by market capitalization, recent news stories, a calendar of upcoming earnings reports, and a list of recent analyst upgrades and downgrades for firms in the industry. Especially valuable are the industry profiles, accessed from a link at the bottom of each industry overview page.

Wards Auto World (www.wardsdealer.com) covers the automobile industry, mostly from the dealers' perspective.

Waste Age (www.wasteage.com) contains news and analysis about the recycling and waste-removal industries.

Wind Power Monthly (http://windpower-monthly.com) contains news and analysis about the wind-power industry from a global perspective.

WorldOil.com (www.worldoil.com) contains news, in-depth reports, current prices, and forecasts. It's hard to imagine what you'd want to know about the oil industry that you couldn't find here.

Appendix B _____

Economic Data

In case you want to try your hand at predicting the economy, this appendix lists free web resources that will help you do the job:

Bureau of Labor Statistics (http://stats.bls.gov) is the best source of data on U.S. employment, consumer spending, and inflation.

Chain Store Age's (www.chainstoreage.com) Weekly Leading Indicator report gives you a timely heads-up on how retail sales are going.

Conference Board (www.conference-board.org) is a source of consumer confidence survey information.

Department of Commerce Bureau of Economic Analysis (www.bea.gov) is a good source of detailed U.S. economic data, including gross domestic product (GDP), personal income, corporate profits, balance of payments, and more.

Economagic.com (www.economagic.com) provides a huge assortment of economic data. Even better, you can graph all the data.

EconomicIndicators.gov (www.economicindicators.gov) lists the next release dates of and gives links to the latest reports for 18 or so economic indicators such as new residential construction and retail e-commerce sales that are compiled by U.S. government agencies. You can also sign up to receive the reports by e-mail the day they are released.

Federal Reserve (www.federalreserve.gov) is the center of the economic universe. You can see the minutes from the discount rate meetings going back to 1996, as well as the legendary Beige Book reports describing economic conditions in each of the 12 Federal Reserve districts.

FedStats (www.fedstats.gov) is a directory of where to find economic statistics collected by more than 100 U.S. government agencies. It's a good place to start your search for the amazing amount of data collected by the feds. It's fun to just poke around.

Financial Forecast Center (http://forecasts.org) features computer-generated forecasts of interest rates, stock market indexes, retail sales, and much more. The six-month forecasts are free, but longer forecasts require a subscription.

Financial Trend Forecaster (www.fintrend.com) is home of the Moore Inflation Predictor, which claims a 90 percent accuracy rate for predicting the inflation rate one year into the future.

Gallup (www.galluppoll.com) measures investor optimism monthly. Many analysts use investor optimism as a contrary indicator. That is, high optimism levels suggest that the market is headed for a fall, and vice versa.

National Association of Home Builders (www.nahb.com) contains monthly housing market forecasts, plus the Housing Market Index. Check out the Traffic of Prospective Buyers component of the index for a look into the future.

U.S. Courts (www.uscourts.gov) lists all bankruptcies, because they must be filed in a federal court. This is the place to find U.S. quarterly bankruptcy statistics.

U.S. Department of Labor (www.ows.doleta.gov) offers weekly unemployment reports.

Appendix C_____

Earnings Reports and Conference Calls

The SEC requires corporations to file quarterly reports within 45 days of each quarter's end and within 90 days of the fiscal year end. However, most companies issue a press release reporting their last quarter's earnings within a few weeks of the quarter's end. So the press release data may be all that you have to go on for some time.

Companies usually conduct an analysts' conference call within hours of the earnings release. Anyone can listen in on the conference call live or listen to a recording (via an Internet browser) for at least a month after the call. You can usually access the live call or the recording from the investors' section of the company's website.

All calls follow the same format. They begin with the CEO and CFO reading the contents of the earnings report, often filling in details not included in the press release, followed by a question-and-answer period. The Q&A session is always the most informative part of the call. Usually only analysts are allowed to ask questions.

Pay attention not only to the answers, but also to how the analyst who asked the question reacts to the answer. Often, the analyst's skepticism will be your first clue that the company's position doesn't compute.

Sometimes an astute question reveals surprising information. For instance, in one call, I learned that a key employee had years earlier been CEO of a company accused of Medicare fraud. That was significant news, because his current employer was then denying the same charge.

Some pundits believe you can get a sense of management quality from how key executives handle tough questions. But that doesn't work. Often the smoothest talkers are the biggest crooks. Don't think you can judge a person's integrity by the tone, timbre, and sincerity conveyed by his or her voice. You can't. You'll do best by focusing on the numbers.

Always analyze the most recent quarter's data, even if the company is also reporting its fiscal year results. Use the analysis strategies described in Chapter 12. The following sections give you some pointers.

Reported Earnings

Many firms report two earnings numbers: pro forma, operating, or similar vague terms, and earnings according to generally accepted accounting principles (GAAP).

Pro Forma

The reported pro forma or operating earnings typically exclude costs or income that management considers nonrecurring. In my experience, most firms are not trying to deceive investors when they report pro forma earnings. Instead, they are presenting numbers they believe are the most useful for evaluating the firm's results and fundamental outlook.

However, that is not always the case. Currently, many firms are excluding employee stock option expenses from pro forma earnings. You may argue whether those are real expenses, but they are certainly recurring costs. Other firms habitually exclude items that to a casual observer sound like part of the normal costs of doing business.

Unfortunately, many analysts accept management's word about what's recurring and what isn't. They compare the firm's pro forma earnings numbers to their forecasts when deciding whether the company beat estimates. In many cases, you'll find that even though the media reported that a company met or exceeded analysts' forecasts, in fact it didn't.

Nevertheless, the share price initially responds to the perceived surprise, which is the difference between analysts' consensus forecasts and the pro forma earnings headlined in the company's press release.

Generally Accepted Accounting Principles (GAAP)

GAAP earnings are calculated using standardized accounting rules called "generally accepted accounting principles." The SEC requires reporting firms to include the GAAP earnings in their quarterly reports. Most earnings report press releases include a complete GAAP income statement and at least some balance sheet items. Some companies even include a statement of cash flows in the release.

Ignore the pro forma reports and focus on the GAAP financial statements. The following sections tell you what to look for.

Sales

Did the reported sales meet forecasts? Compare the just-reported year-over-year sales growth to the year-ago figure. A significant sales growth slowdown is a red flag.

Operating Margin

Compare the just-reported quarter's operating margin to the year-ago margin. The year-ago income statement figures are always listed in a column next to the just-reported quarter.

A significant decline in operating margin is a red flag. Don't be swayed by management's reasonable-sounding excuse for the under-performance. Examine the income statement to determine the reason.

A decline in gross margins signals either rising costs or price cuts triggered by a weakening competitive position. A rise in SG&A (overhead) expense could signal rising advertising costs necessitated by a tougher competitive environment or that costs are spinning out of control.

One of the few justifiable reasons for falling operating margins is higher research and development expenses connected with new-product development.

Receivables and Inventories

Compute the percentages of sales for accounts receivable and inventory levels, and compare them to the year-ago figures. You will probably need to get the year-ago balance sheet items from a financial website. Typically, the press release lists only the recent quarter and last fiscal year-end numbers.

Either receivables or inventories growing significantly faster than sales is a potential red flag that calls for further investigation.

Guidance

Many firms routinely include future quarters' sales and earnings forecasts (guidance) with their earnings reports or in the conference calls that follow. Most analysts change their forecasts accordingly. Compare the new guidance to prior forecasts. Pay particular attention to the next two quarters' sales forecasts. Any significant reduction is a red flag.

Analysts' Research

Analysts following the company usually publish their take on the company's earnings report within a day or two. Most are predictable. They reduce their forecasts in response to bad news and vice versa. However, some point out information you didn't notice or interpret the results in a way that didn't occur to you. Check out as many analysts' reports as possible before reacting to the earnings report.

Summary

Listening to the conference call, carefully analyzing the press release, and reviewing analysts' interpretation of the earnings report can give you a heads-up on potential problems or improving performance weeks before the SEC reports become available.

If your analysis raises red flags, act as soon as you've confirmed your findings. If your analysis is correct, the company may announce reduced guidance well in advance of its next quarterly report.

Appendix D

Detecting Scams, Frauds, and Pump and Dump

If you're like me, you probably get frequent e-mails from people you don't know, advising you to buy stocks you've never heard of. These missives read like research reports from professional stock market analysts, profiling companies that have just developed exciting new products or services with huge market potential.

For instance, recently my new friends sent me tips about the following:

- A "renowned" computer maker that that was just about to introduce a line of laptops with astounding features that no other company could match
- A company about to introduce emergency 911 services for Internet-based long-distance telephone services
- A company that just successfully completed testing of a product that allows shipping of M&Ms candy by UPS instead of by refrigerated truck

I know that these stock-hyping e-mails work, because occasionally sI check the touted stock's trading volume. Typically, the number of shares traded daily jumps by a factor of 5 or more for days after the e-mail.

The stories are always enticing. With dirt-cheap share prices, we could quit our day jobs if we got lucky and just one of those stocks took off. Alas, all too often those exciting stories are just that—stories made up to support a "pump-and-dump" scheme.

In pump and dump, promoters gain control of large blocks of shares of a small, probably dormant public company. The promoters "pump" the stock by issuing copious press releases announcing the firm's entry into a variety of promising businesses.

These press releases become fodder for phony analyst reports circulated via e-mail and on websites that are in the business of publicizing stocks for a fee, regardless of the fundamental prospects.

The resulting publicity creates demand for shares, giving the promoters an opportunity to dump their holdings. Eventually, the promoters sell out and stop "pumping," and the shares again become virtually worthless.

But even if they are not pump-and-dump promotions, many cheap stocks have good stories to tell but little chance of success.

Fortunately, it's easy to spot those risky critters. This appendix describes six checks you can use to quickly rule out dangerous stocks, whether pump-and-dumpers or just bad ideas. You can find the needed data on Yahoo!'s Key Statistics report or on numerous other financial websites. You don't need to tabulate the scores. Rule out any stock that flunks any single check.

Before you start, you should know that many dangerous stocks have never filed financial reports with the Securities and Exchange Commission. If any of the data points required for these checks are unavailable, assume that the company has not filed SEC reports. These are imaginary companies. Rule out all such stocks.

Rule #1: Last Price Is More Than $0.50

Most stocks worth your attention trade at $5 or higher. Stocks trading below that level are called "penny stocks," and risk-averse investors won't touch them.

That said, although it's risky territory, there are solid businesses with stocks trading in the $3 to $4 per share range, and sometimes lower. However, the lower you go in terms of share price, the greater your chances of encountering bad ideas. Once you get down to $0.50 per share, in my experience, the odds are overwhelmingly against you.

There's no point in wasting your time researching these stocks. Rule out all stocks trading below $0.50 per share.

Rule #2: Trailing 12 Months (TTM) Sales of at Least $25 Million

Most bad idea stocks have recorded few or no sales. Instead, they've issued numerous press releases announcing exciting new products and deals with distributors around the world to sell those products. Somehow, those great new products never make it to the marketplace, and the distribution deals never result in significant sales.

Most publicly traded companies with real businesses record annual sales of at least $50 million and usually $100 million or more. Rule out firms with less than $25 million in sales over the four quarters (12 months).

Rule #3: Market Capitalization of at Least $50 Million

Market capitalization is how much you'd have to pay to buy all of a company's outstanding shares. Generally speaking, the lower the market cap, the riskier the stock. Risk-averse investors typically avoid stocks with market caps below $1 billion, and most savvy investors rule out stocks with market caps below $200 million or so.

That said, requiring a minimum $50 million market cap should be sufficient to rule out pump-and-dump stocks and other bad ideas. Avoid stocks with market caps below $50 million.

Rule #4: Institutional Ownership of at Least 5 Percent

Institutions are mutual funds, hedge funds, pension plans, and other large investors. Because they generate huge trading commissions, these big players are more wired into the market than you and I could ever hope to be. No publicly traded stock escapes their attention. Thus, if institutions don't own a stock, it's because most don't think they can make money doing so.

Institutional ownership is the percentage of a firm's outstanding shares held by the big players. Typically it runs in the 30-to-95 percent range. Anything below 25 percent is probably a bad idea. However, setting the minimum at 5 percent is good enough to rule out stocks with imaginary businesses. Avoid stocks with institutional ownership below 5 percent.

Rule #5: Debt/Equity Ratio of Less Than 3

Since they incur expenses but have no income, pump-and-dump stocks and other bad ideas typically carry high debt. The debt/equity ratio compares long-term debt to shareholders' equity. A 0 ratio signals no debt. The higher the ratio, the higher the debt. Usually, ratios above 1.0 signal high debt. However, setting the maximum at 3.0 should be sufficient to rule out dangerous stocks that somehow passed the other tests.

Rule #6: Maximum Price/Book Ratio of 30

The price/book ratio compares the recent share price to book value, which is shareholders' equity expressed on a per-share basis. Since bad idea stocks typically record few or no sales or earnings, the price/book ratio is the only useful valuation gauge. For most stocks, price/book ratios range from below 1 for value-priced stocks to 20 or so for in-favor growth stocks.

Since they have no significant assets, the price/book ratios for dangerous stocks are extraordinarily high. I set the maximum allowable P/B at 30. Stocks with ratios that high are a bad idea. Rule out stocks with a price/book ratio above 30.

Summary

These six tests should rule out stocks that have no real businesses. But that's all they do. Passing these tests doesn't necessarily mean that you would make money owning these stocks. You must read Chapters 1 through 18 to find winning stocks.

Appendix E _____

How to Read Financial Statements

The SEC requires that public corporations submit financial statements four times a year (quarterly). Quarterly reports (10Q) must be filed within 45 days of the end of each quarter, and a 10K (annual) report is required within 90 days of the end of the company's fiscal year.

The SEC reports are filed in electronic format and are immediately available on the SEC's EDGAR database (www.sec.gov). Anyone can access the SEC database directly. You can also access the reports via financial websites, such as Yahoo! and MSN Money.

Data services, such as Reuters, compile the EDGAR data into more user-friendly formats for display on major financial sites. These reports typically display the five most recent quarters or years on one page to facilitate comparisons.

Since many firms file their SEC reports days or weeks after they've issued the quarterly report press release, Reuters and other compilers temporarily update their reports using press release data in the interim.

The SEC requires three financial statements in each quarterly and annual report:

- The **income statement** shows sales, expenses, net income, and per-share earnings for the period.
- The **balance sheet** is a snapshot showing the financial condition as of the last business day of the reporting period.
- The **cash flow statement** shows the year-to-date changes in cash positions.

Income Statement

The income statement, sometimes called the profit-and-loss statement, lists sales and expenses for the quarter or fiscal year and for the year-ago period. The following terms typically appear on the income statement:

- **Revenues** are total sales for the period. Some firms list revenues separately for main business categories.

- **Cost of sales** is the direct material and labor costs of making or acquiring the products sold. For manufacturing firms, cost of sales includes depreciation and amortization of assets used for production. Cost of sales does not include marketing, R&D, or other indirect costs.

- **Gross profit** is revenues minus cost of sales.

- **Research and development** are the costs of developing new products and services.

- **Sales and marketing expenses** often are combined with general and administrative costs.

- **General and administrative** are all other expenses that are not listed separately.

- **Depreciation and amortization** are noncash accounting entries. Depreciation represents the theoretical loss in value of hard assets such as buildings and machinery over the reporting period. Amortization represents the theoretical loss in value of intangible assets such as trade secrets, patents, and trademarks during the reporting period.

- **Interest expense** is interest on loans acquired to finance the firm's main business.

- **Total operating expenses** are the total of all expenses just listed, including cost of sales.

- **Operating income** is revenues less operating expenses, also known as EBIT.

- **Interest income/expense** is interest income or expenses not associated with the company's main business.

- **Income before tax** is operating income less interest expense.

- **Income tax** is taxes (not necessarily paid) due for the period.

- **Net income** is "income before tax" less income tax. This is the bottom-line net profit.
- **Average number of shares** is the average number of shares outstanding during the period.
- **Earnings per share** is net income divided by the average number of shares.

Balance Sheet

The balance sheet includes three separate categories: assets, liabilities, and shareholders' equity. Accounting rules require that assets must equal liabilities plus shareholders' equity. Assets typically exceed liabilities, making shareholders' equity a positive number. However, shareholders' equity is negative when liabilities exceed assets.

Both assets and liabilities are divided into two sections: current and long-term.

Current assets include cash, accounts receivables, inventories, and prepaid expenses. Long-term assets include buildings, equipment, long-term investments, and goodwill.

Current liabilities are short-term debts such as accounts payable, short-term loans, the current portion (due this year) of long-term debts, lease obligations, and the like. Long-term debt includes lease obligations as well as bond obligations and other long-term loans.

Current Assets

- **Cash and equivalents** are cash and highly liquid fixed-income investments with maturities of three months or less.
- **Short-term investments** are stocks and other liquid securities.
- **Accounts receivable** is money owed to the company by customers for products received.
- **Inventory** is raw materials, work in process, and finished products.

Long-Term Assets

- **Property, plant, and equipment** are all hard assets such as buildings, airplanes, and machinery.
- **Goodwill** is a product of an acquisition. Goodwill is the difference between the purchase price and the book value of the acquired company.
- **Intangibles** include intellectul property, such as patents, trademarks, and trade secrets.
- **Long-term investments** are investments that the firm plans to hold for more than one year, such as stocks and bonds of other companies.

Current Liabilities

- **Accounts payable** are amounts owed to suppliers, consultants, contractors, and so on.
- **Accrued expenses** are similar to accounts payable.
- **Short-term debt** is borrowings that must be repaid within one year.
- **Current portion LT debt** is the portion of long-term debt principal and interest due within one year.
- **Capital leases** are lease payments due within one year.

Long-Term Debt

- **Long-term debt** includes bonds, notes, and other long-term credit.
- **Capital lease obligations:** If a company signs a 10-year lease, the entire 12 months' payments are considered a short-term debt, and the remaining 9 years are shown as long-term debt.
- **Deferred income taxes** are taxes due but not yet paid.
- **Deferred anything:** Any income statement expense that hasn't been paid can go here.

- **Other liabilities** are other long-term obligations.
- **Total liabilities** are the total of all short- and long-term liabilities.

Shareholders' Equity

Retained earnings, nominal value of common stock, and a variety of other accounting entries go in this section to make total liabilities plus shareholders' equity equal total assets.

Statement of Cash Flows

This statement shows the cash generated or consumed by the company's business operations, and investing and financing activities. The cash flow statement has three sections:

- Operating activities
- Investing activities
- Financing activities

Unlike the quarterly income statement that lists each quarter's results separately, the quarterly cash flow statement lists fiscal year-to-date totals for each line item.

Operating Activities

The operating cash flow statement lists net income on the top line, adds back noncash accounting entries that reduced reported earnings, and subtracts real cash expenses that, according to accounting rules, weren't deducted from earnings.

- **Net income** is reported after-tax income.
- **Depreciation and amortization** reverses noncash D&A added to operating costs on the income statement. If the D&A charge wasn't listed as a separate line item on the income statement, it was added to cost of sales, thereby reducing the reported gross profit by the D&A amount.

- **Deferred taxes** are taxes deducted from income that have not yet been paid.

- **Stock-based compensation** is employee expenses deducted from income that was paid using company stock.

- **Deferred revenue** is revenues received that were not shown on the income statement, usually because they were for services not yet provided.

- **Accounts receivables and inventories:** These working-capital items are shown as negative numbers (subtracted) if their value increased during the period, and vice versa. If a company sells its receivables to a third party, a process called factoring, the amount received from the third party increases cash from operations.

- **Accounts payable** is added to operating cash flow if the monies owed increased and is subtracted if the accounts payable decreased during the period.

- **Cash from operations** is reported net income adjusted for operating cash flow line items. Some investors consider cash from operations to be the best measure of a firm's real earnings.

Investing Activities

Investing cash flow includes capital expenditures and other investments:

- **Capital expenditures** are net investments in buildings and equipment. Free cash flow, a frequently used term that does not appear on the cash flow statement, is operating cash flow less capital expenditures.

  Software development costs can be capitalized instead of appearing as a charge on the income statement. If that happens, the capitalized software expenditures are listed in investing activities. Companies capitalizing software development will report higher operating cash flow than if they hadn't capitalized those costs.

- **Acquisitions** are cash flows resulting from the acquisition or sale of a subsidiary or partnership.

- **Purchase license:** Cisco Systems and probably others list a separate purchase license line item. Consider these and similar entries the same as capital expenditures when computing free cash flow.
- **Purchase and sales of investments** are investments not directly related to the company's main business.

Financing Activities

This is money raised from the sale of the company's own stock as well as the net of new debt versus paid-down debts and dividends paid out.

Net Change in Cash

This line lists the net effect of operating, investing, and financing activities to the company's total cash position.

Finding the Data

The financial statements included with the SEC reports offer more details than the statements provided on most websites. However, financial websites usually present the data in a format better suited to analysis. For instance, most display several quarters, or years, side by side, making it easier to spot trends.

Smart Money (www.smartmoney.com), Forbes (www.forbes.com), MarketWatch (www.marketwatch.com), and CNN Money (money.cnn.com) all list EBITDA as a separate line item on their income statements. This is a big help when you're analyzing financial strength (see Chapter 10).

Morningstar is the only site I've found that displays trailing 12 months (TTM) operating cash flow, a number needed for our busted cash burner analysis (see Chapter 10).

Pro Forma Accounting Versus GAAP

The income, balance sheet, and cash flow statements included in SEC reports and displayed on financial sites all conform to generally accepted accounting principles (GAAP).

However, many companies headline "pro forma" results in their quarterly report press releases. Originally, pro forma meant "as if" and was mainly employed to present the results of recently merged companies as if they had always been a single company. Now, companies use the term to mean financial statements that they feel more accurately portray their operations than the GAAP numbers. Whether they do or not is subject to discussion. However, most analysts use the pro forma formulas to formulate their earnings forecasts. Thus, at report time, the difference between forecast and actual pro forma earnings determines whether the company met, beat, or fell short of analysts' forecasts. Since the analysts' earnings forecasts don't match GAAP earnings, you can't compare forecast EPS to historical values found on GAAP financial statements.

Appendix F _____

Glossary

accounts receivable
Money owed by customers for received goods or services. Customers must have been billed for items to be included in receivables.

analyst
Someone who publishes buy/hold/sell recommendations and earnings forecasts for a stock. Buy-side analysts work for institutional buyers, and sell-side analysts work for brokerages or investment banking houses.

balance sheet
A financial statement listing a company's assets (what it owns) and liabilities (what it owes) as of a specific date, usually the last day of a company's fiscal quarter.

bond
A long-term promissory note issued by a corporation.

bond rating
A grade evaluating the quality of a bond. AAA is generally the highest or most creditworthy rating.

book value
Total shareholders' equity from the balance sheet divided by the number of shares outstanding.

capitalization-weighted
The largest companies in terms of market capitalization influence an index or other calculation the most.

capitalize

Costs of items such as buildings, equipment, and other items with a useful lifetime exceeding one year are categorized as assets to be depreciated over a number of years, rather than being expensed in the year of purchase.

cash burner

A firm consistently reporting negative operating cash flow.

cash flow

After-tax income minus preferred dividends and general partner distributions plus depreciation, depletion, and amortization. This is probably the definition used when a financial site lists "cash flow" without any other explanation. Not the same as operating cash flow or free cash flow.

conference call

A multiparty telephone call hosted by a company, primarily for analysts, shortly after an earnings announcement is made.

consensus estimate or rating

The average of analysts' individual earnings forecasts or buy/sell ratings.

current ratio

Current assets divided by current liabilities.

debt to equity (long-term)

Total long-term debt divided by total shareholders' equity.

debt to equity (total)

The total of short- and long-term debt divided by shareholders' equity.

dividends

Cash or stock paid to shareholders, typically on a quarterly schedule. However, some firms pay monthly, semiannually, or annually.

downtrend

A stock is in a downtrend when it is mostly moving down in price over time.

earnings per share (EPS)

After-tax annual earnings divided by the number of shares outstanding.

EBITDA
Earnings before interest, taxes, depreciation, and amortization.

fiscal year
Any 12-month period designated by a corporation as its accounting year.

float
Shares outstanding less shares held by insiders. Insiders cannot readily trade shares, so float is considered to be the number of shares available for trading.

free cash flow
Operating cash flow minus cash spent on plants and equipment, and dividends.

GARP
Growth at a reasonable price. A method of valuing stocks by comparing their price/earnings ratio to analysts' annual earnings growth rate forecasts.

generally accepted accounting principles (GAAP)
Accounting rules and procedures established by the Financial Accounting Standards Board, an independent self-regulating organization.

gross margin
The profit a company makes on goods and services considering only the direct costs of producing the goods or services.

growth investor
One who buys stocks of companies expected to grow sales and earnings faster than inflation.

implied growth
The earnings growth rate implied by a stock's price/earnings ratio.

income statement
A record of a company's sales and expenses over a specified year or quarter.

initial public offering (IPO)
The first sale of stock to the public by a corporation.

insider
An officer, director, or anyone else who owns more than 10 percent of shares outstanding.

insider ownership
The number of shares owned or controlled by insiders.

insider trading
Shares bought and sold by company insiders. Can also mean trading by anyone with access to market-moving information that has not yet been made public.

institutional ownership
Shares owned by pension funds, mutual funds, banks, and other large investors. Does not include shares held by hedge funds.

inventory
Raw materials, work in process, and finished goods that haven't been shipped to customers.

investment bank
An organization, usually a stock brokerage firm, involved in taking a new company public (IPO), consulting on mergers and acquisitions, handling corporate borrowing, and the like.

junk bond
A corporate bond with less than an investment-grade rating.

large-cap
A company with market capitalization greater than $8 billion.

leveraged buyout
Takeover of a public corporation using borrowed funds.

liquidity
A measure of the number of shares, or the dollar value of shares traded daily.

market capitalization
The current share price multiplied by the number of shares outstanding (shares issued).

message board
A location on a website dedicated to the discussion of a particular topic, usually a single stock or industry sector. Discussions are not real-time. Someone posts a message, and others respond over a period of hours or days.

micro-cap
A company with market capitalization less than $200 million.

mid-cap
A company with market capitalization between $2 billion and $8 billion.

momentum stock
A highly valued growth stock that is rapidly moving up in price.

most recent quarter (MRQ)
As of the last day of the last reported fiscal quarter.

moving average
A stock's average closing price over a specified period, typically 10 days, 50 days, or 200 days.

net income
Income after considering all costs. Earnings per share is net income divided by the number of outstanding shares.

operating cash flow
Surplus cash generated from a company's basic operations.

operating income
Sales minus all expenses except income taxes, interest expenses, and other items not related to the firm's basic business.

operating margin
Operating income divided by sales.

PEG
Price-to-earnings ratio divided by the forecast annual earnings growth rate. Some growth investors consider a stock fairly valued when its P/E ratio equals its forecast earnings growth rate.

price chart
A chart showing historical prices for a particular stock.

price-to-book ratio (P/B)
The latest share price divided by the book value stated in the latest report.

price-to-cash flow ratio (P/CF)
The latest share price divided by 12 months of operating cash flow.

price-to-earnings ratio (P/E)
The latest share price divided by 12 months of earnings per share.

price-to-sales ratio (P/S)
The latest share price divided by 12 months of sales per share.

profit margin
Bottom-line (after-tax) net income divided by sales.

pro forma earnings
"As if" earnings without considering nonrecurring expenses, extraordinary expenses, or other costs deemed by the reporting company as not representative of its ongoing operations.

receivables
See *accounts receivable*.

return on assets (ROA)
Annual after-tax income divided by total assets.

return on capital (ROC)
Annual after-tax income divided by the total of shareholders' equity plus long-term debt.

return on equity (ROE)
Annual after-tax income divided by shareholders' equity.

revenues
A company's sales.

risk
The probability of losing money.

S&P 500
A capitalization-weighted index of 500 of the largest U.S. corporations.

sales
Services and products sold by a company. Sales and revenues mean the same thing.

same-store sales
Sales at a retail store or restaurant location open at least one year. Same-store sales growth excludes sales gains from recent store openings.

screening
Using programs provided by financial websites that allow you to search for stocks meeting your particular requirements. The American Association of Individual Investors (AAII) also offers a freestanding screening program that runs on PCs.

SEC
The Securities and Exchange Commission. The U.S. government agency created to regulate the stock market.

shareholders' equity
The difference between the total of assets and liabilities shown on a company's balance sheet. Book value is shareholders' equity divided by the number of shares outstanding.

shares outstanding
The total number of shares issued by a corporation.

small-cap
A company with market capitalization less than $2 billion.

surprise
The difference between reported earnings and analysts' consensus forecasts. It's a positive surprise if reported earnings exceed forecasts and a negative surprise when reported earnings come in below forecasts.

trading volume
The number of shares traded during a specified time—usually one day.

trailing twelve months (TTM)
The last four reported quarters.

uptrend
A stock is in an uptrend when it is generally moving up in price over time.

valuation ratio
An expression of how the market values a stock by comparing its recent share price to per-share earnings, sales, book value, or cash flow.

value investor
One who looks for out-of-favor (value-priced) stocks.

working capital
Current assets minus current liabilities.

INDEX

Numbers

401(k) defined-contribution
plans, 208, 312

A

AAA-rated corporate bonds, 73,
151. *See also* bonds
AAII (American Association of
Individual Investors), 44, 137
ABA Banking Online
(www.banking.com/aba), 335
Abercrombie & Fitch, 20
access
distribution, 107, 263, 296
suppliers, 108, 264
Access Control & Security Systems
(www.securitysolutions.com), 335
accounting
clean, 118-120, 265, 298-299
creative, 22
pro forma, 358
rules, 184
accounts receivables, comparing,
197-200
acquisition
growth by, 21, 110-111, 264, 297
spotting serial acquirers, 111-112

activities
financing, 357
investments, 356
operating, 355-356
administrative expenses, 352
Advanced Micro Devices, 168
Advertising Age
(www.adage.com), 335
AIG, 49, 123
allocation, products on, 18
Amazon.com, 161
American Association of
Individual Investors (AAII),
44, 137
American Eagle Outfitters, 20
American Express, 105
American Printer
(www.americanprinter.com), 335
amortization, 352
analysis
business plans, 263-264, 295-297
candidates, 233
earnings reports, 343
reported earnings, 344-346
researching, 346
finances
fitness, 266-267
financial health, 300-301

D

D&A (depreciation and
  amortization), 166
databases, software industry and,
  98-99
Days Sales Outstanding
  (DSO), 197
debt
  calculating, 148
  equity ratios, 350
  long-term, 354
  low-debt companies, 124-125
  measuring, 125-127, 139
debtors, identifying risky, 152
declines in growth, 317
deferred taxes, 184
defined-benefits pension
  plan, 208
Dell Computer, 106, 278
Dental Economics
  (http://de.pennet.com), 336
Department of Commerce
  Bureau of Economic Analysis
  (www.bea.gov), 341
depreciation, 352
  and amortization (D&A), 166
  capital expenses versus, 270
  credits, 209
  growth investor analysis, 312
detailed fiscal fitness exams,
  136-145
detecting red flags, 191-201
deteriorating fundamentals,
  272, 316
Deutsch Bank, 55-56
diminishing sector outlooks,
  19-20
direction, market, 15
disappointing results, 9
Disney, 105

distribution, 263
  access, 107
  growth, 296
  models, 106-107
diversification
  markets, 110
  products, 264, 297
dividends, 80
Dodd, David, 72
downtrends, avoiding, 227
Dreman, David, 45
DrugTopics.com
  (www.drugtopics.com), 336
DSO (Days Sales Outstanding), 197

E

earnings, 51, 241
  growth, 6, 265
    converting to sales growth,
      93-95
    stability, 120-121
  forecasts, 61-65
  history, 242
  long-term growth, 65
  PEG, 76-77
  pro forma, 78, 344
  profits, 155-161
  quality of, 138
  red flags, 270
  reports, 343
    reported earnings, 344-346
    researching, 346
  restating, 19
  shortfalls, 315
  stability, 298-299
  trends, 250-252
Earnings Before Interest, Taxes,
  Depreciation, and Amortization
  (EBITDA), 140, 189-190
Earnings Growth Rate report, 293
earnings per share (EPS), 156

FINANCIAL TIMES

In an increasingly competitive world, it is quality
of thinking that gives an edge—an idea that opens new
doors, a technique that solves a problem, or an insight
that simply helps make sense of it all.

We work with leading authors in the various arenas
of business and finance to bring cutting-edge thinking
and best-learning practices to a global market.

It is our goal to create world-class print publications
and electronic products that give readers
knowledge and understanding that can then be
applied, whether studying or at work.

To find out more about our business
products, you can visit us at www.ftpress.com.